T0201470

VINTAGE

POORNA SWARAJ

M. K. Gandhi was born in 1869 in Porbandar, India. He studied law in London and was admitted to the Inner Temple in 1891. He worked to improve the rights of immigrant Indians in South Africa and returned to India in 1915 to take up the struggle for independence from Britain. Gandhi never wavered in his belief of non-violent protests and in 1947, he succeeded in uniting India with a national movement. In January 1948, Gandhi was assassinated as he walked to take his evening prayers.

Dhananjay Rai is a visiting fellow (2022–24) at the Centre for the Study of Developing Societies, Delhi, and faculty (2011 onwards) at the Centre for Gandhian Thought and Peace Studies, Central University of Gujarat, Gandhinagar.

Celebrating 35 Years of
Penguin Random House India

ADVANCE PRAISE FOR THE BOOK

'This book is a significant and worthy contribution to the discourse on Gandhi's theory and practice, particularly the latter. While considerable critical academic attention has been given to the ideas and principles of Gandhi—what Dhananjay Rai refers to as "philosophy proper", this work, by critically and contextually reading Gandhi's "philosophy practical", his *Constructive Programme*, offers a comprehensive and complete understanding of the idea of poorna swaraj. This book would be of interest to scholars working on Gandhi as well as people interested in the creative possibility of a substantive, open and people-oriented ideal of political democracy'—**Lajwanti Chatani,** professor of political theory, Maharaja Sayajirao University of Baroda, Vadodara, Gujarat

'Dhananjay Rai's engagement with Gandhi's ideas seems to be as thorough as his immersion in political theory. This study doesn't merely present the forgotten half of the Satyagraha coin, namely the *Constructive Programme*; it contributes to current analyses of the health of liberal democracies'—**Rajmohan Gandhi,** University of Illinois Urbana-Champaign

'This work merits attention, as it offers to make sense of Gandhi through the idea of the *Constructive Programme*'—**Gopal Guru,** former editor, *Economic and Political Weekly*, and former professor of political theory, Jawaharlal Nehru University

'Dhananjay Rai has picked an area that is vital for reconstructing Gandhi's non-violent society. Rai has presented and commented on Gandhi's *Constructive Programme* relevant for humanity today in general and Indian society in particular. He calls it "philosophy practical", without which Gandhi's life and work cannot be understood. It is a short novel and a scholarly contribution that gives fresh insights. And [to think] a scholar suggested a moratorium on writing on Gandhi in 1969!'—**Sudarshan Iyengar,** former vice chancellor, Gujarat Vidyapith, and former director, Centre for Social Studies

'A wholistic understanding of Gandhi's *Constructive Programme*, as presented by Dhananjay Rai, is the master key to make sense of the Gandhian way of transformational politics. [The] philosophy of social action is coupled with the politics of sustainable development in this agenda of citizenship development and communitarian nation-building'—**Anand Kumar**, former professor of sociology, Jawaharlal Nehru University

'In this thoughtful book, Rai analyses Gandhi from a rather unusual perspective and relates him to some of the important issues raised but not resolved by liberal theory. [This book] makes an impressive contribution to Gandhian studies and deserves a warm welcome'— **Bhikhu Parekh**, member of the House of Lords

'Gandhi these days is seen at best as the leader of India's anti-colonial political struggle. This however misses the point that the struggle for the liberation of the Indian people—of which the anti-colonial struggle was one crucial element—was an all-encompassing one, involving economic, political and social terrains. Gandhi saw himself as being engaged in this all-encompassing struggle that he felt had to be ethically informed and to eschew the pursuit of capitalist development (for which he used the term "English system"). Dhananjay Rai has done a great service in drawing attention to the integrity of Gandhi's thought and, through that, to the condition for the liberation of the Indian people. This is an extremely valuable and timely work'—**Prabhat Patnaik**, Professor Emeritus of Economics, Jawaharlal Nehru University, and former vice chairman, Kerala State Planning Board

'The well-tested *Constructive Programme* in Gandhi is wonderfully connected by Dhananjay Rai to the ideals of swaraj, thereby bridging the gap between theory and practice. He also examines Gandhi's political theory, both within and outside the liberal political theory, highlighting its distinctness'—**A. Raghuramaraju**, professor of philosophy, Indian Institute of Technology Tirupati

'The book constructs a long trajectory (1917–48) of Gandhi's constructive programmes involving continuous churning and evolution of ideas. Liberal political theorists have differently conceptualized these programmes. Dhananjay Rai very ably sums up these interpretations and provides his critique. The significant contribution of this book to Gandhian studies and liberal political theory is Rai's refreshing interpretation of the constructive programmes as "extraparliamentary" bringing people's everyday politics to the centre of democracy for social transformation. This book would interest scholars and students of Gandhian thoughts for social transformation to construct a non-violent society'—**Ghanshyam Shah**, former professor, Jawaharlal Nehru University, and former director, Centre for Social Studies, Surat

POORNA SWARAJ

Constructive Programme:
Its Meaning and Place

M.K. GANDHI

Introduced by Dhananjay Rai

VINTAGE
An imprint of Penguin Random House

VINTAGE

USA | Canada | UK | Ireland | Australia
New Zealand | India | South Africa | China | Singapore

Vintage is part of the Penguin Random House group of companies
whose addresses can be found at global.penguinrandomhouse.com

Published by Penguin Random House India Pvt. Ltd
4th Floor, Capital Tower 1, MG Road,
Gurugram 122 002, Haryana, India

Penguin
Random House
India

First published in Vintage by Penguin Random House India 2023

Copyright of Preface, Introduction, Afterword, Notes
and References © Dhananjay Rai 2023

All rights reserved

10 9 8 7 6 5 4 3 2 1

ISBN 9780670098279

Typeset in Adobe Garamond Pro by Manipal Digital Systems, Manipal
Printed at Thomson Press India Ltd, New Delhi

www.penguin.co.in

CONTENTS

PREFACE

In the *Constructive Programme*, M.K. Gandhi uses the phrase 'Poorna Swaraj'* (complete freedom or comprehensive change) twice—each time with complementary meanings. In the first sense, it appears as a 'truthful and non-violent means for winning Poorna Swaraj'. In the second sense, the constructive programme is the construction of Poorna Swaraj. The first is a continuum towards achieving the second. This continuum is multi-layered and multidimensional. Hence, the construction of Poorna Swaraj is contingent on the continuum. Herein, Gandhi offers one of the original insights towards conceptualizing the political community. There is no compromise on the continuum, yet finality is also envisaged. Therefore, achieving finality (Poorna Swaraj) does not deplete or discontinue the continuum (constant presence of constructive programmes). On the other hand, there cannot be finality without the continuum's expansion in the form of the constructive programme. The continuum

---

* The phrase 'Purna Swaraj' is also commonly heard. Poorna Swaraj as well as Purna Swaraj can be found in Gandhi's works. The *Constructive Programme* uses the former.

constructs the necessary space and substantive notions of politics.

Poorna Swaraj encapsulates both *philosophy proper* (Hind Swaraj/Swaraj postulation) and *philosophy practical* (constructive programmes). It is informed by swaraj *per se* and attainable by a slew of principally informed and categorically identifiable activities known in Gandhi's lexicon as constructive programmes. Poorna Swaraj is unthinkable without constructive programmes and thereby, both become indivisible. The swaraj apotheosis, or *Hind Swaraj* (1909/1910) and associated writings, conjoined with substantive interpretations, have invited substantive attention globally. Discourse on swaraj's engagement, interpretation and understanding are also linked with the severity of crises in human civilization.

The *Constructive Programme* (1941/1945/1948)—a concise document of fewer than 10,000 words—has not received the same level of attention as *Hind Swaraj*. It has not been able to get the book-length treatment since Independence. Most scholarly papers are essentially scattered remarks, notwithstanding the initial excitement. Recently, it has been used more as an informational booklet.

This is the state of sheer irony. There is a celebration of philosophy proper (*Hind Swaraj/Swaraj*) and the neglect of philosophy practical (*Constructive Programme*). It is to be stated categorically that philosophical proper is unattainable without philosophical practical—both constitute Poorna Swaraj. In the absence of philosophical practical, philosophical proper remains a mere scholastic exercise since the former makes it an attainable ideal.

More than just a way to bring back the *Constructive Programme*'s importance, this book draws attention to eighteen programmes in the text for public discussion and action by showing how its history, philosophical values and theoretical contribution have developed over time. The book is split into three parts: an introduction, the text (*Constructive Programme*) and an afterword.

The introduction discusses the biography of the text from 1917 to 1948. This is a rare occasion in the life of a text where a marathon discussion ensues before the text's finalization. The introduction also maps out the trajectory of the inclusion of items in the *Constructive Programme*. The introduction construes the *Constructive Programme* as an extraparliamentary and immanent text. The immanent text entails immediacy and adopts a centrifugal approach. It does not work from the outside to envisage the outside world.

On the contrary, the *Constructive Programme* works within to go outside, attaining the transformative world. It becomes essential against the *normalization of paradox* and *inattention towards contradictions*. Extraparlimentary is discussed in detail in the Afterword. Briefly, extraparliamentary overcomes two limitations of liberal political theory and liberal democracy. Liberal democracies operate through a definite space of politics and a particular way of representation. A definite space of politics and a particular way of representation are converted into a sphere of legitimate politics and delegation.

A definite space of politics (legitimate politics) and constrained representation (delegation) limit the scope and practice of politics for people.

Reading the *Constructive Programme* as extraparliamentary helps us to understand the de-definite space of politics (every space is political) and de-constrained representation (everyone is a participant). The introduction also points out why the *Constructive Programme* is not 'Satyagraha' or 'beyond parliamentary'. The *Constructive Programme* needs to be discussed as an evolutionary episteme (constantly learning and adding up the issues) and a horizontal struggle (struggle directed and participated by people). The *Constructive Programme* prioritizes *politics as participation* over *politics as mobilization*.

The text (*Constructive Programme*) is the second part, where eighteen items (or chapters) along with two appendices are given with annotations.

The Afterword is the book's third part, focusing on the extraparliamentary. At the outset, it analyses the nature of reading the *Constructive Programme*. Next, it locates the notion of politics (or a definite space of politics) and representation (or constrained representation) in liberalism or liberal political theory. After that, it debates and defines extraparliamentary. In the end, it proposes that reading the *Constructive Programme* overcomes the above-mentioned limitations prevalent in modern democracies.

The book uses a March 1948 reprinted edition (Navajivan Publishing House, Ahmedabad) due to the two added appendices. These two appendices were not part of the second edition published in December 1945. The 'constructive programme' will be referred to as a slew of activities defying the idea of rigid political space. The *Constructive Programme* will be referred to as the text written by Gandhi. *CWMG* refers to the *Collected Works of Mahatma Gandhi* (100 volumes), published by the Publication Division, Ministry of Information and Broadcasting, Government of India. *CWMG* is an important source for Gandhian Studies and for comprehending the churning during the Independence movement. Ninety volumes contain Gandhi's writings, speeches and letters from 1884 to 30 January 1948. Volumes 91–97 are supplementary volumes. Volumes 98 and 99 contain the 'Index of Subjects and Persons for Volumes up to XC'. Volume 100 contains a 'compilation of prefaces' written for numerous publications.

I am to blame for any mistakes or oversights that may have occurred.

Poorna Swaraj
Evolution of *Constructive Programme:*
Its Meaning and Place

Item Number	1941	1944	1945	1948
			Foreword (13 November)	Foreword
1	Communal unity	Communal unity	Communal Unity	Communal Unity
2	Removal of untouchability	Removal of untouchability	Removal of Untouchability	Removal of Untouchability
3	Prohibition	Prohibition	Prohibition	Prohibition
4	Khadi	Khadi	Khadi	Khadi
5	Other village industries	Other village industries	Other Village Industries	Other Village Industries
6	Village sanitation	Village sanitation	Village Sanitation	Village Sanitation
7	New or Basic Education	New or basic education	New or Basic Education	New or Basic Education
8	Adult education	Adult education	Adult Education	Adult Education
9	Uplift of women	Uplift of women	Women	Women
10	Education in health and hygiene	Service of the so-called aboriginals	Education in Health and Hygiene	Education in Health and Hygiene
11	Propaganda of rashtrabhasha	Education in health and hygiene	Provincial Languages	Provincial Languages
12	Love of one's own language	Propaganda of rashtra bhasha	National Language	National Language
13	Working for economic equality	Love of one's own language	Economic Equality	Economic Equality
14		Working for economic equality	Kisans	Kisans
15			Labour	Labour
16			Adivasis	Adivasis
17			Lepers	Lepers
18			Students	Students
19 (Appendix I)				Improvement of Cattle
20 (Appendix II)				Congress Position

INTRODUCTION

Gandhi's *Constructive Programme: Its Meaning and Place* (1941, 1945, 1948) calls for people's attention and participation in eighteen issues in preparation for the arrival of Poorna Swaraj. Poorna Swaraj is unthinkable without addressing the people's eighteen issues and their participation. Gandhi brings about significant change by elevating people's issues to the forefront of politics and making people a legitimate space for politics and representation. As a result, the *Constructive Programme* must be widely re-read for collective action to occur.

The biography of the *Constructive Programme: Its Meaning and Place* (hereafter the *Constructive Programme*) summarizes marathon experiments and the theoretical evolution of multiple ideas and alternatives.

The text encapsulates thirty-one years (1917–48) of intensive churning and continuous evolution of ideas and inclusion of issues.[1] Gandhi, the author of this atypical text, unleashed massive discussion and innumerable suggestions, playing the anchor role in these processes. This text can be called the first text, booklet or pamphlet whose codification or finality preceded massive discussions, making the content omnipresent.

The most protracted process is imbued with multi-layered discussion and intervention by Gandhi and a slew of known and unknown interlocutors and institutions. Reading the onward method (such as reading the *Constructive Programme* 1941 and 1945 editions onwards while forgetting the process) does not aid in understanding the forgotten historical development of extraparliamentary theory. On the contrary, a theory of extraparliamentary not only enlarges the scope of politics but also improves its rhythm. Gandhi's intervention was unique—he was engaging with the programme or writing the programme for the Congress workers but not on behalf of the Congress. It is also a deep irony that he wrote a programme for the Congress workers whose party he had left (severing connection, or retirement in Gandhi's words) in 1934 (CWMG LVIII, 1974: 403–06; CWMG LIX, 1974: 3–12; Sarkar, 2014: 297). Before and after his departure, the idea of political action, which defies the logic of the constrictive political by way of particular space and representative, had become a known entity.

One of the earliest and modest beginnings of 'constructive work' can be located in the public domain of *Champaran Satyagraha* in 1917. It became the substantive reference point for disobedience against unjust laws. Herein, Gandhi not only reversed the processes of the standard practising of the trial of people by the government into 'government on trial'[2] but also emphasized the 'voice of conscience'.[3] In addition to offering substantive criticism of the duality of liberal laws (laws for the subject, laws by the master), Gandhi was also offering, in his own words, 'constructive work' (village education, sanitary principles, medical relief [castor oil, quinine and sulphur ointment], women's question, communal welfare) (Gandhi, 2018: 637–57; Tendulkar, 1957). Besides Gandhi's Satyagraha, Champaran ' . . . also marked Gandhi's first attempt in the country to link political activism with a constructive programme . . .'(Das, 2022: 25–26).

In the *Congress Resolution on Non-Cooperation*, Nagpur session, 30 December 1920 (*Report of the Thirty-fifth Session of the Indian National Congress*), an implicit recognition of constructive work could be explored. The resolution was an important beginning and document for understanding a unique method of non-cooperation in the form of *withdrawal,* and working in those spheres that are not necessarily initiated by the institutionalized spaces. Public associations were called upon to work on Hindu–Muslim unity, settling disputes between Brahmins and non-Brahmins, and removing untouchability (CWMG XIX, 1966: 578).

In 1921, Gandhi, in an article 'To Gujaratis' (*Navjivan*, 1 May 1921), while highlighting the membership of the Congress and the monetary contribution to it in advanced areas, pondered over applying similar principles to the spinning wheel for the arrival of an 'easy to understand' and 'easy to implement' programme. 'Where there is greater capacity for work and greater enlightenment, we ought to succeed in introducing a greater number of spinning-wheels. It is only thus by helping one another in every way that we can succeed in implementing our modest, simple and easy-to-understand programme' (CWMG XX, 1966: 50).

Though this was an initial and rudimentary use of the programme, the use of extraparliamentary elements like the spinning wheel in association with the political realm is noticeable. The Bardoli Resolution (11–12 February 1922), in which Gandhi played an important role, had cancelled the mass civil disobedience and substituted it with 'a constructive programme of spinning, temperance, social reforms and educational activities'[4] (CWMG XXIII, 1967: 4). While the cancellation of civil disobedience remained much debated and controversial, the commencement of the constructive programme was an important addition.

Against this backdrop, on 3 March 1922, Gandhi indicated his discomfort with 'majoritarianism', a mainstay of modern democratic political space. He wrote that at Bardoli, '[t]he All-India Congress Committee gave me a majority, but I could see that very few really liked the Bardoli resolutions. I got the votes because I was Gandhi and not because people were convinced' (CWMG XXIII, 1967: 4–5). Gandhi treated violence herein not only as an act of violence but also as majoritarianism. After that, he searched for non-violence and its components. The components of non-violence could be the spinning wheel and Hindu–Muslim unity. 'Both grow in the soil of non-violence' (CWMG XXIII, 1967: 6).

He proposed the constructive work/constructive programme in the context of releasing prisoners. The eightfold constructive works are as follows:

1. Every man and woman should take the Congress pledge and get his or her name enrolled at a Congress office paying four annas.
2. Contributions should be collected for the Tilak Swaraj Fund.
3. National schools should be started and run.
4. The homes of liquor-addicts should be visited.
5. People who wear foreign cloth should be persuaded to wear khadi and the spinning-wheel should be introduced into every home.
6. *Antyajas* [untouchables] should be helped.
7. Panchayats should be set up.
8. Any person who suffers from a disease or injury should be nursed, irrespective of whether he be white or black (CWMG XXIII, 1967: 8).

Herein, Gandhi combined both mainstream political space and the extraparliamentary realm. Barring the first, the rest can be easily put in the extraparliamentary realm. Methodologically, Gandhi was not missing the crux of extraparliamentary that is immediacy. For him, '[t]here is not a single item among these which will require ages for implementation, unless public opinion is against our activities' (CWMG XXIII, 1967: 8).

It was also important to de-spatalize (decentring) the idea of swaraj in terms of defining it as mass education and de-constrained from urban spaces. 'Swaraj movement means mass education which you cannot impart directly through a few cities perfecting and achieving independent government' (CWMG XXII, 1966: 405).

Gandhi was, probably for the first time, using and concretely defining the constructive programme in his *Speech at Public Meeting*, Calcutta, on 2 May 1925. From this onwards, he started giving importance to constructive programmes. Amidst the debate between giving importance to the political programme and the constructive programme, he affirmed his support for the latter.

Nevertheless, it was not a binary but a possibility regarding expansion or reclaiming the space of everydayness politics. 'I swear by,' Gandhi reminded, 'the constructive programme; the more I examine myself the more I feel that I am more fitted for handling the constructive programme for developing our own power from within . . .'(CWMG XXVII, 1968:6). He ' . . . propose[d] . . . [his] . . . best ability to concentrate solely and exclusively upon the constructive programme . . .' (CWMG XXVII, 1968:6).

He called upon making the constructive programme a living entity for dropping fetters. He offered an elaboration of three items by way of explaining the constructive programme: Hindu–Muslim unity, untouchability, charkha (spinning wheel) and khaddar. ' . . . Hindu-Muslim unity, meaning unity between all the races . . .'(CWMG XXVII, 1968:6). He linked the untouchability question with the attainment of swaraj. 'So long as untouchability disfigures Hinduism, so long do I hold the attainment of swaraj to be an utter impossibility . . . If we do not get rid of this curse, it would be a curse added to curse, swaraj without the freedom of the untouchables' (CWMG XXVII, 1968:7). He warned Sanatani Hindus of Calcutta that Hinduism '. . . will go down to perdition if you do not get rid of this untouchability' (CWMG XXVII, 1968:7). The emphasis on the charkha and khaddar was to highlight the need of a supplementary industry for the agricultural economy along with reliance on local production (CWMG XXVII, 1968:7).

Gandhi further discussed Hindu–Muslim unity, untouchability, charkha and khaddar at the All-Bengal Hindu Sammelan on 2 May 1925. For Gandhi, 'Hindu-Muslim unity is a vital question . . .' (CWMG XXVII, 1968:10). Regarding untouchability, Gandhi made the difference between untouchability and *varnashrama* (fourfold division of society or four varnas). This is the beginning of one of the fiercely contested debates around untouchability as varna, or varna as untouchability or untouchability, not varna. For Gandhi, untouchability '. . . is a great sin and has no religious sanction behind it . . . [R]emove the blot of untouchability and induce others to do so. The removal of untouchability does never mean destruction of *varnashrama* dharma which is a very beautiful and beneficial thing and never a bad one' (CWMG XXVII, 1968: 10). Highlighting the significance of charkha, he associated it with the fight against poverty. He advocated for wearing khaddar as it was produced locally.

Gandhi also compared charkha and khaddar to *Sudarshan Chakra* and *Kamdhenu* (CWMG XXVII, 1968:10).

Again, he placed the significance of Hindu–Muslim unity, removal of untouchability and the spinning wheel in his speech at Bengal Provincial Conference, Faridpur, on 3 May 1925 (*The Searchlight,* 8 May 1925) (CWMG XXVII, 1968: 32). Accordingly, Gandhi's 'Talk with Untouchables', Faridpur (*Young India,* 14 May 1925) defined the national programme as 'removal of untouchability by the Hindus, khaddar and Hindu-Muslim unity' (CWMG XXVII, 1968: 14). Gandhi in his 'Letter to the Statesman', 31 July 1925 (*The Statesman,* 8 August 1925), states his position on 'civil resistance against wrong'. For Gandhi, the idea is not new. It was an integral part of life. 'To prepare the country for civil resistance is to prepare it for non-violence. To prepare the country for non-violence is to organize it for the constructive work which . . . is synonymous with the spinning-wheel (CWMG XXVII, 1968: 462), Hindu–Muslim unity, khaddar and the removal of untouchability' (CWMG XXVII, 1968: 464).

In 1926, at the Kathiawar Political Conference, he stated that '. . . there can be no conference or other politics outside of such constructive activities' (CWMG XXXII, 1969:422). Moreover, constructive work became a place of mutual relationship for all (CWMG XXXII, 1969:423). Here onwards, Gandhi started expanding the constructive programme. He discussed issues like 'fighting not the only work' (i.e. fighting alone cannot bring swaraj; more emphasis on constructive work), 'repair and reconstruction', 'village sanitation', 'temperance', 'Hindu–Muslim unity', 'khadi', 'removal of untouchability', 'organic swaraj', 'remember of "skeletons"', 'work in faith' and 'true soldiers' in his speech at Bardoli on 12 August 1928 (CWMG XXXVII, 1970: 162–69).

For Gandhi, this was the first comprehensive engagement with constructive work issues. He linked swaraj with labour ('fighting not the only work'). For him, replacing the structure with something similar would not be sufficient for swaraj's arrival, but changing the contour was crucial. 'Driving out the English will not by itself establish swaraj in India' (CWMG XXXVII, 1970: 165). Acting outside the government was also crucial to Gandhi (repair and reconstruction). 'The Government has no doubt many a grievous sin to answer for. Let us not impute our sins also to the Government or use the latter's lapses to justify ours. Enough unto the day is the evil thereof' (CWMG XXXVII, 1970: 165). Village sanitation provided an idea of the neighbourhood. Gandhi's shift from 'other' to 'self' is important. 'We shall be unfit for swaraj if we are unconcerned about our neighbour's insanitation and are content merely to keep our own surroundings clean' (CWMG XXXVII, 1970: 166). He asked for the sacrifice of life for Hindu–Muslim unity and offered satyagraha amidst the 'high of the communal passions' (CWMG XXXVII, 1970: 166). And '. . . there is no other way to swaraj than this' (CWMG XXXVII, 1970: 167). The question of untouchability became important for attaining swaraj (CWMG XXXVII, 1970: 167).

Gandhi also remained sceptical regarding 'heart unity' amidst communal tension ('not enough'). In place of 'constitutional swaraj', 'swaraj of the masses' was preferred (organic swaraj). Gandhi also needed to differentiate between 'constitutional swaraj' and 'real swaraj/swaraj of the masses'. He linked an act of Parliament with constitutional swaraj (CWMG XXXVII, 1970: 168). In the act of 'extraparliamentary', reckless expenditure or extravagance is rejected. In the realm of extraparliamentary, identification with the masses and their suffering becomes crucial. 'Have you completely identified yourselves with them and their sufferings?' (CWMG XXXVII, 1970: 169). 'True soldiers' entails committed volunteers.

The Nehru Report (1928) was a crucial battleground which would eventually shape the contour and acceptance of the constructive programme. The battle line was drawn primarily between groups supporting or opposing Dominion Status or Independence. Gandhi's speeches during deliberation brought another aspect: passing a resolution on the constructive programme. In his speech on 'Resolution on Nehru Report', Calcutta Congress, 26 December 1928 (*Amrita Bazar Patrika,* 27 December 1928), Gandhi defended the Nehru Report for the Dominion Status. He also proposed ten-fold works to be done by the Congress as a part of its activities during achieving dominion status or debate over independence. These were:

a) In the legislatures and outside, every attempt will be made to bring about total prohibition of intoxicating drugs and drinks; picketing of liquor and drug shops shall be organized wherever desirable and possible.

b) Inside and outside legislatures, methods suited to respective environments shall be immediately adopted to bring about boycott of foreign cloth by advocating and stimulating production and adoption of hand-spun and hand-woven khaddar.

c) Specific grievances, wherever discovered and where people are ready, shall be sought to be redressed by non-violent action as was recently done at Bardoli.

d) Members of legislatures returned on Congress tickets shall devote the bulk of their time to the constructive work settled from time to time by the Congress Committee.

e) Congress organizations shall be perfected by enlisting members and enforcing [the] strictest discipline.

f) Measures shall be taken to rid the country of social abuses.

g) Measures shall be taken to remove disabilities of women and they will be invited and encouraged to take their due share in national upbuilding.

h) It will be the duty of all Congressmen, being Hindus, to do all they can to remove untouchability and help the so-called untouchables in every possible way in their attempt to remove their disabilities and better their condition.

i) Volunteers shall be enlisted to take up village reconstruction in addition to what is being done through the spinning-wheel and khaddar.

j) Such other work as may be deemed advisable in order to advance nation-building in all its departments and in order to enable the Congress to secure co-operation in national efforts of the people engaged in different pursuits.

In order to finance the activities mentioned in the foregoing programme, every Congressman with a monthly income of Rs 100 and over shall contribute five per cent of his monthly income provided that in special cases exemption may be granted at the discretion of the Working Committee (CWMG XXXVIII, 1970: 268–69).

These were important not only for encompassing issues related to the constructive work but also for strengthening the idea of extraparliamentary, particularly when legislatures were asked to devote time to constructive work. However, due to constant disagreement and proposed amendments over the Dominion Status and Independence, Gandhi withdrew the above resolution and introduced a new one.

In his 'Speech on Resolution on Nehru Report, Calcutta Congress-II' at the Subjects Committee,[5] Calcutta Congress, 28 December 1928 (*Amrita Bazar Patrika,* 29 December 1928; *Forward,* 29 December 1928), and his compromised resolution, 'Speech on Resolution on Nehru Report, Calcutta Congress-III', at the Open Session, Calcutta Congress, 31 December 1928 (*Amrita Bazar Patrika,* 1 January 1929; *Aaj,* 2 January 1929) did not refer to the constructive work (CWMG XXXVIII, 1970: 283–96; 307–10).

This was due to the insistence on passing two separate resolutions meant for Nehru Report and constructive programme in the Calcutta Congress by the Subjects Committee. Gandhi's 'Speech on Constructive Programme', Calcutta Congress, 1 January 1929 (published as *Report of the Forty-third Session of the Indian National Congress, 1928*) contained the resolution of the constructive programme. There were primarily two suggestions which were incorporated in the latest resolution.

Regarding the suggestion given by Satyamurthi on the organization of the peasantry and workers, Gandhi suggested that '. . . village reconstruction work is nothing but the organization of the peasantry and workers upon an economic basis' (CWMG XXXVIII, 1970:311). However, he was also aware that city workers were not mentioned in the resolution, therefore, they would be included. 'I do not want it for one moment to be understood that the city workers and labourers are to be neglected . . . So I have no hesitation in accepting . . . [this] . . . part' (CWMG XXXVIII, 1970: 312). The second amendment was regarding tax. In place of the earlier 5 per cent of income, if the income was above Rs 100, the contribution now was decided as per the ability (CWMG XXXVIII, 1970: 312).

Sr. No.	Gandhi's Speech Resolution on Nehru Report, Calcutta Congress, 26 December 1928	Speech on Constructive Programme, Calcutta Congress, 1 January 1929 (*Report of the Forty-third Session of the Indian National Congress, 1928*)	Remarks
1	In the legislatures and outside every attempt will be made to bring about total prohibition of intoxicating drugs and drinks; picketing of liquor and drug shops shall be organized wherever desirable and possible.	In the Legislatures and outside every attempt will be made to bring about total prohibition of intoxicating drugs and drinks; picketing of liquor and drug shops shall be organized wherever desirable and possible.	
2	Inside and outside legislatures methods suited to respective environments shall be immediately adopted to bring about boycott of foreign cloth by advocating and stimulating production and adoption of hand-spun and hand-woven khaddar.	Inside and outside the legislatures, methods suited to respective environment shall be immediately adopted to bring about boycott of foreign cloth by advocating and stimulating production and adoption of hand-spun and hand-woven khaddar.	
3	Specific grievances, wherever discovered and where people are ready, shall be sought to be redressed by non-violent action as was recently done at Bardoli.	Specific grievances, wherever discovered and where people are ready, shall be sought to be redressed by non-violent action as was done recently at Bardoli.	

Sr. No.	Gandhi's Speech Resolution on Nehru Report, Calcutta Congress, 26 December 1928	Speech on Constructive Programme, Calcutta Congress, 1 January 1929 (*Report of the Forty-third Session of the Indian National Congress, 1928*)	Remarks
4	Members of legislatures returned on Congress tickets shall devote the bulk of their time to the constructive work settled from time to time by the Congress Committee.	Members of Legislatures returned on the Congress tickets shall devote the bulk of their time to the constructive work settled from time to time by the Congress Committee.	
5	Congress organizations shall be perfected by enlisting members and enforcing strictest discipline.	The Congress organization shall be perfected by enlisting members and enforcing stricter discipline.	
6	Measures shall be taken to rid the country of social abuses.	Measures shall be taken to remove the disabilities of women and they will be invited and encouraged to take their due share in national upbuilding.	It was point seven in the previous resolution.
7	Measures shall be taken to remove disabilities of women and they will be invited and encouraged to take their due share in national upbuilding.	Measures shall be taken to rid the country of social abuses.	It was point six in the previous resolution.

Sr. No.	Gandhi's Speech Resolution on Nehru Report, Calcutta Congress, 26 December 1928	Speech on Constructive Programme, Calcutta Congress, 1 January 1929 (*Report of the Forty-third Session of the Indian National Congress, 1928*)	Remarks
8	It will be the duty of all Congressmen, being Hindus, to do all they can to remove untouchability and help the so-called untouchables in every possible way in their attempt to remove their disabilities and better their condition.	It will be the duty of all Congressmen, being Hindus, to do all they can to remove untouchability and help the so-called untouchables in every possible way in their attempt to remove their disabilities and better their condition.	
9	Volunteers shall be enlisted to take up village reconstruction in addition to what is being done through the spinning-wheel and khaddar.	Volunteers shall be enlisted to take up the work among the city labourers and village reconstruction in addition to what is being done through the spinning-wheel and khaddar.	City labourers were included in the last resolution.
10	Such other work as may be deemed advisable in order to advance nation-building in all its departments and in order to enable the Congress to secure co-operation in national efforts of the people engaged in different pursuits.	Such other work as may be deemed advisable in order to advance nation-building in all its departments and in order to enable the Congress to secure co-operation in the national effort of the people engaged in different pursuits.	

Sr. No.	Gandhi's Speech Resolution on Nehru Report, Calcutta Congress, 26 December 1928	Speech on Constructive Programme, Calcutta Congress, 1 January 1929 (*Report of the Forty-third Session of the Indian National Congress, 1928*)	Remarks
Generic Comments	In order to finance the activities mentioned in the foregoing programme every Congressman with a monthly income of Rs 100 and over shall contribute five per cent of his monthly income provided that in special cases exemption may be granted at the discretion of the Working Committee (CWMG XXXVIII, 1970: 268–69)	In order to finance the activities mentioned in the foregoing programme, the Congress expects every Congressman to contribute to the Congress coffers a certain percentage of his or her income according to his or her ability. (CWMG XXXVIII, 1970:313–14)	In the last resolution, the tax is as per ability.

The noticeable omission in both resolutions was Hindu–Muslim unity.[6] This was the *only* omission of it in significant drafts or resolutions, or writings.

Just after the Calcutta Congress, Gandhi (*Young India,* 17 January 1929) rejected the charge that the constructive programme was a tame pursuance. He claimed '. . . that the programme is so catholic as to satisfy all tastes and to occupy the whole nation' (CWMG XXXVIII, 1970:355). Soon after, his definition of constructive work included Hindu–

Muslim unity. '. . . [C]onstructive work means the spinning-wheel and khadi, eradication of untouchability, propaganda against the drink-evil and Hindu-Muslim unity' (CWMG XLVII, 1971: 105).

It is noticeable that along with Hindu–Muslim unity, constant engagement with untouchability was an important part of Gandhi's constructive programme. He believed that constructive work was crucial for removing untouchability in a 'Letter to Ambalal' on 10 November 1932 (CWMG LI, 1972: 396). His 'Statement on Untouchability- X'(*Bombay Chronicle,* 10 December 1932) was the first major and independent illustration of this oppressive mechanism. In this statement, Gandhi also used the terms 'untouchable' and 'Harijan' interchangeably. At the outset, he answered the question, 'Why not work among the caste Hindus first?' He said that he had 'repeatedly declared in unequivocal terms that caste Hindus are sinners who have sinned against those who are called untouchables. Caste Hindus are responsible for the present condition of the untouchables' (CWMG LII, 1972: 151).

He proposed that '. . . the first and foremost items in the programme of work should be a whirlwind propaganda for educating and canvassing opinion among caste Hindus' (CWMG LII, 1972: 152). Personal visits and extensive use of literature became vital components. For him, 'perform literature' was crucial since 'shastras' were invoked to justify untouchability linked with birth. '. . . [A]s there is a body of learned men who invoke the aid of Shastras in order to justify untouchability by reason of mere birth, it would be well for workers to arm themselves with pro-reform literature' (CWMG LII, 1972: 152).

Some of Gandhi's suggestions also appeared to be 'paternalistic'. For example, his suggestion to the caste Hindus was to 'take one Harijan at least per family either as member or at least as domestic servant' (CWMG LII, 1972: 153). The following proposition was to share a meal with 'untouchables'. His suggestion for sharing meals with untouchables was construed as *yajna* (sacrifice). 'I cannot conceive of a better mode of offering this *yajna* than that of having a Harijan to share the meal with us' (CWMG LII, 1972: 153). After that, he cautioned them not to confuse it with interdining. '. . . [I]nterdining means dining with those who may touch your food and whose food you may touch but dining together under the roof without the mutual touch does not mean interdining' (CWMG LII, 1972: 153). He also suggested that in case of removal of untouchability, there cannot be any objection to sharing the family meal 'precisely on the same terms as other castes' (CWMG LII, 1972: 153).

However, Gandhi's critique of caste Hindus was sharp and categorical. Caste Hindus never invited untouchables into their social functions and ceremonies. 'Their cattle and other domestic animals may share their joys and sorrows but not Harijans, or if they do, these are occasions when they are pointedly reminded that they are not the same sort of human beings as caste Hindus' (CWMG LII, 1972: 153). For Gandhi, it was important to remind the caste men to differentiate between 'teachers/donors' and 'debtors'. His advice for the caste men was to meet Dalits '. . . as debtors going to their creditors to discharge their obligations . . .' (CWMG LII, 1972: 153).

Gandhi rejected the charge that the constructive programme was expensive. Moreover, if it causes universal awakening, it '. . . will not prove expensive' (CWMG LII, 1972: 154). Regardless of whether slow or fast, expensive or inexpensive, the constructive programme must be an integral part of society (CWMG LII, 1972: 154). Gandhi opposed the imposition of 'additional norms' for Dalits' temple entry. '. . . [N]o special condition should be laid down for the entry of Harijans that is not applicable to every other Hindu worshipper' (CWMG LII, 1972: 155). Between new regulations and the freedom of Dalits, he preferred the latter. 'New regulations may undoubtedly be framed after freedom of Harijans is honestly declared and assured to them' (CWMG LII, 1972: 155).

One can read that he underlined the significance of propaganda and *real* constructive work for expanding the 'extraparliamentary' realm in *Propaganda v. Construction* (*Harijanbandhu*, 26 March 1933). In this, he writes that propaganda is crucial to the entire schema. Nevertheless, mere propaganda is not sufficient. Effective propaganda is possible only if pure constructive work takes place. Due to the impossibility of a pure constructive programme, propaganda becomes vital to supplement the constructive programme. 'Pure constructive work means constructive activities by men and women workers of character who have perfect faith in the cause and who do their work in a missionary spirit. We, however, are imperfect. We may, therefore, sincerely do the best we can by way of constructive work and simultaneously carry on propaganda too' (CWMG LIV, 1973: 207). He made it clear that '[p]ropaganda work should be self-supporting' (CWMG LIV, 1973: 207). Self-supporting propaganda would promote constructive work (CWMG LIV, 1973: 208).

The idea of self-supporting propaganda is to avoid meddling or the interventions of those who are not attached to or interested in the work.

After withdrawing from the Congress membership in 1934, his assertion about the constructive programme became more vocal. In 1936, Gandhi stated that his '. . . faith in the constructive programme is probably ten times [what] it was then' (CWMG LXII, 1975: 229).

In August 1937, Gandhi discussed seven issues with workers of Kathiawar (his guidance, political conference, the Prajamandal and the conference, injustices to the states, labour improvement, constructive work for khadi and harijan, and carrying these activities under one organizations or independently) (*Harijanbandhu,* August 1937). Three issues were important for the constructive programme. Issues five and six were related to 'improvement of labour condition' and 'constructive work like khadi' and 'service of Harijan etc.' (CWMG LXVI, 1976: 22). In the subsequent pages, he suggested that '[i]n order to improve its condition labour must get organized' (CWMG LXVI, 1976: 23). He gave '. . . the highest place to khadi, eradication of untouchability, service of Harijans, village industries and prohibition' (CWMG LXVI, 1976: 23). The third crucial issue was 'whether these activities should be carried on independently or under one organization' (CWMG LXVI, 1976: 22). Gandhi's answer was categorical regarding 'independence'/'decentralization' of the programme. 'I see no harm in each activity being carried on wholly independently. Even if these are being carried on under the same authority, each should become self-sufficient, and people should be allowed to be absorbed in the particular sphere which they have chosen' (CWMG LXVI, 1976: 24).

During the 'Answers to Questions at Gandhi Seva Sangh Meeting' at Brindaban on 5 May 1939, constructive programme was linked with non-violence. He outlined four components (Hindu–Muslim unity, removal of untouchability, prohibition, and charkha) of the constructive programme and linked all four with non-violence (CWMG LXIX, 1977: 214). Constructive programme travelled through many paths, including several religious references. However, Gandhi also made charkha an important component by way of linking it with non-violence, swaraj and economic independence (CWMG LXIX, 1977: 215). He also unequivocally made the constructive programme a part of satyagraha (CWMG LXIX, 1977: 217). On 7 May 1939, his speech at the All-India Village Industries Board Meeting, Brindaban, highlighted the significance of village industries for bringing swaraj quicker than the election and also solving Hindi–Muslim tension by way of providing full wages (CWMG LXIX,1977: 239).

Gandhi also proposed a fourfold constructive programme which included spinning wheel, literacy, prohibition and hygiene in his 'Talks with Co-Workers' at Rajkot on 17 May 1939. He treated the spinning wheel meticulously as to '. . . no haphazard programme of spinning but scientific understanding of every detail, including the mechanics and the mathematics of it, study of cotton and its varieties, and so on' (CWMG LXIX, 1977: 275). Literacy was a new item added to the constructive programme. 'There is the programme of literacy. You must concentrate exclusively on it and not talk of any other thing. The work should be systemic and according to time table' (CWMG LXIX, 1977: 275). He coined 'the mass constructive programme' for 'going on endlessly' (CWMG LXIX, 1977: 276). He also reminded not to know '. . . other programme than the fourfold constructive programme of 1920' (CWMG LXIX, 1977: 324) and that civil resistance is only effective if it is backed by constructive effort on a mass scale (CWMG LXXIII, 1978: 388).

In 1940, Gandhi published a thirteen-point constructive programme titled 'Implications of Constructive Programme' (originally published in *Harijanbandhu* on 17 August 1940) with a pithy illustration of each item. This could be called an outline of the Constructive Programme. The thirteen-point items were as follows:

1. Hindu–Muslim or communal unity;
2. Removal of untouchability;
3. Prohibition;
4. Khadi;
5. Other village industries;
6. Village sanitation;
7. New or basic education;
8. Adult education;
9. Uplift of women;
10. Education in hygiene and health;
11. Propagation of Rashtrabhasha;
12. Cultivating love of one's own language;
13. Working for economic equality (CWMG LXXII, 1978: 378).

Up to now, the Congress-led All India Village Industries Association and the Basic Education Board were created (CWMG LXXII, 1978: 378). Gandhi did not discuss the issues '. . . in order of importance' (CWMG LXXII, 1978: 379). Khadi was important for him '. . . because millions of people can take their share in this work, and progress can be arithmetically measured' (CWMG LXXII, 1978: 379). Communal unity and the removal of untouchability must become part of everyday life. Once it is done, individuals need to do nothing. Gandhi used communal unity in two senses: for the attainment of swaraj and the wider unity of Hindus, Sikhs, Muslims, Christians, Parsis and Jews. They all constituted Hindustan. The removal of untouchability was linked to the attainment of non-violent swaraj. Interestingly and correlatedly, Gandhi suggested that 'under non-violent swaraj it will be impossible to conceive of any country as an enemy country' (CWMG LXXII, 1978: 379). It could be construed either as an organic unity or a non-territorial partition of human beings.

Prohibition was emphasized for moral sense. Returning to khadi he further linked it with the 'resurrection' of ruined Indian village artisans and the arrival of self-contained villages. Other village industries were equally crucial as khadi due to their interdependence with each other. Gandhi offered interconnecting methods in general and linkages to all constructive programmes in particular. 'All things in the universe are interdependent' (CWMG LXXII, 1978: 380).

Rural sanitation, basic education and women were given serious attention thereafter. Gandhi described discrimination against women in terms of not having equal rights in law as men, as a sign of 'partial paralysis' which India was suffering. He also used 'relational language' to treat women as mothers, sisters or daughters. Village workers must be aware of the 'general principles of health'. His conception of a common language came in the form of *Rashtrabhasha,* which both Hindus and Muslims could understand. Gandhi drew attention to the provincial language (CWMG LXXII, 1978: 380–381). In the end, he linked the constructive programme successfully to the 'foundation of economic equality'. 'The whole of this programme will, however, be a structure on sand if it is not built on the solid foundation of economic equality' (CWMG LXXII, 1978: 381).

Here, he defined his idea of economic equality not in terms of '. . . possession of an equal amount of worldly goods by everyone' (CWMG LXXII, 1978: 381) but in terms of '. . . everyone will have a proper house to live in, sufficient and balanced food to eat, and sufficient khadi with which to cover himself' (CWMG LXXII, 1978: 381). Gandhi, however, did not explain his choice of *second* preference over the first option.

More or less, Gandhi reiterated this 'Thirteen-Point-Programme' on 8 September 1940 (in Hindi, *Harijan Sevak*, dated 14 September 1940). At point four, khadi became 'Charkha and Khadi'. 'New or basic education' was replaced by 'Nayee Talim or Basic Education' (point 7). 'Propagation of Rashtrabhasha' was replaced with 'Propagation of the national language (Hindustani)' (point 11). 'Cultivating love for one's own language' was rephrased as 'Cultivating love for mother tongue' (CWMG LXXII, 1978: 451).

These thirteen-point items were as follows:

1. Hindu–Muslim or communal unity;
2. Removal of untouchability;
3. Prohibition;
4. Charkha and khadi;
5. Other village industries;
6. Village sanitation;
7. Nayee Taleem or Basic Education;

8. Adult education;
9. Uplift of women;
10. Education in health and hygiene;
11. Propagation of the national language (Hindustani);
12. Cultivating love for mother language;
13. Working for economic equality (CWMG LXXII, 1978: 451).

In 1940, Gandhi made constructive work round-the-clock engagement in 'Fragment of Letter to Abdul Ghaffar Khan'. '. . . [A] non-violent man has to keep himself engaged usefully during all waking hours and, therefore, *constructive work is for him what arms are for the violent men*' (CWMG LXXIII, 1978: 36). In November 1940 (*Discussion with Kishorelal Mashruwala*, 13 November 1940; *Harijan,* 18 January 1941), Gandhi stressed on thirteen different activities of the constructive programme. However, he accorded maximum importance to three items (khadi, eradication of untouchability and Hindu–Muslim unity). These three items were '. . . pregnant with revolutionary possibilities' (CWMG LXXIII, 1978: 175).

The year 1941 turned out to be the defining year for concretizing the *Constructive Programme*. In 'Statement to the Press' (28 October 1941), he reiterated the significance of the constructive programme. He suggested that '[e]ven parliamentary programme without it is a mere farce' (CWMG LXXV, 1979: 61). He defended the programme aggressively. 'There is communal unity. It is worth much more than the whole parliamentary programme. Without it, the latter is useless. It becomes a field for interminable wrangling' (CWMG LXXV, 1979: 61). Concerning untouchability, he '... repeat[ed] that if untouchability lives, Hinduism and with it India dies. Is that not a programme worth living for, dying for?' (CWMG LXXV, 1979: 61). Moreover, 'the programme gives ample scope for public meetings, demonstrations, exhibitions and the like' (CWMG LXXV, 1979: 62).

Just before the publication of the 1941 edition of the *Constructive Programme*, Gandhi made the constructive programme an integral part of civil disobedience for achieving independence in 'Statement to the Press' on 7 December 1941 (CWMG LXXV, 1979: 137). The first edition of *Constructive Programme: Its Meaning and Place* was published in December 1941. His treatment of the Constructive Programme is both descriptive and prescriptive. The CWMG (footnotes 1 and 2) relies on *Mahatma,* Vol. VI, and a letter by Gandhi to Mirabehn (13 December 1941) for suggesting that Gandhi started writing the Constructive Programme on the train from Sevagram (Wardha)(9 December 1941) to Bardoli (10 December 1941) and completed it at Bardoli. The publication date of the *Constructive Programme* and the communication date to Mirabehn remain the same: 13 December 1941 (CWMG LXXV, 1979: 146). It was completed between 9 December 1941 and 13 December 1941.

D.G. Tendulkar's edited Volume Six (*Mahatma: Life of Mohandas Karamchand Gandhi;* first edition 1953; revised version 1962) also sheds light on the text while reproducing the entire text of the *Constructive Programme* (1941). In this, Gandhi's arrival date to Bardoli is mentioned as 8 December 1941 (Tendulkar, 1962: 17). But the journey date should be 9 December 1941 as Gandhi wrote a letter to Nehru on the same date, stating his departure to Bardoli from Sevagram, Wardha: 'My Dear Jawaharlal . . . I am off to Bardoli tonight with Rajen Babu' (CWMG LXXV, 1979: 145).

However, *Mahatma Volume VI* becomes important for giving three concrete pieces of information. Firstly, the *Constructive Programme* was completed during his train journey from Sevagram to Bardoli. Secondly, his arrival in Bordoli meant spending a month at Sardar's Ashram. He met a slew of people who discussed their problems. Thirdly, in the middle of December 1941, he issued a twenty-five-page booklet. The booklet was needed in the context of the suspension of *Harijan* (Tendulkar, 1962: 17). Taking cognizance of both sources of information (CWMG and *Mahatma*), it can be stated that the *Constructive Programme* was completed during his visit (train journey included) and stay at Bardoli.

Volume 75 of CWMG does not give the 1941 edition (inserted as *227, 'Constructive Programme: Its Meaning and Place'*) of the *Constructive Programme*. Instead, '[t]he version reproduced here was "thoroughly revised" and date-lined "Poona, 13-11-1945"' (CWMG LXXV, 1979: 146). However, the footnotes allude to the first edition and its relevant portion. Tendulkar's *Mahatma Volume VI* gives the *Constructive Programme* (1941) along with a paragraph introduction and a few interconnected sentences (Tendulkar, 1962: 17–32). In the text, Gandhi calls the constructive programme the construction of Poorna Swaraj by way of truthful and non-violent means. Earlier, the thirteen-point programmes remained intact in the 1941 edition with some significant changes. 'Hindu-Muslim or communal unity' (1940 version; point 1) is rewritten as 'Communal unity' (1941 version; point 1). 'Charkha and khadi' (1940 version; point 4) appeared as 'Khadi' (1941 version; point 4). 'Nayee Taleem or Basic Education' (1940 version; point 7) was rephrased as 'New or Basic Education' (1941 version; point 7). 'Propagation of the national language (Hindustani)' (1940 version; point 11) was rewritten as 'Propagation of *rashtrabhasha*' (1941 version; point 11). 'Cultivating love for mother tongue' (1940 version; point 11) became 'Love of one's own language' (1941 version; point 12).

In addition to the thirteen points, the 1941 edition also mentioned 'Kisans', 'Labour' and 'Students'. He asked these three groups to work on thirteen points, which were 'issues' to be worked upon. 'They have to work the thirteen items the same as any other worker in the cause' (Tendulkar, 1962: 28). For these three groups, the reference comes in the form of 'instructions'. The epilogue of the *Constructive Programme* elaborated the three definite functions of civil disobedience: 'redressal of local wrong'; 'offering without regarding effect'; and 'issue being definite' (Tendulkar, 1962: 28). The 1941 version is vital for treating all thirteen plus three issues in a full-fledged manner. Gandhi elaborated on each point substantially.

Soon after the publication of the *Constructive Programme*, Gandhi's attention was drawn to a significant omission. Gandhi alludes to Thakkar Bapa's complaint regarding Adivasi's omission from the *Constructive Programme* in 'Notes' (written on Train Bardoli-Wardha, 9 January 1942; published in *Harijan,* 18 January 1942) (CWMG LXXV, 1979: 210).

Against this backdrop, Gandhi wrote that '[t]he *Adivasis* are the original inhabitants whose material position is perhaps no better than that of Harijans and who have long been victims of neglect on the part of the so-called high classes. The *Adivasis* should have found a special place in the constructive programme. Non-mention was an oversight' (CWMG LXXV, 1979: 210). This was the first time Adivasis were referred to as inclusion in the constructive programme/ *Constructive Programme.* He immediately mentioned it in the constructive programme as fourteen-fold on 27 January 1942 (Constructive Programme, *Harijan,* February 1942) (CWMG LXXV, 1979: 263).

Sharpening the issue and the inclusion of more items were constant pursuance. In the former case, Gandhi stated his preference for *dhanush takli* (bow-shape spindle) in the constructive programme over the spinning wheel due to cost-effective reasons. Manufacturing spinning wheels by thousands require '. . . plenty of money which we do not have . . . That leaves only the *dhanush takli* which can be made with little labour and less money' (CWMG LXXV, 1979: 272).

On 9 February 1942, Gandhi declared that *'Adivasis* have become the fourteenth item in the constructive programme' (published as 'Adivasis', *Harijan*, 15 February 1942) (CWMG LXXV, 1979: 299).

Against this backdrop, questions were raised concerning government and constructive programme relationships. He suggested avoiding conflict between the two since both are supposed to work for people ('Constructive Programme and Government', *Harijan*, 25 January 1942). His additional caveat gave the constructive programme additional sharpness. 'I expect every Congress worker to do his best to avoid it. But there is no help for it, if the Government prohibit[s] such activities because they are undertaken by Congressmen who believe that the working of the constructive programme will bring swaraj' (CWMG LXXV, 1979: 236). In July 1944, Gandhi's 'Statement to the Press' (28 July 1944; published in the *Bombay Chronicle* on 29 July 1944) confirmed the conversion of the thirteen-point programme into the fourteen-point programme. As discussed previously, the new addition was 'Service of the so-called aboriginals' (version 1944; point 10) (CWMG LXXVII, 1979: 430).

In the same year, Gandhi sent a message, 'Hints for Constructive Workers' (22 October 1944; Sevagram), to the Worker's Conference, Bombay, on 28–29 October 1944. This address or message was meaningful due to multiple reasons. The constructive programme was construed as a non-violent and truthful way to achieve poorna swaraj (complete independence). What could be more fruitful than the engagement of 40 crore people to build the nation from the below? It was independence in the absolute sense, including freedom from foreign domination. Against the critics' prognosis about non-cooperation among people, he remained sanguine about cooperation. He suggested that it was a worthy attempt. Individual and collective civil disobedience were aided in the constructive effort. Training in the constructive effort was crucial for civil resistance. Readiness in a constructive effort defied the defeat. Khadi and its use could not be defeated if both became universal by not being imposed on the people but cultivated as a necessary item in the freedom struggle, and working through the villages as units. There could be suffering to attain swaraj because the latter was not delinked from the former. It was important to remember that the items of the *Constructive Programme* were not exhaustive but illustrative. 'Local circumstances' were crucial for the programme, which might not be part of the printed programme. Some items needed fuller emphasis. The kisan does come first. As the son of the soil, land should belong to peasants, not absentee landlords or zamindars. Regarding labour, capital should not be the master of the labour but the servant of them. In a concrete form, labour needed to have unions, education, children's education, hospitals, crèches, maternity homes and sustainability during strikes. All workers were feasible only when they had a union. Regarding students, they should be kept aloof from political turmoil (CWMG LXXVIII, 1979: 218–21).

On 24 March 1945 (Speech at A.I.S.A. Meeting-I*)*, Gandhi asserted the independence of the constructive programme for doing full justice to it. 'I entirely concur with the view that for full justice to be done to constructive work it must stand on its own feet and should not be tied to political work' (CWMG LXXIX, 1980: 297).

He gave additional information. The *Constructive Programme* was now a fifteen-point programme. However, the fifteenth point was not mentioned. On 31 March 1945, Gandhi, in 'Statement to the Press' (*Bombay Chronicle*, 1 April 1945), emphasized khaddar fondly and linked it with the fifteen constructive programmes. 'Let it be noted that khaddar has attained a wider connotation than before. It has become the central sun round which other village industries revolve like so many planets. Moreover, it now represents the fifteenfold constructive programme. Khaddar itself has after much experience got its proper value and thus has received a dignity never before given to it' (CWMG LXXIX, 1980: 334). His 'Speech at Prayer Meeting', 6 April 1945 (*Bombay Chronicle*, 7 April 1945) referred to 'the fifteen-point programme' (CWMG LXXIX, 1980: 348–50).

On all three occasions (24 March, 31 March and 6 April 1945), only once *was* khaddar mentioned, which 'represented the fifteenfold constructive programme' (31 March 1945). Previous and succeeding dates had not contained a reference to khaddar.

There are two puzzles in this regard. First, the difference between khadi and khaddar needed to be delineated. Second, since khadi was always a part of the constructive programme, adding the term 'khaddar' as one of the fifteenth programmes was inexplicable due to the absence of a substantive difference between khadi and khaddar. This was resolved in November 1945 when 'khaddar' as a term was dropped in the new edition of the *Constructive Programme*.

Gandhi also discussed the *Constructive Programme* with R.G. Casey, the Governor of Bengal. He sent a proof copy of the revised edition, which he had received from Jivanji Desai for proof correction, to Casey on 6 December 1945 (CWMG LXXXII, 1980: 167). The next day, Gandhi wrote a letter to Jivanji Desai ('Letter to Jivanji D. Desai', 7 December 1945, Sodepur) suggesting several *stylistic* changes. 'You have given a heading to my preface but there is no heading on the page on which the pamphlet itself begins . . . [E]ighteen headings which you have given in the pamphlet should be reproduced on the cover in their proper order, with the page number given against each other' (CWMG LXXXII, 1980: 174). Other suggestions are topics to be shown in the form of a circle; a spinning wheel in the centre, and printed headings around the circle like the planets and the sun. He finally gives up the idea of a circle due to the most critical complexities, like how communal unity is presented as a planet. 'How can communal unity be represented as a planet? If it is so represented, my original conception, would be vitiated, for the basic conception is that khadi is the chief handicraft and that the other industries take their place and revolve round khadi like planets round the sun. If now we can find a place in this scheme for Adivasi, *kisans,* students and communal unity, then the conception will have been worked out. It might be better, therefore, to give up the idea of the circle or to form the circle only with khadi and cottage industries' (CWMG LXXXII, 1980: 175).

Gandhi requested 'another copy of proof'. Gandhi received 'the booklet on the constructive programme' on 4 January 1946, as acknowledged in his 'Letter to Jivanji D. Desai' (5 January 1946, Sodepur). He expressed his discomfort with giving the price on the back page of the booklet in place of the cover page since readers would see the cover page and look for the price. He also asked why there was no signature at the end of the preface (CWMG LXXXII, 1980: 348). He acknowledged receiving the new edition of the *Constructive Programme* ('Letter to Jivanji D. Desai', 16 January 1946, Sodepur) along with Jivanji Desai's '. . . full explanation about the preface, as also about the price'[7] (CWMG LXXXII, 1980: 429).

Accordingly, Gandhi's 'thoroughly revised edition' of the *Constructive Programme* was published in December 1945. The foreword, 'specially written' for this edition, highlights the significance of complete independence.[8] Engagement of all (40 crore people) in the constructive programme is envisaged for complete freedom in which freedom from foreign domination, among other things, is included. The constructive programme is the *training* of civil disobedience. By way of khadi, he proposes the idea of decentralization. ' . . . [C]entralized *khadi* can be defeated by the Government, but no power can defeat individual manufacture and use of *khadi*. The manufacture and use of *khadi* must not be imposed upon the people, but it must be intelligently and willingly accepted by them as one of the items of the freedom movement' (Constructive Programme: Its Meaning and Place, 1948: 6).

Gandhi discussed the major part of the two-page content of the Foreword in 'Hints for Constructive Workers', 22 October 1944, Sevagram (discussed in previous pages). The following contents (by way of paraphrasing/changing word or extension of the sentence) from the address were incorporated in the Foreword:

> . . . the constructive programme is the non-violent and truthful way of winning *purna* swaraj. Its wholesale fulfilment is complete independence. Imagine all the forty crores of people engaged in the constructive programme which is designed to build up the nation from the very bottom upward. Can anybody dispute the proposition that it must mean complete independence in every sense of the expression, including the ousting of foreign domination? When the critics laugh at the proposition, what they mean is that forty crores of people will never co-operate in the effort to fulfil the programme. No doubt there is considerable truth in the scoff. My answer is, it is worth the attempt. Given an indomitable will on the part of a band of earnest workers, the programme is as workable as any other and more so than most. Anyway, I have no substitute for it, if it is to be based on non-violence (CWMG LXXVIII, 1979: 218).

Civil disobedience, mass or individual, is an aid to constructive effort and is a full substitute for armed revolt. Just as military training is necessary for armed revolt, training in constructive effort is equally necessary for civil resistance. And just as the use of arms becomes necessary only when an occasion demands it, even so is the use of civil resistance only occasional. Therefore, workers will never be on the lookout for civil resistance. They will hold themselves in readiness, if the constructive effort is sought to be defeated. To take one or two illustrations, effort for communal friendship cannot be defeated, political pacts can (CWMG LXXVIII, 1979: 219).

But political pacts are required because of the previous lack of friendship. Similarly, manufactured khadi and its use cannot be defeated if both become fairly universal. The manufacture and use are not to be brought about by imposing them upon the people, but they have to be intelligently accepted by them as some of the necessary items of the freedom movement, when it is worked from the villages as units. Pioneers even in such programmes are likely to be obstructed. They have had to go through the fire of suffering throughout the world. There is no swaraj without suffering. In violence truth is the greatest sufferer; in non-violence truth is ever triumphant (CWMG LXXVIII, 1979: 219).

The tabular format of *Hints for Constructive Workers* and
Foreword is as follows:
Precursor of *Foreword*

Hints for Constructive Workers (22 October 1944, Sevagram)	*Foreword of Constructive Programme: Its Meaning and Place (1945)*	Rephrasing/adding/ changing word or extension of the sentence
. . . the constructive programme is the non-violent and truthful way of winning *purna* swaraj.	. . . the constructive programme is the truthful and non-violent way of winning Poorna Swaraj.	truthful and non-violent; Poorna Swaraj
Its wholesale fulfilment is complete independence.	Its wholesale fulfilment *is* complete independence.	*is*
Imagine all the forty crores of people engaged in the constructive programme which is designed to build up the nation from the very bottom upward.	Imagine all the forty crores of people busying themselves with the whole of the constructive programme which is designed to build up the nation from the very bottom upward.	busying themselves with the whole of the

Hints for Constructive Workers (22 October 1944, Sevagram)	*Foreword* of *Constructive Programme: Its Meaning and Place* *(1945)*	Rephrasing/adding/ changing word or extension of the sentence
Can anybody dispute the proposition that it must mean complete independence in every sense of the expression, including the ousting of foreign domination?	Can anybody dispute the proposition that it must mean complete Independence in every sense of the expression, including the ousting of foreign domination?	Independence
My answer is, it is worth the attempt.	My answer is, it is still worth the attempt.	still
Civil disobedience, mass or individual, is . . .	Civil Disobedience, mass or individual, is . . .	Disobedience
Just as military training is necessary for armed revolt, training in constructive effort is equally necessary for civil resistance.	Training is necessary as well for civil disobedience as for armed revolt. Only the ways are different.	Rephrased
And just as the use of arms becomes necessary only when an occasion demands it, even so is the use of civil resistance only occasional.	Action in either case takes place only when occasion demands.	Rephrased

Hints for Constructive Workers (22 October 1944, Sevagram)	*Foreword* of *Constructive Programme: Its Meaning and Place* *(1945)*	Rephrasing/adding/changing word or extension of the sentence
Therefore workers will never be on the look-out for civil resistance.	Therefore, workers will never be on the look-out for civil resistance.	This sentence starts as a new paragraph.
To take one or two illustrations, effort for communal friendship cannot be defeated, political pacts can.	From one or two illustrations it will be seen where it can be and, where it cannot be, offered. Political pacts we know have been and can be, but personal friendship with individuals cannot be, prevented. Such friendships, selfless and genuine, must be the basis for political pacts.	Rephrased
But political pacts are required because of the previous lack of friendship.	----do---	-------do----
Similarly khadi manufacture and its use cannot be defeated if both become fairly universal.	Similarly, centralized *khadi* can be defeated by the Government, but no power can defeat individual manufacture and use of *khadi*.	Rephrased

Hints for Constructive Workers (22 October 1944, Sevagram)	*Foreword* of *Constructive Programme: Its Meaning and Place (1945)*	Rephrasing/adding/ changing word or extension of the sentence
The manufacture and use are not to be brought about by imposing them upon the people, but they have to be intelligently accepted by them as some of the necessary items of the freedom movement, when it is worked from the villages as units.	The manufacture and use of *khadi* must not be imposed upon the people, but it must be intelligently and willingly accepted by them as one of the items of the freedom movement. This can be done only from the villages as units.	Rephrased
Pioneers even in such programmes are likely to be obstructed.	Pioneers even in such programmes can be obstructed.	Rephrased
There is no swaraj without suffering.	There is no Swaraj without suffering.	Swaraj
In violence truth is the greatest sufferer; in non-violence truth is ever triumphant.	In violence, truth is the first and the greatest sufferer; in non-violence it is ever triumphant.	Rephrased
(CWMG LXXVIII, 1979: 218–21).	(Gandhi, 1948: 5–6)	

Gandhi's assertion of 1945 as 'a thoroughly revised edition' of the 1941 edition must be understood as 'a point of emphasis' rather than the addition of new items. In fact, Gandhi gives full treatment to both the 1941 and 1945 versions.

Content of the *Constructive Programme: Its Meaning and Place*

Item Number	1941	1944	1945	1948
			Foreword (13 November)	Foreword
1	Communal unity	Communal unity	Communal Unity	Communal Unity
2	Removal of untouchability	Removal of untouchability	Removal of Untouchability	Removal of Untouchability
3	Prohibition	Prohibition	Prohibition	Prohibition
4	Khadi	Khadi	Khadi	Khadi
5	Other village industries	Other village industries	Other Village Industries	Other Village Industries
6	Village sanitation	Village sanitation	Village Sanitation	Village Sanitation
7	New or Basic Education	New or basic education	New or Basic Education	New or Basic Education
8	Adult education	Adult education	Adult Education	Adult Education
9	Uplift of women	Uplift of women	Women	Women
10	Education in health and hygiene	Service of the so-called aboriginals	Education in Health and Hygiene	Education in Health and Hygiene

Item Number	1941	1944	1945	1948
11	Propaganda of *rashtrabhasha*	Education in health and hygiene	Provincial Languages	Provincial Languages
12	Love of one's own language	Propaganda of *rashtra bhasha*	National Language	National Language
13	Working for economic equality	Love of one's own language	Economic Equality	Economic Equality
14		Working for economic equality	Kisans	Kisans
15			Labour	Labour
16			Adivasis	Adivasis
17			Lepers	Lepers
18			Students	Students
19 (Appendix I)				Improvement of Cattle
20 (Appendix II)				Congress Position

Four changes are discernible between the 1941 and 1945 versions: 'foreword', rephrasals, breaking existing points into more points and addition of new points. For the first time, a foreword was added to the *Constructive Programme* based on the 1944 content. Regarding the second (rephrasing), 'Uplift of women' (1941, 1944) was changed to 'Women' (1945). 'Propaganda of rashtrabhasha' and 'Love of one's own language' (points 11 and 12 in 1941; 12 and 13 points in 1944) were rephrased as 'Provincial languages' and 'National language' (points 11 and 12 in 1945) respectively. In the third (breaking of existing points), 'Propaganda of rashtrabhasha' in the 1941 version (point 11) contained two paragraphs. In the 1945 revision, only the first paragraph was retained under point 11 ('Provincial language'). Point 12 ('Love of one's own language') of 1941 was entirely removed in the 1945 edition. The last paragraph of point 11 of the 1941 version was split into two paragraphs and placed under the title 'National Language' (point 12) in the 1945 edition. Some of the grammatical corrections are as follows:

1941: Point 11	1945: Point 12		Remarks
Para Two	Para One	Para Two	
It is called Urdu when it is written in the Persian character.	It is called Urdu when it is written in the Urdu character.		The Persian character was rewritten as Urdu character.
And since that time, in theory at least, Hindustani has been the *rashtrabhasha*.	And since that time, in theory at least, Hindustani has been the Rashtra Bhasha.		
I say. . . the Congressmen . . . as they should have.	I say. . . Congressmen . . . as they should have.		'the' removed.
The picture I have drawn in this paragraph is true to life as it was before 1920.			The entire sentence was removed.

1941: Point 11	1945: Point 12		Remarks
Para Two	Para One	Para Two	
From 1920 a deliberate attempt began to be made to recognize the importance of Indian languages for the political education of the masses, as also of an all-India common speech which the politically-minded India could easily speak and which the Congressmen from the different provinces could understand at annual sessions as also at the meetings of the A.I.C.C.	In 1920 a deliberate attempt was begun to recognize the importance of Indian languages for the political education of the masses, as also of an all-India common speech which politically-minded India could easily speak and which Congressmen from the different provinces could understand at all-India gatherings of the Congress.		Added: 'In 1920. . .'. removed: 'be made to'. Removed: 'which politically' removed: 'the'. Removed: 'the'. Added: 'at all-India gatherings of the Congress.'
	Such National language should enable one to understand and speak both forms of speech and write in both the scripts.		The entire sentence was added.

1941: Point 11	1945: Point 12		Remarks
Para Two	Para One	Para Two	
But I am sorry to have to say that many Congressmen have failed to carry out the resolution.		I am sorry to have to say that many Congressmen have failed to carry out that resolution.	Deleted: 'but'; Rephrased 'the' as 'that'
And so we have the shameful spectacle of Congressmen insisting on speaking in English and compelling others to do likewise for their sakes.		And so we have, in my opinion, the shameful spectacle of Congressmen insisting on speaking in English and compelling others to do likewise for their sakes.	Added 'in my opinion'

New Points added in 1945

1941 (Post-Point 13)	Common Points	1945 (Points 14, 15, 16,17, 18	Remarks
Kisan			Kisan, labour and students were part of the 1941 version but given without subheadings; Adivasis as a part of the programme was added in 1944.
Labour			
		Adivasis	
		Lepers	
Students			

There was a thirteen-point programme in the 1941 edition of the *Constructive Programme*. Gandhi added the Adivasis question in a page summary extending points from thirteen to fourteen in 1944. The 1945 edition was an eighteen-point programme. In comparison to the 1941 edition, specific headings for the 1945 version appeared as 'Kisans' (point 14), 'Labour' (point 15), 'Adivasis' (point 16), 'Lepers' (point 17) and 'Students' (point 18). These specific headings were new, but the content was borrowed from the 1941 edition regarding 'Kisans, Labours, and Students'. In the 1941 version, Gandhi mentioned 'Kisans, Labour, and Students' after the end of the thirteenth point of the programme. (Tendulkar, 1962: 27–31). He rearranged the content of the 1941 version while adding required sentences for continuity in the 1945 edition into three more headings. Since 'Kisans, Labour, and Students' (1941) and 'Adivasis' (1944) were already discussed by him, the 1945 version added *only* one new item, i.e. 'Lepers' (point 17).

In a 'Letter to Jivanji D. Desai'[9] (16 January 1946), Gandhi responded to Desai's request for adding cow protection to the *Constructive Programme*. 'Your suggestion for adding something more to the paragraphs on cow-protection in *The Constructive Programme* seems a good one. I would describe it as "improvement of livestock". I agree that it should not have been left out' (CWMG LXXXII, 1980: 429).

On 27 January 1948, he stated his position on Congress titled *Congress Position* (CWMG XC, 1984: 497–98). The reprint of the *Constructive Programme* in 1948 contained these two appendices. The first appendix reproduced the 'Extract from a letter written by Gandhiji to Shri Jivanji Desai' (Gandhi, 1948: 30), which was also a response to Desai. This extract was based on the letter provided by Jivanji Desai. In the first appendix (which also mentions the date as 16 January 1946), two changes can be identified in contrast to the *original* letter, which is referred to in the CWMG LXXXII (1980: 428–30) (dated 16 January 1946).

The first change was regarding the title of the appendix. Gandhi proposed it as 'Improvement of Livestock' in 1946. The 1948 reprint was titled 'Improvement of Cattle'. The second change was concerning words and sentences. The extract produced herein of 1948 was as follows: '. . . You are right; cow service (*goseva)* should be included as one more item in the *Constructive Programme*. I would phrase it as improvement of cattle. I think it should not have been left out' (Gandhi, 1948: 30). In addition to sentence formation change, earlier 'cow protection' was replaced with 'cow service'. 'Improvement of Livestock' was replaced with 'Improvement of Cattle'.

Post-publication of the *Constructive Programme* (1945 edition), Gandhi, during 'Discussion with Midnapur Political Workers' on 2 January 1946 (*Anand Bazar Patrika*, 5 January 1946), valued the *Constructive Programme* more than swaraj in two definite senses, i.e. making it multi-religious and non-metaphysical affairs. Firstly, the constructive programme meant '. . . *Ramarjaya, Khudai Sultanat or* the divine kingdom' (CWMG LXXXII, 1980: 334).

After making multi-religious affairs, it became necessary to convert such inclusivity into demystifying postulations. The demystifying postulation took place subtly. Gandhi added that '[he is] . . . thirsting after such *Ramarajya*. My God does not reside up above. He has to be realised on earth. . . You need not think of the world beyond. If we can do our duty here, the "beyond" will take care of itself' (CWMG LXXXII, 1980: 334). Unfortunately, a demystifying postulation like this had/has not invited substantive attention in Gandhian Studies.

On 27 January 1946, Gandhi made a difference between the parliamentary and constructive programmes in 'Answers to Questions at Constructive Worker's Conference, Madras' (*The Hindu*, 29 January 1946). 'The parliamentary programme was like building from the top. Their aim must be to build from below so that the foundation would be strong and the structure good. If any mistake occurred while building from the bottom, it could be rectified immediately, and the harm done would not be much' (CWMG LXXXIII, 1981: 39). He maintained this standpoint throughout. In response to a letter which highlighted the delinking of the Government of India and the constructive programme on 4 September 1947 (*Harijan*, 14 September 1947), he defended the constructive programme and appealed for the involvement of all to make it successful (CWMG LXXXIX, 1983: 144–47).

Furthermore, Gandhi advised in 'A Letter' (17 July 1947; *Bihar Pachchi Dilhi*; Gujarati) '. . . that constructive workers should not take part in politics. If they take interest in both, they will be able to do justice to neither' (CWMG LXXXVIII,

1983: 355). This must be construed in the context of Gandhi's consideration of the constructive programme as an inalienable part of swaraj. There was no meaning of swaraj without the constructive programme. He linked present malaise to the earlier insufficiency of the constructive programme (CWMG LXXXIX, 1983: 364).

Gandhi's 'Discussion at Constructive Works Committee Meeting', 11–12 December 1947, offered important insights regarding the role of constructive workers, their participation in politics, the government's obstruction, the need for overall organization or not, work done through Congress and functional representation in A.I.C.C. In addition, they offered important standpoints along with ongoing churning at that time. A few excerpts are reproduced below.

J.B. KRIPALANI: . . . The question has been raised what the constructive workers should do?

GANDHIJI: The first thing we have to do is to improve our national character. No revolution is possible till we build our character. The pity is that though swaraj is so recent an achievement, there is already a slackness in constructive efforts . . .

QUESTION: Should constructive workers take part in politics?

GANDHIJI: . . . [L]eave politics to Rajendra Babu, Jawaharlal and Vallabhbhai. You confine yourselves to constructive work . . .

All the Sangh, except the Harijan Sevak Sangh, were brought into being by the Congress. Why is it then that the workers of these Sanghs lack the power to make the Government go the whole hog with them? . . .

There should be rapport between the constructive workers and the institution . . . The Congress has always had the constructive programme. Now it has the power. Why is it then that our work is not progressing? . . . I have had a hand in the formation of all these various institutions, and I can say that things are in such a state because our hearts are not pure. A current was generated. The people caught on to the idea that that was the way to overcome the British . . . The fight being over, our interest in the constructive programme waned. Constructive work is not a strategy or a technique of fighting. Constructive work connotes a way of life. It can be carried on only by . . . [those] . . . who have adopted it by the heart as well as by the intellect.

To set our own house [Sanghs/constructive workers/ associations] in order is the first indispensable requisite, if we want to influence political power . . .

The objective of the constructive works organizations is to generate political power. But if we say that political power having come, it must be ours as a price for our labours, it would degrade us and spell our ruin . . .

. . . The Charkha Sangh is the biggest Sangh. It has funds. It is pursuing the policy of decentralization . . . The workers of the Charkha Sangh are not there merely to earn a living for themselves or merely to distribute some wages to the spinners and weavers, etc., by way of poor relief. The only goal worthy of their ambition is to create a non-violent order of society. But, in this they have not made much headway. If our khadi workers are there for wages only, then we had better bid good-bye to the dream of realizing a non-violent social order . . .

QUESTION: The people are with us, but the Government obstruct[s] our effort. What are we to do?

GANDHIJI: If the people are with you, the Government[s] are bound to respond. If they do not, they will be set aside and another installed in their place . . .

QUESTION: Should there not be an overall organization, which would include and co-ordinate all the Sanghs' activities?

GANDHIJI: A separate organization is not necessary for that purpose . . .[10]

QUESTION: Why cannot we get it done through the Congress?

GANDHIJI: Because the Congressmen are not sufficiently interested in constructive work . . .[11] (CWMG XC, 1984: 215–21).

On 23 January 1948, Gandhi reflected on a scathing letter received by one Kanti Gandhi, who questioned several positions of Gandhi, particularly on Hindu–Muslim unity and the constructive programme (*Harijan,* February 1948). Regarding communal unity, Gandhi pointed out that it '. . . is not a new one. It has always been before the country as one of the pillars of national independence. Without it independence cannot last. This has been regarded as more or less axiomatic' (CWMG XC, 1984: 480). Unity is based on constructive work, which everyone must remember. The realization of it is possible through inclusion in every life, making it interesting by the way explaining it scientifically and discarding unintelligent mechanical work (CWMG XC, 1984: 480).

At the end of the biography of the text, the last item added to the *Constructive Programme*, 'Congress Position', needs some explanation. After writing 'Congress Position' on 27 January 1948, Gandhi also wrote/gave thirty-six letters/interviews till 30 January 1948, as per records available in CWMG XC. However, in neither the 'Congress Position' nor the subsequent thirty-six letters/interviews, Gandhi had explained Congress Position vis-à-vis the Constructive Programme or assured/promised to include it in the *Constructive Programme.*

Since the *Constructive Programme* is located outside the *defined space*, it is inconceivable to include 'Congress Position' in the *Constructive Programme*. At least Gandhi did not give any specific indication between 27 January 1948 and 30 January 1948 (the day of his assassination). The month of reprinting 10,000 copies is mentioned as March 1948. In other words, two appendices were included in the

Constructive Programme, which was published posthumously. Gandhi indicated the inclusion of the first appendix, with a slight variation and change in heading.

Regarding the second appendix, Gandhi did not give any indication but was included by the publisher in 1948. The Gandhi Heritage Portal provides the Gujarati version of the *Constructive Programme*[12] (રચનાત્મક કાર્યક્રમ : તેનું રહસ્ય અને સ્થાન, 1941) which was translated from the 1941 edition of the *Constructive Programme* written in English. The Hindi version appeared in 1946. The second edition was published in 1951, replicating the *Constructive Programme*'s English version, including appendices.[13] Gandhi's 'Congress Position' was soon followed by 'Draft Constitution' drafted by Gandhi.

Gandhi's 'Draft Constitution of Congress', 29 January 1948 (*Harijan,* 15 February 1948) was an interesting take on the political and the extraparliamentary.[14] In it, he puts forward some of the subtlest propositions. Congress was defined as a 'propaganda vehicle' and 'parliamentary machine' which had achieved political independence, thus outliving its use. India was yet to achieve 7,00,000 villages' social, moral and economic independence. The constrictive political space, which had 'outlived its utility' due to the exclusion of maximum people's social, moral and economic independence, needed to be replaced by 'maximum political', i.e. ascendancy of people. India's progress towards the democratic goal was linked with the ascendancy of the civil over the military and a rejection of unhealthy competition with political parties and communal bodies.

Remarkably, Gandhi did two things herein. Firstly, in the form of *Lok Sevak Sangh*, he proposed the democratization of political space by offering substantive grassroots democracy in which Panchayats had to synchronize themselves for massive election, selection and representation. Secondly, he did not abdicate the idea of everyday political or extra-institutional politics in the form of proposing ten rules for a member of the Lok Sevak Sangh. Some of the important signifiers for a member were 'khadi wearer, anti-untouchability, promoter of inter-communal unity, equality of all religions, equality of opportunity and status without recognition of race, creed and sex', 'maintaining personal contact with villagers', 'enrolling and training workers from villagers', 'developing self-sufficient villages through agriculture and handicrafts', 'educating sanitation and hygiene', and 'promotion of Nayee Talim in villages', 'helping to acquire legal and franchise rights' (CWMG XC, 1984: 526–28).

The crucial aspect of the 'draft' was its expansion of political space horizontally, which was impossible in liberal political space due to reliance on vertical political space.

The biography of the Constructive Programme unravels a slew of distinctive features. It can be called an immanent text.

Gandhi has been primarily understood by his three major texts (*Hind Swaraj or Indian Home Rule* (1909/1910);[15] *Satyagraha in South Africa* (1928); *An Autobiography Or, The Story of My Experiments with Truth* (1927/1929/1940).[16]

Several corresponding allusions are referred to from the corpora of writings known as *The Collected Works of Mahatma Gandhi 100 volumes*. Indeed, a holistic analysis of his postulations remains incomplete without his 'major' texts and further references to 'fragmentary' writings. These are accepted as a 'discourse' meant for the everlasting desire to achieve 'utopia' but will not be allowed by the state's infrastructure and superstructure as 'utopia' is possible and *required* only in the 'future' but not immediately and in the present. Nevertheless, the political right celebrates 'Gandhi discourse' as an unflinching signature of 'native greatness'.

More often than not, the liberal state and liberal political theory constantly refer to Gandhi's discourse for 'liberalism discourse' to declare institutional violence as an 'aberration' for the arrival of 'aesthetics' in democracy.[17] However, amidst major texts supported by fragmentary writings, another form is also available: *immanent text.* The immanent text appeals to *political action.*

Nevertheless, unlike the major texts, it remains marginalized due to its advocacy of immediacy in the course of political action. The *Constructive Programme* is an immanent text which offers an idea of 'extraparliamentary' in the form of political action in those areas which are not even considered sites of political action. In other words, liberal political theory designates some places as political sites in the form of institutionalisation/institutions wherefrom political action is supposed to be implemented. Gandhi's *Constructive Programme* breaks this *sui generis* pedestal of liberal political theory employing the extraparliamentary but also faces 'referential marginality'.

The distinction between major, fragmentary and immanent texts is crucial to invite attention to the subtle differences. Moreover, this division is crucial for mapping the significance of the *Constructive Programme*. In the endeavour of major texts, three postulations, among other things, acquire significance. These are 'narration of human condition', 'transformation of the human condition' and 'foundational principle of desired society/political community'. Even the engagement with *either one* could be the objective/pursuit of writers.

The vantage point of the 'narration of the human condition' is to explicate the severe deficiency in human beings' philosophical and empirical locations. The transformation of the human condition is about overcoming deficiency by using the most appropriate method or act. The ideation about transformation is *intrinsically* linked with identifying deficiencies in the human condition. Major texts also engage with foundational principles of desired society or nature of the political community.

In such texts, philosophical/intellectual integrity is presented rather than pursuing descriptive content or empirical detailing in the form of 'outlining bare laws'.

Fragmentary texts are either reflective writings or extensions of major texts. Both reflectivity and extension are written to highlight the major theoretical points or encapsulate minor issues in the larger framework. Due to hands-on philosophical needs, fragmentary writings may also appear as separate epithets. It may also be misleading due to very generic statements. Fragmentary writings are more or less generally epistemological than engaging with epistemological queries. It may be presented as an 'epistemological departure' of writers. This appends due to the 'delinked theorization' of writers from major texts. It must be noted that fragmentary writings have no independent existence without major texts. Major texts do exist with or without fragmentary writings, but it cannot be stated about fragmentary writings.

For the sustenance of the structure, normalization of paradox and inattention towards contradictions are required.

Immanent texts are engaged with fundamental questions. In an immanent text, the inner contradiction of the political community is surfaced. The surfacing of contradictions is meant to resolve the contradictions. Nevertheless, contradictions exist due to the presence of the structure.

For the sustenance of the structure, *normalization of paradox* and *inattention towards contradictions* are required. We live in a world where everyday paradoxes are normalized, and attention towards society's contradictions is in a forlon condition. These two become extremely important in the backdrop of the functioning of modern democracies. The contemporary world is one of the testimonies of the site of modern democracies. There are promises and struggles for pledges. Modern democracies acquire significance due to the greater need to fulfil concerted aspirations and democratize all walks of life.

The offer of liberal political theory and modern liberal democracies produces a complex phenomenon. There is an emphasis on the choice principle. The choice principle is mediated in the realm of political equality. However, even political equality is conditional. The choice principle is not available in the domain of socio-economic inequalities. Equality backed by the choice principle in the socio-economic domain is unconditionally denied. This happens through the *normalization of paradox* and *inattention towards contradictions.*

The normalization of paradox must invite attention.
Conditional choice in political equality is categorical. The political structure mediates people's aspirations by assigning itself disproportionate significance to decide the weightage of their aspirations. The choice principle is based on the need for the political structure to transmit people's aspirations into concrete outcomes. The political community is envisaged for the undiluted translation and transmission of people's aspirations. The problem starts when the political structures acquire a lexical significance over people's aspirations while asserting themselves in the form of a concrete and all-powerful domain.

Theoretically, people's aspiration is supreme. Nevertheless, an almighty political structure backed by socio-economic differential becomes an effective tool for people's life.

The people's aspirations undergo a mandatory regulatory framework in political equality. People's aspirations become valuable and legitimate only when it is proposed by a definite space and through constrained representation (both are crucial in liberal democracy and liberal political theory).

This is the classic case when 'political structure' (a definite space and constrained representation) becomes more significant than people's aspirations. In other words, issues are not important *ipso facto* (by the fact itself) but acquire value only by the outlined method of a definite space and constrained representation. Instead, the person and platform become crucial for the wider legitimacy of matters raised about the people by the people. A definite space and constrained representation syndrome have been intertwined with liberalism cogently since its inception. Therefore, the contemporary problem is not of *recent* origin, but the difference lies in degrees. The endorsement of the choice principle in political equality and methodological defence by the practice of a definite space and constrained representation is an important paradox. It has been normalized by not reminding the unbridgeable gap between the two.

In modern times, inattention to contradictions is celebrated.

By and large, modern democracies, particularly those with a liberal democratic framework, do not pay deliberate attention to contradictions. Concerning the contradictions, procedural political equality and socio-economic inequality coexist in modern liberal democracies. It does not invite questions about bringing parity between the two within liberal political theory. The fault line of this division is not discussed forthwith due to meticulous taking care of the non-deliberation by a definite space and constrained representation methodology. There is a separation between procedural political equality and socio-economic inequalities. Moreover, circumventing socio-economic inequalities in procedural political equality by a definite space and constrained representation creates the seeming condition for inattention towards contradictions.

The *normalization of paradox* and *inattention to contradictions* prevent the postulation and actualization of an egalitarian world by emphasizing mobilized being over participatory being. Reading the *Constructive Programme,* an immanent text and extraparliamentary is towards exploring this cogent possibility.

The immanent text makes it possible for two developments to take place.

Firstly, since the contradiction of the political community or the state/structure affects multi-layered realms, an emphasis on resolving the contradiction immediately activates a slew of realms. This leads to the creation of multi-spaces of politics. In other words, multi-spaces are being converted into political due to igniting the contradiction. Immanent text's immense contribution lies in treating political institutions as political and treating every sphere as a political sphere. The immanent text urges us to perceive everything in life as political, including the defined spaces of politics. This is the immense contribution of the immanent text.

Secondly, since contradictions are 'immanent' in the capitalist state, immanent texts *methodologically* adopt the centrifugal approach. In other words, it moves away from the system while engaging with the contradiction. The thrust is after converting several spaces into political spaces, and the issue is going out of the state. The immediacy in the immanent text is threatening in terms of latent potentiality for threatening the structure 'from within'.

Major texts and immanent texts must be read together. However, there is a fundamental difference between the two. Major texts represent a neat and clean presentation of alternative worlds. The ideational of an alternative political community is delineated in major texts. It appears almost a different system or a system which is juxtaposed to the existing political community. It appears to be a system from the outside or 'ideal outside'. The existing political system perceives the 'ideal outside' as a distant project; thus, 'rhetorical obeisance' becomes one harmless endeavour. On the other hand, major texts are being converted into 'utopia', which is likeable but not achievable. Therefore, 'likeable unachievable' becomes a rhetorical ploy for deferment of the question of much-needed transformation.

On the contrary, the immanent text, due to its immediacy, which constructs the numerous realms of the political along with the possibility of going out of the system, is sharp and obviously cannot be ignored by the state apparatus. Moreover, immanent texts cannot be construed as utopian texts as immediate concerns are put in place. Immanent texts are nothing but philosophy simplified of major texts in everydayness. The engagement with everydayness by an immanent text becomes a serious problem due to its cascading effect on the structure. Therefore, belittling or ignoring immanent texts becomes a tested method in the statist discourse.

Gandhi's three major texts are not only a necessary persistence but also a lifetime commitment. Therefore, despite the usual method of disdaining, rejecting or negating major texts, ruling classes also celebrate it for the constant postponement of the texts. The 'utopia' is celebrated not for the text's arrival but for the text's appropriation. The political right is a champion in this regard as to the celebration of 'swaraj' by divesting its meaning and practice. However, in the case of immanent text, even a reference is avoided due to its potential to create the political space and political subject immediately during the *imminent* crippling of the structure 'from within'.

Put differently, immanent text contravenes the liberal political theory or statist discourse. In the liberal political theory or statist discourse, contradictions are saved by the protracted realm of politics in terms of theory and practice. The accessibility to politics is limited to not engaging with paradoxes and contradictions. Conversely, the immanent text becomes the significant representation and carrier of extraparliamentary politics for the following reasons. It stresses 'thinking immediacy'. It appeals to 'resurfacing the contradictions'. The creation of multi-site or multiple space-led politics is proposed and pursued adamantly. Herein, every sphere is political in rejecting the binaries of 'inside' and 'outside' based notion of politics for legitimacy.

Most importantly, it adopts the centrifugal approach. The structure is attempted to be revamped incessantly from within while ensuring every possible move goes out of the structure and is replaced with the new one. In the case of the *Constructive Programme*, it is swaraj.

One of Gandhi's crucial and perhaps forgotten ideas is the extraparliamentary postulation which questions 'the sublime rigidities' of institutions.

Reading Gandhi's *Constructive Programme* as an extraparliamentary one becomes crucial to rejecting the constrictive principles of liberal political theory. The constrictive tendency of liberalism/liberal political theory allows democracy while normalizing fundamentalism, violence, communalism, caste atrocities, gendering and exploitation.

In other words, liberalism and illiberalism can coexist. There can be a liberal democracy and institutions with all illiberal practices. This is the paradox of liberal democracy. Sometimes, democracy is used for anti-democratic practices. This mismatch must be answered unequivocally. One of the ways could be to understand the manifestation of politics. In other words, *how often politics is manifested* and *by what means politics is manifested* must become guiding norms for critical analysis. Rigidities of deliberate protocols, norms and guarding rigidities of representation mar these two spaces in liberalism. Manifestation of politics becomes an occasional engagement. Means of manifestation of politics become the only 'authorized' and 'authenticated voice'. This is a sign of a constrictive tendency of politics that provides the 'occasional opportunity' for politics and permanent negation of non-authorized versions of politics.

Engaging with the *Constructive Programme* as the extraparliamentary offers to cement the idea of permanent opportunity for 'politics' and inclusion of a non-authorized (heterodox) version of politics. In other words, the construal of the *Constructive Programme* as extraparliamentary offers the permanency of politics, which does not require only occasions and authorized means of politics. Thus, rejecting the constrictive programme of politics becomes crucial in this schema.

Gandhi's *Constructive Programme* is based on a non-binary universalistic normative emphasis. The non-binary universalistic normative concerns the issues to be expressed for addressing and readdressing in a dialectical sense. The issues and contradictions cannot be status quo or relapsed. This can be done on an everyday basis and by everyone. The contents of the *Constructive Programme* may need a substantive addition or revision in the context of a slew of changes and alternatives. However, the idea of everydayness/everyone is an important component par excellence for rejecting the occasional manifestation of politics and authorized notion of politics—the idea and practice of extraparliamentary offer such opportunities.

The idea of extraparliamentary is generally associated with social movements or activities associated with non-state actors. The extraparliamentary is subject to a slew of interpretations. This study uses the concept in a definite sense where extraparliamentary does not work in isolation from parliamentary politics. Engagement, however, is aimed at changing the latter by exposing serious limitations and politizising everydayness. Extraparliamentary is 'political everydayness' for transformation.[18]

Can extraparliamentary be equated with satyagraha?

According to Gandhi, '[n]on-co-operation and civil disobedience are but different branches of the same tree called satyagraha' (CWMG XXV, 1967: 489). As a substantive and analytical category, satyagraha subsumes civil disobedience. The former is more elaborative and comprehensive, whereas the latter is more focused and limited.[19] Gandhi outlines 'the place of civil disobedience' in the *Constructive Programme*. Civil disobedience has three definite functions: redress local wrongs, self-immolation to rouse local consciousness and conscience and focus on definite issues. An elaborative constructive programme is not required for the first and the second.

Regarding the third, particularly in the context of independence, the constructive programme is crucial. In Gandhi's schema, civil disobedience or satyagraha is an organized endeavour. It must start and end with a specific concern or achievement. The constructive programme is an ongoing process. It is a process, not a finality. Gandhi conjoins the *Constructive Programme* and civil disobedience to make the latter more successful and effective. Civil disobedience cannot be effective without envisaging a slew of constructive programme activities. However, constructive programme as the process is also available with or without satyagraha/civil disobedience. Therefore, in place of naming it satyagraha/ civil disobedience, it can be called 'extraparliamentary' due to its overall presence in everyday political.

Can extraparliamentary be called beyond-parliamentary?

Gandhi's major texts offer substantive and required utopia. These texts offer a systematic critique and corresponding alternatives. Reading these texts suggests the arrival of a new world which could be superimposed on liberalism or liberal constitutionalism. Major texts do not wish to operate 'from within and disengage the existing structure'. Instead, they construct and fight for the 'valuable utopia' which needs to be materialized. In this way, major texts offer 'beyond parliamentary' formulation.

On the other hand, the immanent text engages existing structure from within in terms of continuous disrupting the centre while going out of the system in terms of metamorphosing it. It engages for change. It is immediately available. The extraparliamentary is not outside the parliamentary but is present to change the contour of it while going outside of the essence and substance of the parliamentary per se. In a nutshell, the engagement is towards transformational politics while going out from the centre.

The Constructive Programme *is based on the evolutionary episteme and horizontal struggles.*

The constructive programme must be understood regarding the 'evolutionary epistemic' and horizontal expansion. Extraparliamentary of constructive programme offers de-definite space and de-constrained representation. This means both must be informed by the evolutionary epistemic and horizontal expansion of struggle. Evolutionary epistemic end the incessant inclusion of issues responsible for human exploitation and humiliation. New venues of exploitation and means of humiliation must be included for an egalitarian world.

Issues cannot be static. The real purpose of the constructive programme is to overcome the limitation of liberal democracy. The purpose must be backed by bringing attention to new values of the neoliberal state and majoritarianism. Therefore, the inclusion of people in the *Constructive Programme* must be more horizontal regarding diversity and degree of engagement. Moreover, the dynamics of the *Constructive Programme* must be available for the everyday changing world. In other words, under changing circumstances, history, technology and world order, the constructive programme would have to evolve imaginatively to address old and new problems differently.[20]

The Constructive Programme *catapults politics as participation over politics as mobilization.*

The contemporary crisis of modern democracies is also due to the irresolution of the perpetual mechanism of keeping people away from participatory beings. Modern democracies, particularly in post-colonial societies, did not struggle enough to overcome the fault lines of liberal political theory and liberal polity. The liberal political theory offers a constrictive programme. The core of the constrictive programme is dividing people into participatory and mobilized beings. While making the socio-economic status quo comfortable, unchanged and unchallenged, the state prefers mobilized being over participatory being. The contour of polity likes mobilized being over participatory being for several reasons. The mobilized being is bereft of agency. The participatory being asserts its political agency. For mobilized beings, *politics as participation* is replaced by *politics as mobilzation.*

In this way, politics as participation is always kept away from mobilized beings. Separating mobilized beings and political structure is not innocuous but deliberate and categorical. This is to debar mobilized beings' role in the political structure. Mobilized being is required not only to protract the structure but also to sustain the structure. To put it more precisely, this polity has been divided into definite space and constrained representation. All forms of political activities must be channelized in this way. In other words, legitimate politics is through a definite space and constant representation. Though people may defy this logic, this method/model is accepted practice and expects hope from the state.

This is a severe lacuna in modern democracies. Earlier, the severity was not sufficiently realized due to the nature of political leadership shaped by exposure to some fragments of non-Weberian modern constitutionalism (curbing the state for unleashing violence legitimately or otherwise incessantly), which preaches the notion of restraint against its own people. The 'notion' of restraint against own people also remained disciplinary and ideological. The 'restraint' is also proposed as both benevolence and limit. Benevolence is conditional based on the 'limited' role of people. In the case of encroachment of the limit or threshold, the benevolence may be compromised. The transitory period of benevolence and compromised benevolence is a fundamental ideological weapon of the state for proposing a caring *res publica* (the state or related to the state).

The proposed caring contour results in restraints informed by minimum moralism. The seriousness is compounded when minimum moralism is stripped away by the res publica. The political leadership bereft of minimum moralism altogether abdicates the practice of 'restraint'. This creates the ubiquitous condition of the heebie-jeebies towards an anti-status quo political standpoint. Due to the enormous condition of the heebie-jeebies, the political per se or the contrary political perspective is not articulated. Therefore, the state of the heebie-jeebies paves the way for the condition of acquiescence. This is one of the verifiable components in the theatre of democracy. This ubiquitous concern is the elephant in the room which can be addressed *only* by asking, 'What happens to democracy when fear eclipses heterodox opinions?'.

The issue is more complicated. Since the beginning of liberal political theory, postulation and practice of definite space and constrained representation have kept people at bay from becoming participatory beings. People have become procedural consented being-cum-delegated being. The rigidities of definite space and constrained representation have done two enormous harms. First, it has created a large pool of people *only* available for mobilizing without realizing the significance of participation. Secondly, the condition of acquiescence obstructs the rejection/resistance of the subservient role in the res publica. Concerning the first harm, the un-realization of participatory values prevents taking a cogent standpoint on many issues. Some of the crucial issues can be located in Gandhi's *Constructive Programme* are communal unity, removal of untouchability, khadi, other village industries, village sanitation, basic education, adult education, women's question, education in health and hygiene, language question, economic equality, farmers, working-class, Adivasis, lepers and so on.

Concerning the second harm, the lack of political agency/political power and the absence of the urge to resist exploitation and humiliation for the alternative world paves the way for permanent entrapment—the sustenance of the status quo.

Such enormous complexities of liberal democracies need constant collective contemplation. The idea of de-definite political space and de-constrained representation is towards democratizing the polity and ameliorating the socio-economic condition. Against this backdrop, the extraparliamentary aphorism helps expand the space of politics and the ambit of representation.

Therefore, reading the immanent text, the *Constructive Programme*, helps us to understand the immense significance of activating participation immediately on substantive issues. Gandhi's extraparliamentary is neither based on civilizational superiority-led action nor binaries of 'us' vs 'they'. It activates everydayness.

Reading Gandhi's Constructive Programme *offers the opportunity to activate the idea of extraparliamentary for three specific purposes.*

Firstly, it does not keep people out of politics. Rather, in a substantive sense, politics become part of people in terms of participatory endeavours. This is not a lesser achievement in the backdrop of extreme centralization led by capital and state.

Secondly, the condition of the heebie-jeebies from politics is replaced by politics by participation. The heebie-jeebies from politics is inherent in the structure of modern democracies. This is inherent in mobilization per se. In the realm of mobilization realm, mobilization is an end itself. It is itself a process and also an end. It is both a beginning and an ending. This method and model have successfully generated legitimacy by the condition of the heebie-jeebies in place of consensual legitimacy through the participatory process. The fear of politics, specifically heterodox opinion, is not a new development. However, it has been accentuated on a larger scale. Participatory politics germinates the condition for the political self, which emphasizes unlimited space for doing politics and thinking of representation by themselves.

Thirdly, socio-economic inequalities and hierarchies invite everydayness, politicization and representation. Definite space and constrained representation obstruct the required attention and possibly undermine he issues of socio-economic disparities. The *Constructive Programme*-led extraparliamentary politics resurrects the issues by making people legitimate owners of political space and the substantive notion of representation. This serves the purpose of deliberative and participatory democracy.

It must be stated that the *Constructive Programme* is an immanent text which offers a significant understanding of the extraparliamentary. Being an immanent text, it provides immediacy. The conversion of immediacy takes place by rejecting a definite space of politics and constrained representation, which defines the liberal theory of politics. Instead, it offers a de-definite space of politics (expansion of political and interlinking with everydayness) and de-constrained representation (self-representation in place of 'technical representation').

CONSTRUCTIVE PROGRAMME

ITS MEANING AND PLACE

BY

M. K. GANDHI

CONTENTS

FOREWORD

This is a thoroughly revised edition of the "Constructive Programme" which I first wrote in 1941. The items included in it have not been arranged in any order, certainly not in the order of their importance. When the reader discovers that a particular subject though important in itself in terms of Independence does not find place in the programme, he should know that the omission is not intentional. He should unhesitantingly add to my list and let me know. My list does not pretend to be exhaustive; it is merely illustrative. The reader will see several new and important additions.

Readers, whether workers and volunteers or not, should definitely realize that the constructive programme is the truthful and non-violent way of winning Poorna Swaraj. Its wholesale fulfilment *is* complete Independence. Imagine all the forty crores of people busying themselves with the whole of the constructive programme which is designed to build up the nation from the very bottom upward. Can anybody dispute the proposition that it must mean complete Independence in every sense of the expression, including the ousting of foreign domination? When the critics laugh at the proposition, what they mean is that forty crores of people will never co-operate in the effort to fulfil the programme. No doubt, there is considerable truth in the scoff. My answer is, it is still worth the attempt. Given an indomitable will on the part of a band of earnest workers, the programme is as workable as any other and more so than most. Anyway, I have no substitute for it, if it is to be based on non-violence.

Civil Disobedience, mass or individual, is an aid to constructive effort and is a full substitute for armed revolt. Training is necessary as well for civil disobedience as for armed revolt. Only the ways are different. Action in either case takes place only when occasion demands. Training for military revolt means learning the use of arms ending perhaps in the atomic bomb. For civil disobedience it means the Constructive Programme.

Therefore, workers will never be on the look-out for civil resistance. They will hold themselves in readiness, if the constructive effort is sought to be defeated. From one or two illustrations it will be seen where it can be and, where it cannot be, offered. Political pacts we know have been and can be, but personal friendship with individuals cannot be, prevented. Such friendships, selfless and genuine, must be the basis for political pacts. Similarly, centralized *khadi* can be defeated by the Government, but no power can defeat individual manufacture and use of *khadi*. The manufacture and use of *khadi* must not be imposed upon the people, but it must be intelligently and willingly accepted by them as one of the items of the freedom movement. This can be done only from the villages as units. Pioneers even in such programmes can be obstructed. They have had to go through the fire of suffering throughout the world. There is no Swaraj without suffering. In violence, truth is the first and the greatest sufferer; in non-violence it is ever triumphant. Moreover, men composing the Government are not to be regarded as enemies. To regard them as such will be contrary to the non-violent spirit. Part we must, but as friends.

If this preliminary observation has gone home to the reader, he will find the constructive programme to be full of deep interest. It should prove as absorbing as politics so-called and platform oratory, and certainly more important and useful.

Poona, 13-11-1945   M.K. GANDHI

INTRODUCTORY

The constructive programme may otherwise and more fittingly be called construction of Poorna Swaraj or complete Independence by truthful and non-violent means.

Effort for construction of, Independence so called through violent and, therefore, necessarily untruthful means we know only too painfully. Look at the daily destruction of property, life, and truth in the present war.

Complete Independence through truth and non-violence means the independence of every unit, be it the humblest of the nation, without distinction of race, colour or creed. This independence is never exclusive. It is, therefore, wholly compatible with inter-dependence within or without. Practice will always fall short of the theory, even as the drawn line falls short of the theoretical line of Euclid. Therefore, complete Independence will be complete only to the extent of our approach in practice to truth and non-violence.

Let the reader mentally plan out the whole of the constructive programme, and he will agree with me that, if it could be successfully worked out, the end of it would be the Independence we want. Has not Mr. Amery[1] said that an agreement between the major parties, translated in my language, any agreement *after* communal unity which is only one item in the constructive programme, will be respected? We need not question his sincerity, for, if such unity is honestly, i.e., non-violently, attained, it will in itself contain the power to compel acceptance of the agreed demand.

On the other hand there is no such thing as an imaginary or even perfect definition of Independence through violence. For, it presupposes only ascendancy of that party of the nation which makes the most effective use of violence. In it perfect equality, economic or otherwise, is inconceivable.

But for my purpose, which is to convince the reader of the necessity of following out the constructive programme in the non-violent effort, the acceptance of my argument about the ineffectiveness of violence for the attainment of Independence is not required. The reader is welcome to the belief that Independence of the humblest unit is possible under a scheme of violence, if this effort enables him also to admit it is a certainty through the complete execution of the programme by the nation.

Let us now examine the items.

1

COMMUNAL UNITY[1]

Everybody is agreed about the necessity of this unity. But everybody does not know that unity does not mean political unity which may be imposed. It means an unbreakable heart unity. The first thing essential for achieving such unity is for every Congressman, whatever his religion may be, to represent in his own person Hindu, Muslim, Christian, Zoroastrian, Jew, etc., shortly, every Hindu and non-Hindu. He has to feel his identity with every one of the millions of the inhabitants of Hindustan.[2] In order to realize this, every Congressman will cultivate personal friendship with persons representing faiths other than his own. He should have the same regard for the other faiths as he has for his own.

In such a happy state of things there would be no disgraceful cry at the stations such as "Hindu water" and "Muslim water" or "Hindu tea" and "Muslim tea". There would be no separate rooms or pots for Hindus and non-Hindus in schools and colleges, no communal schools, colleges and hospitals. The beginning of such a revolution has to be made by Congressmen without any political motive behind the correct conduct. Political unity will be its natural fruit.

We have long been accustomed to think that power comes only through Legislative Assemblies. I have regarded this belief as a grave error brought about by inertia or hypnotism. A superficial study of British history has made us think that all power percolates to the people from parliaments. The truth is that power resides in the people and it is entrusted for the time being to those whom they may choose as their representatives. Parliaments have no power or even existence independently of the people. It has been my effort for the last twentyone years to convince the people of this simple truth. Civil Disobedience is the storehouse of power. Imagine a whole people unwilling to conform to the laws of the legislature, and prepared to suffer the consequences of non-compliance! They will bring the whole legislative and executive machinery to a standstill. The police and the military are of use to coerce minorities however powerful they may be. But no police or military coercion can bend the resolute will of a people who are out for suffering to the uttermost.

And parliamentary procedure is good only when its members are willing to conform to the will of the majority. In other words, it is fairly effective only among compatibles.

Here in India we have been pretending to work the parliamentary system under separate electorates which have created artificial incompatibles. Living unity can never come out of these artificial entities being brought together on a common platform.[3] Such legislatures may function. But they can only be a platform for wrangling and sharing the crumbs of power that may fall from rulers whoever they may be. These rule with a rod of iron, and prevent the opposing elements from flying at one another's throats. I hold the emergence of complete Independence to be an impossibility out of such a disgrace.

Though I hold such strong views, I have come to the conclusion that so long as there are undesirable candidates for elective bodies, Congress should put up candidates in order to prevent reactionaries from entering such bodies.

2

REMOVAL OF UNTOUCHABILITY[1]

At this time of the day it is unnecessary to dilate upon the necessity of the removal of this blot and curse[2] upon Hinduism. Congressmen have certainly done much in this matter. But I am sorry to have to say that many Congressmen have looked upon this item as a mere political necessity and not something indispensable, so far as Hindus are concerned, for the very existence of Hinduism[3]. If Hindu Congressmen take up the cause for its own sake, they will influence the so-called *Sanatanis* far more extensively than they have hitherto done. They should approach them not in a militant spirit but, as befits their non-violence, in a spirit of friendliness. And so far as the Harijans[4] are concerned, every Hindu should make common cause with them and befriend them in their awful isolation—such isolation as perhaps the world has never seen in the monstrous immensity one witnesses in India.[5] I know from experience how difficult the task is. But it is part of the task of building the edifice of Swaraj. And the road to Swaraj is steep and narrow. There are many slippery ascents and many deep chasms. They have all to be negotiated with unfaltering step before we can reach the summit and breathe the fresh air of freedom.[6]

3

PROHIBITION[1]

Although like communal unity and removal of untouchability prohibition has been on the Congress programme since 1920, Congressmen have not taken the interest they might have taken in this very vital social and moral reform. If we are to reach our goal through non-violent effort, we may not leave to the future government the fate of lakhs of men and women who are labouring under the curse of intoxicants and narcotics.

Medical men can make a most effective contribution towards the removal of this evil. They have to discover ways of weaning the drunkard and the opium-addict from the curse.

Women and students have a special opportunity in advancing this reform. By many acts of loving service they can acquire on addicts a hold which will compel them to listen to the appeal to give up the evil habit.

Congress committees can open recreation booths where the tired labourer will rest his limbs, get healthy and cheap refreshments, find suitable games.[2] All this work is fascinating and uplifting. The non-violent approach to Swaraj is a novel approach. In it old values give place to new. In the violent way such reforms may find no place. Believers in that way, in their impatience and, shall I say, ignorance, put off such things to the day of deliverance. They forget that lasting and healthy deliverance comes from within, i.e. from self-purification. Constructive workers make legal prohibition easy and successful even if they do not pave the way for it.

4

KHADI[1]

Khadi is a controversial subject. Many people think that in advocating *khadi* I am sailing against a head-wind and am sure to sink the ship of Swaraj and that I am taking the country to the dark ages. I do not propose to argue the case for *khadi* in this brief survey. I have argued it sufficiently elsewhere. Here I want to show what every Congressman, and for that matter every Indian, can do to advance the cause of *khadi*. It connotes the beginning of economic freedom and equality of all in the country.[2] "The proof of the pudding is in the eating".[3] Let everyone try, and he or she will find out for himself or herself the truth of what I am saying. *Khadi* must be taken with all its implications. It means a wholesale swadeshi mentality, a determination to find all the necessaries of life in India and that too through the labour and intellect of the villagers.[4] That means a reversal of the existing process. That is to say that, instead of half a dozen cities of India and Great Britain living on the exploitation and the ruin of the 700,000 villages of India, the latter will be largely self-contained, and will voluntarily serve the cities of

India and even the outside world in so far as it benefits both the parties.

This needs a revolutionary change in the mentality and tastes of many. Easy though the non-violent way is in many respects, it is very difficult in many others. It vitally touches the life of every single Indian, makes him feel aglow with the possession of a power that has lain hidden within himself, and makes him proud of his identity with every drop of the ocean of Indian humanity. This non-violence is not the inanity for which we have mistaken it through all these long ages; it is the most potent force as yet known to mankind and on which its very existence is dependent. It is that force which I have tried to present to the Congress and through it to the world. *Khadi* to me is the symbol of unity of Indian humanity, of its economic freedom and equality and, therefore, ultimately, in the poetic expression of Jawaharlal Nehru, "the livery of India's freedom".[5]

Moreover, *khadi* mentality means decentralization of the production and distribution of the necessaries of life. Therefore, the formula so far evolved is, every village to produce all its necessaries and a certain percentage in addition for the requirements of the cities.[6]

Heavy industries will needs be centralized and nationalized. But they will occupy the least part of the vast national activity which will mainly be in the villages.

Having explained the implications of *khadi*, I must indicate what Congressmen can and should do towards its promotion. Production of *khadi* includes cotton growing, picking, ginning, cleaning, carding, slivering, spinning, sizing, dyeing, preparing the warp and the woof, weaving, and washing. These, with the exception of dyeing, are essential processes. Every one of them can be effectively handled in the villages and is being so handled in many villages throughout India which the A.I.S.A. is covering.[7] According to the latest report the following are the interesting figures:

275,146 villagers, including 19,645 Harijans and 57,378 Muslims, scattered in at least 13,451 villages, received, as spinners, weavers, etc. Rs. 3,485,609 in 1940. The spinners were largely women.[8]

Yet the work done is only one-hundredth part of what could be done if Congressmen honestly took up the *khadi* programme. Since the wanton destruction of this central village industry and the allied handicrafts, intelligence and brightness have fled from the villages, leaving them inane, lustreless, and reduced almost to the state of their ill-kept cattle.

If Congressmen will be true to their Congress call in respect of *khadi*, they will carry out the instructions of the A.I.S.A. issued from time to time as to the part they can play in *khadi* planning. Only a few broad rules can be laid down here:

1. Every family with a plot of ground can grow cotton at least for family use. Cotton growing is an easy process. In Bihar the cultivators were by law compelled to grow indigo on 3/20 of their cultivable land. This was in the

interest of the foreign indigo planter.[9] Why cannot we grow cotton voluntarily for the nation on a certain portion of our land? The reader will note that decentralization commences from the beginning of the *khadi* processes. Today cotton crop is centralized and has to be sent to distant parts of India. Before the war it used to be sent principally to Britain and Japan. It was and still is a money crop and, therefore, subject to the fluctuations of the market. Under the *khadi* scheme cotton-growing becomes free from this uncertainty and gamble. The grower grows what he needs. The farmer needs to know that his first business is to grow for his own needs. When he does that, he will reduce the chance of a low market ruining him.

2. Every spinner would buy—if he has not his own—enough cotton for ginning, which he can easily do without the hand-ginning roller frame. He can gin his own portion with a board and an iron rolling pin. Where this is considered impracticable, hand-ginned cotton should be bought and carded. Carding for self can be done well on a tiny bow without much effort. The greater the decentralization of labour, the simpler and cheaper the tools. The slivers made, the process of spinning commences. I strongly recommend the *dhanush takli*.[10] I have used it frequently. My speed on it is almost the same as on the wheel. I draw a finer thread and the strength and evenness of the yarn are greater on the *dhanush takli* than on the wheel. This may not,

however, hold good for all. My emphasis on the *dhanush takli* is based on the fact that it is more easily made, is cheaper than and does not require frequent repairs like the wheel. Unless one knows how to make the two *mals*[11] and to adjust them when they slip or to put the wheel right when it refuses to work, the wheel has often to lie idle. Moreover, if the millions take to spinning at once, as they well may have to, the *dhanush takli*, being the instrument most easily made and handled, is the only tool that can meet the demand. It is more easily made even than the simple *takli*. The best, easiest and cheapest way is to make it oneself. Indeed one ought to learn how to handle and make simple tools. Imagine the unifying and educative effect of the whole nation simultaneously taking part in the processes up to spinning! Consider the levelling effect of the bond of common labour between the rich and the poor!

Yarn thus produced may be used in three ways: by presenting it to the A.I.S.A for the sake of the poor, by having it woven for personal use, or by getting as much *khadi* for it as it can buy. It is clear enough that the finer and better the yarn the greater will be its value. If Congressmen will put their heart into the work, they will make improvements in the tools and make many discoveries. In our country there has been a divorce between labour and intelligence.[12] The result has been stagnation. If there is an indissoluble marriage between the two, and that in the manner here suggested, the resultant good will be inestimable.

In this scheme of nation-wide spinning as a sacrifice, I do not expect the average man or woman to give more than one hour daily to this work.

5

OTHER VILLAGE INDUSTRIES[1]

These stand on a different footing from *khadi*: There is not much scope for voluntary labour in them. Each industry will take the labour of only a certain number of hands. These industries come in as a handmaid to *khadi*. They cannot exist without *khadi*, and *khadi* will be robbed of its dignity without them. Village economy cannot be complete without the essential village industries such as hand-grinding, hand-pounding, soap-making, paper-making, match-making, tanning, oil-pressing, etc. Congressmen can interest themselves in these and, if they are villagers or will settle down in villages, they will give these industries a new life and a new dress. All should make it a point of honour to use only village articles whenever and wherever available. Given the demand there is no doubt that most of our wants can be supplied from our villages. When we have become village-minded, we will not want imitations of the West or machine-made products, but we will develop a true national taste in keeping with the vision of a new India in which pauperism, starvation and idleness will be unknown.[2]

6

VILLAGE SANITATION[1]

Divorce between intelligence and labour[2] has resulted in criminal negligence of the villages. And so, instead of having graceful hamlets dotting the land, we have dung-heaps. The approach to many villages is not a refreshing experience. Often one would like to shut one's eyes and stuff one's nose; such is the surrounding dirt and offending smell.[3] If the majority of Congressmen were derived from our villages, as they should be, they should be able to make our villages models of cleanliness in every sense of the word.[4] But they have never considered it their duty to identify themselves with the villagers in their daily lives. A sense of national or social sanitation is not a virtue among us. We may take a kind of a bath, but we do not mind dirtying the well or the tank or the river by whose side or in which we perform ablutions. I regard this defect as a great vice which is responsible for the disgraceful state of our villages and the sacred banks of the sacred rivers and for the diseases that spring from insanitation.[5]

7

NEW OR BASIC EDUCATION[1]

This is a new subject. But the members of the Working Committee felt so much interested in it that they gave a charter to the organizers of the Hindustani Talimi Sangh which has been functioning since the Haripura session.[2] This is a big field of work for many Congressmen. This education is meant to transform village children into model villagers. It is principally designed for them. The inspiration for it has come from the villages.[3] Congressmen who want to build up the structure of Swaraj from its very foundation dare not neglect the children. Foreign rule has unconsciously, though none the less surely, begun with the children in the field of education. Primary education is a farce designed without regard to the wants of the India of the villages and for that matter even of the cities. Basic education links the children, whether of the cities or the villages, to all that is best and lasting in India. It develops both the body and the mind, and keeps the child rooted to the soil with a glorious vision of the future in the realization of which he or she begins to take his or her share from the very commencement of his or her career in school. Congressmen would find it of absorbing interest benefiting themselves equally with the children with whom they come in contact. Let those who wish, put themselves in touch with the Secretary of the Sangh at Sevagram.[4]

8

ADULT EDUCATION[1]

This has been woefully neglected by Congressmen. Where they have not neglected it, they have been satisfied with teaching illiterates to read and write. If I had charge of adult education, I should begin with opening the minds of the adult pupils to the greatness and vastness of their country. The villager's India is contained in his village. If he goes to another village, he talks of his own village as his home. Hindustan is for him a geographical term. We have no notion of the ignorance prevailing in the villages. The villagers know nothing of foreign rule and its evils. What little knowledge they have picked up fills them with the awe the foreigner inspires. The result is the dread and hatred of the foreigner and his rule. They do not know how to get rid of it. They do not know that the foreigner's presence is due to their own weaknesses and their ignorance of the power they possess to rid themselves of the foreign rule. My adult education means, therefore, first, true political education of the adult by word of mouth. Seeing that this will be mapped out, it can be given without fear. I imagine that it is too late in the day for authority to interfere with this type of education; but if there is interference, there must be a fight for this elementary right without which there can be no Swaraj. Of course, in all I have written, openness has been assumed. Non-violence abhors fear and, therefore, secrecy. Side by side with the education by the mouth will be the literary education. This is itself a specialty. Many methods are being tried in order to shorten the period of education. A temporary or permanent board of experts may be appointed by the Working Committee to give shape to the idea here adumbrated and guide the workers. I admit that what I have said in this paragraph only points the way but does not tell the average Congressman how to go about it. Nor is every Congressman fitted for this highly special work. But Congressmen who are teachers should find no difficulty in laying down a course in keeping with the suggestions made herein.[2]

9

WOMEN[1]

I have included service of women in the constructive programme, for though *satyagraha* has automatically brought India's women out from their darkness, as nothing else could have in such an incredibly short space of time, Congressmen have not felt the call to see that women became equal partners in the fight for Swaraj. They have not realized that woman must be the true helpmate of man in the mission of service. Woman has been suppressed under custom and law for which man was responsible and in the shaping of which she had no hand. In a plan of life based on non-violence, woman has as much right to shape her own destiny as man has to shape his. But as every right in a non-violent society proceeds from the previous performance of a duty, it follows that rules of social conduct must be framed by mutual co-operation and consultation. They can never be imposed from outside. Men have not realized this truth in its fullness in their behaviour towards women. They have considered themselves to be lords and masters of women instead of considering them as their friends and co-workers. It is the privilege of Congressmen to give the women of India a lifting hand. Women are in the position somewhat of the slave of old who did not know that he could or ever had to be free. And when freedom came, for the moment he felt helpless. Women have been taught to regard themselves as slaves of men. It is up to Congressmen to see that they enable them to realize their full status and play their part as equals of men.

This revolution is easy, if the mind is made up. Let Congressmen begin with their own homes. Wives should not be dolls and objects of indulgence, but should be treated as honoured comrades in common service. To this end those who have not received a liberal education should receive such instruction as is possible from their husbands. The same observation applies, with the necessary changes, to mothers and daughters.[2]

It is hardly necessary to point out that I have given a one-sided picture of the helpless state of India's women. I am quite conscious of the fact that in the villages generally they hold their own with their men folk and in some respects even rule them. But to the impartial outsider the legal and customary status of woman is bad enough throughout and demands radical alteration.[3]

10

EDUCATION IN HEALTH AND HYGIENE[1]

Having given a place to village sanitation, the question
may be asked why give a separate place to education
in health and hygiene? It might have been bracketed with
sanitation, but I did not wish to interfere with the items.
Mention of mere sanitation is not enough to include
health and hygiene. The art of keeping one's health and the
knowledge of hygiene is by itself a separate subject of study
and corresponding practice. In a well-ordered society the
citizens know and observe the laws of health and hygiene. It
is established beyond doubt that ignorance and neglect of the
laws of health and hygiene are responsible for the majority of
diseases to which mankind is heir. The very high death rate
among us is no doubt due largely to our gnawing poverty,
but it could be mitigated if the people were properly educated
about health and hygiene.

Mens sana in corpore sano is perhaps the first law for
humanity. A healthy mind in a healthy body is a self-evident
truth. There is an inevitable connection between mind and
body. If we were in possession of healthy minds, we would

shed all violence and, naturally obeying the laws of health, we would have healthy bodies without an effort. I hope, therefore, that no Congressman will disregard this item of the constructive programme. The fundamental laws of health and hygiene are simple and easily learnt. The difficulty is about their observance. Here are some:

Think the purest thoughts and banish all idle and impure thoughts.

Breathe the freshest air day and night.

Establish a balance between bodily and mental work.

Stand erect, sit erect, and be neat and clean in every one of your acts, and let these be an expression of your inner condition.

Eat to live for service of fellow-men. Do not live for indulging yourselves. Hence your food must be just enough to keep your mind and body in good order. Man becomes what he eats.

Your water, food and air must be clean, and you will not be satisfied with mere personal cleanliness, but you will infect your surroundings with the same threefold cleanliness that you will desire for yourselves.[2]

11

PROVINCIAL LANGUAGES[1]

Our love of the English language in preference to our own mother tongue has caused a deep chasm between the educated and politically-minded classes and the masses. The languages of India have suffered impoverishment. We flounder when we make the vain attempt to express abstruse thought in the mother tongue. There are no equivalents for scientific terms. The result has been disastrous. The masses remain cut off from the modern mind. We are too near our own times correctly to measure the disservice caused to India by this neglect of its great languages. It is easy enough to understand that, unless we undo the mischief, the mass mind must remain imprisoned. The masses can make no solid contribution to the construction of Swaraj.[2] It is inherent in Swaraj based on non-violence that every individual makes his own direct contribution to the Independence movement. The masses can not do this fully unless they understand every step with all its implications.[3] This is impossible unless every step is explained in their own languages.[4]

12

NATIONAL LANGUAGE[1]

And then for all-India intercourse we need, from among the Indian stock, a language which the largest number of people already know and understand and which the others can easily pick up. This language is indisputably Hindi. It is spoken and understood by both Hindus and Muslims of the North. It is called Urdu when it is written in the Urdu character. The Congress, in its famous resolution passed at the Cawnpore session in 1925, called this all-India speech Hindustani.[2] And since that time, in theory at least, Hindustani has been the Rashtra Bhasha. I say 'in theory' because even Congressmen have not practised it as they should have. In 1920 a deliberate attempt was begun to recognize the importance of Indian languages for the political education of the masses, as also of an all-India common speech which politically-minded India could easily speak and which Congressmen from the different provinces could understand at all-India gatherings of the Congress. Such National language should enable one to understand and speak both forms of speech and write in both the scripts.

I am sorry to have to say that many Congressmen have failed to carry out that resolution. And so we have, in my opinion, the shameful spectacle of Congressmen insisting on speaking in English and compelling others to do likewise for their sakes. The spell that English has cast on us is not yet broken. Being under it, we are impeding the progress of India towards her goal. Our love of the masses must be skin-deep, if we will not take the trouble of spending over learning Hindustani as many months as the years we spend over learning English.[3]

13

ECONOMIC EQUALITY[1]

This last is the master key to non-violent Independence. Working for economic equality means abolishing the eternal conflict between capital and labour. It means the levelling down of the few rich in whose hands is concentrated the bulk of the nation's wealth on the one hand, and the leveling up of the semi-starved naked millions on the other. A non-violent system of government is clearly an impossibility so long as the wide gulf between the rich and the hungry millions persists. The contrast between the palaces of New Delhi and the miserable hovels of the poor labouring class nearby cannot last one day in a free India in which the poor will enjoy the same power as the richest in the land. A violent and bloody revolution is a certainty one day unless there is a voluntary abdication of riches and the power that riches give and sharing them for the common good.

I adhere to my doctrine of trusteeship in spite of the ridicule that has been poured upon it. It is true that it is difficult to reach. So is non-violence. But we made up our minds in 1920 to negotiate that steep ascent. We have found it worth the effort. It involves a daily growing appreciation of the working of non-violence. It is expected that Congressmen will make a diligent search and reason out for themselves the why and the wherefore of non-violence. They should ask themselves how the existing inequalities can be abolished violently or non-violently. I think we know the violent way. It has not succeeded anywhere.

This non-violent experiment is still in the making. We have nothing much yet to show by way of demonstration. It is certain, however, that the method has begun to work though ever so slowly in the direction of equality. And since non-violence is a process of conversion, the conversion, if achieved, must be permanent. A society or a nation constructed non-violently must be able to withstand attack upon its structure from without or within. We have moneyed Congressmen in the organization. They have to lead the way. This fight provides an opportunity for the closest heart-searching on the part of every individual Congressman. If ever we are to achieve equality, the foundation has to be laid now. Those who think that the major reforms will come after the advent of Swaraj are deceiving themselves as to the elementary working of non-violent Swaraj. It will not drop from heaven all of a sudden one fine morning. But it has to be built up brick by brick by corporate self-effort. We have travelled a fair way in that direction. But a much longer and weary distance has to be covered before we can behold Swaraj in its glorious majesty. Every Congressman has to ask himself what he has done towards the attainment of economic equality.[2]

14

KISANS

The programme is not exhaustive. Swaraj is a mighty structure. Eighty crores of hands have to work at building it. Of these *kisans*, i.e. the peasantry are the largest part. In fact, being the bulk of them (probably over 80%) the *kisans* should be the Congress. But they are not. When they become conscious of their non-violent strength, no power on earth can resist them.

They must not be used for power politics. I consider it to be contrary to the non-violent method. Those who would know my methods of organizing *kisans* may profitably study the movement in Champaran when *satyagraha* was tried for the first time in India with the result all India knows. It became a mass movement which remained wholly non-violent from start to finish. It affected over twenty lakhs of *kisans*. The struggle centred round one specific grievance which was a century old. There had been several violent revolts to get rid of the grievance. The *kisans* were suppressed. The non-violent remedy succeeded in full in six months. The *kisans* of Champaran became politically conscious without any direct effort. The tangible proof they had of the working of non-violence to remove their grievance drew them to the Congress, and led by Babu Brijkishoreprasad and Babu Rajendraprasad they gave a good account of themselves during the past Civil Disobedience campaigns.[1]

The reader may also profitably study the *kisan* movements in Kheda,[2] Bardoli[3] and Borsad.[4] The secret of success lies in a refusal to exploit the *kisans* for political purpose outside their own personal and felt grievances. Organization round a specific wrong they understand. They need no sermons on non-violence. Let them learn to apply non-violence as an effective remedy which they can understand, and later when they are told that the method they were applying was non-violent, they readily recognize it as such.

From these illustrations Congressmen who care could study how work can be done for and among *kisans*. I hold that the method that some Congressmen have followed to organize *kisans* has done them no good and has probably harmed them. Anyway they have not used the non-violent method. Be it said to the credit of some of these workers that they frankly admit that they do not believe in the non-violent method. My advice to such workers would be that they should neither use the Congress name nor work as Congressmen.

The reader will now understand why I have refrained from the competition to organize *Kisans* and Labour on an all-India basis. How I wish that all hands pulled in the same direction! But perhaps in a huge country like ours it is impossible. Anyway, in non-violence there is no coercion.

Cold reason and demonstration of the working of non-violence must be trusted to do the work.

In my opinion, like labour, they should have under the Congress, a department working for their specific questions.[5]

15

LABOUR

Ahmedabad Labour Union[1] is a model for all India to copy. Its basis is non-violence, pure and simple. It has never had a set-back in its career. It has gone on from strength to strength without fuss and without show. It has its hospital, its schools for the children of the mill-hands, its classes for adults, its own printing press and *khadi* depot, and its own residential quarters. Almost all the hands are voters and decide the fate of elections. They came on the voters' list at the instance of the Provincial Congress Committee. The organization has never taken part in party politics of the Congress. It influences the municipal policy of the city. It has to its credit very successful strikes which were wholly non-violent. Millowners and labour have governed their relations largely through voluntary arbitration. If I had my way, I would regulate all the labour organizations of India after the Ahmedabad model. It has never sought to intrude itself upon the All-India Trade Union Congress and has been uninfluenced by that Congress. A time, I hope, will come when it will be possible for the Trade Union Congress to accept the Ahmedabad method and have the Ahmedabad organization as part of the All-India Union. But I am in no hury. It will come in its own time.[2]

16

ADIVASIS[1]

The term *adivasi*, like *raniparaj*, is a coined word. *Raniparaj* stands for *kaliparaj* (meaning black people, though their skin is no more black than that of any other). It was coined, I think by Shri Jugatram. The term *adivasi* (for Bhils, Gonds, or others variously described as Hill Tribes or aboriginals) means literally original inhabitants[2] and was coined, I believe, by Thakkar Bapa.[3]

Service of *adivasis* is also a part of the constructive programme. Though they are the sixteenth number in this programme, they are not the least in point of importance. Our country is so vast and the races so varied that the best of us cannot know all there is to know of men and their condition. As one discovers this for oneself, one realizes how difficult it is to make good our claim to be one nation, unless every unit has a living consciousness of being one with every other.

The *adivasis* are over two crores in all India. Bapa began work among the Bhils years ago in Gujarat. In about 1940

Shri Balasaheb Kher threw himself with his usual zeal into this much-needed service in the Thana District. He is now President of the Adivasi Seva Mandal.

There are several such other workers in other parts of India and yet they are too few. Truly, "the harvest is rich but the labourers are few".[4] Who can deny that all such service is not merely humanitarian but solidly national, and brings us nearer to true independence?[5]

17

LEPERS[1]

Leper is a word of bad odour. India is perhaps a home of lepers next only to Central Africa. Yet they are as much a part of society as the tallest among us. But the tall absorb our attention though they are least in need of it. The lot of the lepers who are much in need of attention is studied neglect. I am tempted to call it heartless, which it certainly is, in terms of non-violence. It is largely the missionary who, be it said to his credit, bestows care on him. The only institution run by an Indian, as a pure labour of love, is by Shri Manohar Diwan near Wardha. It is working under the inspiration and guidance of Shri Vinoba Bhave. If India was pulsating with new life, if we were all in earnest about winning independence in the quickest manner possible by truthful and non-violent means, there would not be a leper or beggar in India uncared for and unaccounted for. In this revised edition I am deliberately introducing the leper as a link in the chain of constructive effort. For, what the leper is in India, that we are, if we will but look about us, for the modern civilized world. Examine the condition of our brethren across the ocean and the truth of my remark will be borne home to us.[2]

18

STUDENTS[1]

I have reserved students to the last. I have always cultivated close contact with them. They know me and I know them. They have given me service. Many ex-collegians are my esteemed co-workers. I know that they are the hope of the future. In the heyday of non-co-operation they were invited to leave their schools and colleges. Some professors and students who responded to the Congress call have remained steadfast and gained much for the country and themselves.[2] The call has not been repeated for there is not the atmosphere for it. But experience has shown that the lure of the current education, though it is false and unnatural, is too much for the youth of the country. College education provides a career. It is a passport for entrance to the charmed circle. Pardonable hunger for knowledge cannot be satisfied otherwise than by going through the usual rut. They do not mind the waste of precious years in acquiring knowledge of an utterly foreign language which takes the place of the mother tongue. The sin of it is never felt. They and their teachers have made up their minds that the indigenous languages are useless for gaining access to modern thought and the modern sciences. I wonder how the Japanese are faring. For, their education, I understand, is all given in Japanese. The Chinese Generalissimo[3] knows very little, if anything, of English.[4]

But such as the students are, it is from these young men and women that the future leaders of the nation are to rise. Unfortunately they are acted upon by every variety of influences. Non-violence offers them little attraction. A blow for a blow or two for one is an easily understandable proposition. It seems to yield immediate result though momentary. It is a never-ending trial of brute strength as we see in time of war among brutes or among human beings. Appreciation of non-violence means patient research and still more patient and difficult practice. I have not entered the list of competitors for the students' hand, for the reasons that have dictated my course about Kisans and Labour. But I am myself a fellow student, using the word in its broader sense. My university is different from theirs. They have a standing invitation from me to come to my university and join me in my search. Here are the terms:

1. Students must not take part in party politics. They are students, searchers, not politicians.[5]
2. They may not resort to political strikes. They must have their heroes, but their devotion to them is to be shown by copying the best in their heroes, not by going on strikes, if the heroes are imprisoned or die or are even sent to the gallows. If their grief is unbearable and if all the students feel equally, schools or colleges may be closed on such

occasions, with the consent of their principals. If the principals will not listen, it is open to the students to leave their institutions in a becoming manner till the managers repent and recall them. On no account may they use coercion against dissentients or against the authorities. They must have the confidence that, if they are united and dignified in their conduct, they are sure to win.

3. They must all do sacrificial spinning in a scientific manner. Their tools shall be always neat, clean, and in good order and condition. If possible, they will learn to make them themselves. Their yarn will naturally be of the highest quality. They will study the literature about spinning with all its economic, social, moral and political implications.

4. They will be *khadi*-users all through and use village products to the exclusion of all analogous things, foreign or machine-made.

5. They may not impose *Vande Mataram* or the National Flag on others. They may wear National Flag buttons on their own persons but not force others to do the same.

6. They can enforce the message of the tricolour flag in their own persons and harbour neither communalism nor untouchability in their hearts. They will cultivate real friendship with students of other faiths and with Harijans as if they were their own kith and kin.

7. They will make it a point to give first aid to their injured neighbours and do scavenging and cleaning in the neighbouring villages and instruct village children and adults.

8.   They will learn the national language, Hindustani, in its present double dress, two forms of speech and two scripts, so that they may feel at home whether Hindi or Urdu is spoken and *nagari* or *urdu* script is written.

9.   They will translate into their own mother tongue every thing new they may learn, and transmit it in their weekly rounds to the surrounding villages.

10. They will do nothing in secret, they will be above board in all their dealings, they will lead a pure life of self-restraint, shed all fear and be always ready to protect their weak fellow-students, and be ready to quell riots by non-violent conduct at the risk of their lives. And when the final heat of the struggle comes they will leave their institutions and, if need be, sacrifice themselves for the freedom of their country.

11. They will be scrupulously correct and chivalrous in their behaviour towards their girl fellow-students.

For working out the programme I have sketched for them, the students must find time. I know that they waste a great deal of time in idleness. By strict economy, they can save many hours. But I do not want to put an undue strain upon any student. I would, therefore, advise patriotic students to lose one year, not at a stretch but spread it over their whole study. They will find that one year so given will not be a waste of time. The effort will add to their equipment, mental, moral and physical, and they will have made even during their studies it substantial contribution to the freedom movement.[6]

PLACE OF CIVIL DISOBEDIENCE[1]

I have said in these pages that Civil Disobedience is not absolutely necessary to win freedom through purely non-violent effort, if the co-operation of the whole nation is secured in the constructive programme. But such good luck rarely favours nations or individuals. Therefore, it is necessary to know the place of Civil Disobedience in a nation-wide non-violent effort.

It has three definite functions:

1. It can be effectively offered for the redress of a local wrong.
2. It can be offered without regard to effect, though aimed at a particular wrong or evil, by way of self-immolation in order to rouse local consciousness or conscience. Such was the case in Champaran when I offered Civil Disobedience without any regard to the effect and well knowing that even the people might remain apathetic. That it proved otherwise may be taken, according to taste, as God's grace or a stroke of good luck.

3. In the place of full response to constructive effort, it can be offered as it was in 1941. Though it was a contribution to and part of the battle for freedom, it was purposely centered round a particular issue, i.e. free speech. Civil Disobedience can never be directed for a general cause such as for Independence. The issue must be definite and capable of being clearly understood and within the power; of the opponent to yield. This method properly applied must lead to the final goal.

I have not examined here the full scope and possibilities of Civil Disobedience. I have touched enough of it to enable the reader to understand the connection between the constructive programme and Civil Disobedience. In the first two cases, no elaborate constructive programme was or could be necessary. But when Civil Disobedience is itself devised for the attainment of Independence, previous preparation is necessary, and it has to be backed by the visible and conscious effort of those who are engaged in the battle. Civil Disobedience is thus a stimulation for the fighters and a challenge to the opponent. It should be clear to the reader that Civil Disobedience in terms of Independence without the co-operation of the millions by way of constructive effort is mere bravado and worse than useless.[2]

CONCLUSION

This is not a thesis written on behalf of the Congress or at the instance of the Central Office. It is the outcome of conversations I had with some co-workers in Sevagram. They had felt the want of something from my pen showing the connection between constructive programme and Civil Disobedience and how the former might be worked. I have endeavoured to supply the want in this pamphlet. It does not purport to be exhaustive, but it is sufficiently indicative of the way the programme should be worked.

Let not the reader make the mistake of laughing at any of the items as being part of the movement for Independence. Many people do many things, big and small, without connecting them with non-violence or Independence. They have then their limited value as expected. The same man appearing as a civilian may be of no consequence, but appearing in his capacity as General he is a big personage, holding the lives of millions at his mercy. Similarly, the *charkha* in the hands of a poor widow brings a paltry pice to her, in the hands of Jawaharlal it is an instrument of India's freedom. It is the office which gives the *charkha* its dignity.

It is the office assigned to the constructive programme which gives it an irresistible prestige and power.

Such at least is my view. It may be that of a mad man. If it makes no appeal to the Congressman, I must be rejected. For my handling of Civil Disobedience without the constructive programme will be like a paralysed hand attempting to lift a spoon.

Poona,13-11-1945

APPENDICES

I

IMPROVEMENT OF CATTLE

[This is what Gandhiji wrote sometime ago about adding *Goseva* as one more item in the Constructive Programme.

—J.DESAI]

Extract from a letter written by Gandhiji to Shri Jivanji Desai:

Sodepur
16.1.46

" . . . ..You are right; cow service (*goseva*) should be included as one more item in the Constructive Programme. I would phrase it as improvement of cattle. I think it should not have been left out. We shall see about it when the next edition is out."[1]

II

CONGRESS POSITION

Indian National Congress which is the oldest national political organization and which has after many battles fought her non-violent way to freedom cannot be allowed to die. It can only die with the nation. A living organism ever grows or it dies, The Congress has won political freedom, but it has yet to win economic freedom, social and moral freedom. These freedoms are harder than the political, if only because they are constructive, less exciting and not spectacular. All-embracing constructive work evokes the energy of all the units of the millions.

The Congress has got the preliminary and necessary part of her freedom. The hardest has yet to come. In its difficult ascent to democracy, it has inevitably created rotten boroughs leading to corruption and creation of institutions, popular and democratic only in name. How to get out of the weedy and unwieldy growth?[2]

The Congress *must* do away with its special register of members, at no time exceeding one crore, not even then easily identifiable. It had an unknown register of millions who could never be wanted. Its register should now be co-extensive with all the men and women on the voters' rolls in the country. The Congress business should be to see that no faked name gets in and no legitimate name is left out.

On its own register it will have a body of servants of the nation who would be workers doing the work allotted to them from time to time.

Unfortunately for the country they will be drawn chiefly for the time being from the city dwellers, most of whom would be required to work for and in the villages of India. The ranks must be filled in increasing numbers from villagers.

These servants will be expected to operate upon and serve the voters registered according to law, in their own surroundings. Many persons and parties will woo them. The very best will win. Thus and in no other way can the Congress regain its fast ebbing unique position in the country. But yesterday the Congress was unwittingly the servant of the Nation, it was *khudai khidmatgar*–God's servant. Let it now proclaim to itself and the world that it is only God's servant – nothing more, nothing less. If it engages in the ungainly skirmish for power, it will find one fine morning that it is no more. Thank God, it is now no longer in sole possession of the field.

I have only opened to view the distant scene. If I have the time and health, I hope to discuss in these columns what the servants of the Nation can *do* to raise themselves in the estimation of their masters, the whole of the adult population, male and female.

New Delhi, 27-1-48   M.K. GANDHI

AFTERWORD

REJECTION OF THE DOUBLE REJECTION

Reading of *Constructive Programme*

After Gandhi's theory and practice of the constructive programme became popular, the text and practice elicited some critical and enthusiastic responses, which eventually faded except for a few. The initial responses, which were confined to Gandhians, to the *Constructive Programme* had invited attention to the 'close link of it with the struggle for freedom' (Prasad, 1942: 32), the compilation for aggregate understanding (Singh, 1944), 'importance for students and congressmen' (Agarwal, 1945 and 1953) and 'revolutionary significance of the programme' (Datta, 1946: 5). In 1944 and 1945, a collection of articles on the constructive programme was also published (Singh, 1944; Kulkarni, Swami and Khan, 1945).

Manmohan Choudhary proposes the trinity of Gramdan, khadi and Shanti Sena. These three are crucial to countering the three maladies of the world—capitalism, bureaucratism and militarism. Gramdan paves the way for decentralized planning and administration, thereby controlling bureaucratization. Khadi and village industries counter capitalism. Shanti Sena makes the need for military and police forces irrelevant (Choudhary, 1966: 63). However, a slew of writings, either indirectly or subsumed under or along with other Gandhian categories, kept rekindling the debate. For M. L. Gujaral, Lok Sevak Sangh is for the fulfilment of the constructive programme (Gujaral, 1985).

Though full-fledged treatment of the *Constructive Programme* has evaded attention in political theory and the social sciences, some crucial interpretations are available. Arne Naess had one of the earliest nuanced methodological interpretations and scholarly engagements. He refers to the constructive programme as 'the course of a Systematisation of Gandhian Ethics of Conflict Resolution'. Participation and trustworthiness are two required methods herein. 'The norms saying that one should contribute to the implementation of the constructive program make up an integral part of the Gandhian ethics of group struggle. It is not a mere accessory' (Naess, 1958:148).

Moreover, 'Gandhi requires methods whereby the constructive intent is made completely clear and trustworthy to the skeptical opponent' (Naess, 1958: 148). In fact, the constructive programme implements many norms (Naess, 1958: 149). The constructive programme was the anticipation of *poorna swaraj*. Therefore, it cannot be reduced to the mere absence of British dominance. 'Actually, the constructive work was a kind of partial anticipation of the condition

Gandhi called *purna swaraj*, real independence, an ideal state of society. The political independence was not, as such, a constructive goal for him, since it was defined as *absence* of British domination' (Naess, 1958: 149). In other words, it is not a negative envision.

Likewise, Judith Brown also perceives the *Constructive Programme* as making *swaraj* (Brown, 2008: 161–84). In Ved Mehta, spiritual socialism is a *qua* constructive programme (Mehta, 2013: 177). There are two specific arguments in Bhikhu Parekh regarding the constructive programme— alternative thinking/strategy and failure to establish coherent relationships between conventional politics, satyagraha and constructive programme. Regarding the first, Bhikhu Parekh views the constructive programme as a comprehensive syllabus of national regeneration (Parekh, 1989; 1997: 11). 'Gandhi's programme for Indian regeneration was highly complex and involved a cluster of interrelated strategies of which cultivating the *swadeshi* spirit, *satyagraha* and the Constructive Programme were the most important' (Parekh, 1989: 56). Regarding the second, he points that ' . . . since Gandhi had not clearly worked out the relationship between conventional politics, satyagraha, and the Constructive Programme . . . his overall strategy remained somewhat incoherent' (Parekh, 1997: 14).

Despite the limited impact of several items of the *Constructive Programme*, its symbolic and pedagogical value was significant for the following reasons: Indians were provided for the first time a clear statement on social-economic objectives; these were achievable; political independence was worthily in aligning with national regeneration; the arrival of dedicated grass-root workers built for mobilizing people (Parekh, 1989: 62–63). The argument is further extended by Ajit K. Dasgupta, who understands the constructive programme where from Gandhi proposes an alternative path to economic development, equality and efficacy and decentralization for rural development (Dasgupta, 1996: 66, 95, 178).

According to David Hardiman, it is alternative modernity wherein rational and scientific approaches are imbued with moral principles, thus not a rejection of the former (Hardiman, 2003:77). For Thomas Weber, the constructive programme is 'working not just *for* the people, but *with* them' (Weber, 2004:121). Ronald Terchek perceives constructive programme as power dispersion (Terchek, 2011: 131). For Richard Johnson, civil disobedience is a political revolution, whereas the constructive programme is a social revolution (Johnson, 2006: 92). Dennis Dalton construes the *Constructive Programme* as an 'agenda of social reforms' (Dalton, 2012). In Tridip Suhrud, the *Constructive Programme* is a quintessential cynosure of interlinkages of the several ideas of Gandhi. 'The relationship between swadeshi and swaraj, between freedom and the creation of a non-violent social order, and between sacrifice and swaraj become clear when we read a small tract *Constructive Programme: Its Meaning and Place*' (Suhrud, 2011: 79).

Anthony Parel argues that Gandhi reminds any sound philosophy to have its own constructive programme for the betterment of members of civil society (Parel, 1997: 170). Moreover, even in Gandhi's schema, a coercive state is necessary for a non-violent social order. This state is reflected in *Hind Swaraj*. *Constructive Programme* argues that for a less violent, more peaceful and prosperous India, the constructive programme is carried out by numerous non-coercive organizations. Along with the state, India's social reconstruction is done through voluntary civil society organizations (Parel, 2011: 167). In other words, *Programme* represents non-government organizations. 'The focal point of *Constructive Programme* is Non-Governmental Organisations (NGOs) of civil society' (Parel, 2011: 154). Parel argues that it is a mistaken interpretation that Gandhi is arguing for an alternative to the coercive state. 'What it is arguing for is that if India is to become less violent and more peaceful and prosperous, it should have a coercive state that accepts, both in principle and in practice, the need for the 'constructive work' carried out by a multitude of non-coercive organizations. That is to say, in addition to the *state*, voluntary organizations of *civil society* should also get involved in India's social reconstruction' (Parel, 2011: 167).

For Anuradha Veeravalli, the *Constructive Programme* is 'the structure of non-violent society'. After that, she links the constructive programme with civil disobedience and its preparedness. 'Gandhi saw the constructive programme as primary training in building and maintaining a non-violent army in continual preparedness for civil disobedience' (Veeravalli, 2016: 43). Non-violent civil disobedience, like military training, also needs training. The constructive programme has to be understood in terms of the foundation of a sovereign nation based on non-violence, which is 'the law of human existence' (Veeravalli, 2016: 43). Civil disobedience aims at conducting experiments for the transfiguration of ' . . . the very institutions, structure and culture of society into a civilisational experiment in non-violence' (Veeravalli, 2016: 43). It is also important to note that it is not action but 'sense of office' attached to action. It collapses the separation of subject and object in determining truth and 'the meaning of a sign' and several binaries of modern states. Veeravalli puts it into two definite ways. Firstly, ' . . . what the constructive programme signifies is determined not merely by what it is objectively, but by what we perceive it to be, and the office attached to it' (Veeravalli, 2016:25). Regarding binaries, secondly, ' . . . it addresses the divide between the public sphere and private sphere, universalism and individualism, the divorce between the role of the individual and that of the citizen that is the mainstay of the modern nation state' (Veeravalli, 2016: 45). Returning to the civil disobedience, she points out that 'civil dissent in the constructive programme and a notion of office lays the ground for the fundamental distinction between power and [t]ruth on which the discourse of *swaraj* is based' (Veeravalli, 2016: 45).

M.V. Naidu states that the *Constructive Programme* laid the foundation for future democracy, democratisation and peacebuilding (Naidu, 2006: 88). K.N. Pannikar links

cultural consciousness with the *Constructive Programme*.
This was ' . . . a form of cultural struggle to equip the people
for higher social and political efforts' (Panikkar, 2009: 36).
For Karuna Mantenna, means and ends are two central
components of the *Constructive Programme*. Coming these
two (means and ends) are crucial for the transformation
of mistrust and domination. It is a non-violent revolution,
having the centrality of non-violent politics. Despite having
national scope, it is to be implemented at the village level
(Mantenna, 2012: 462–66). Bindu Mathew considers the
Constructive Programme not a departure from mainstream
politics. It cannot be comprehended within the domain of
philanthropic and moralistic domains. It was a sign of an
emerging nation. It created political energy reserves for many
radical policies and their implementation. It offers a different
mode of politics to enrich mainstream politics. Indirect
politics (the different modes of politics) creates tremendous
political energy. Gandhi pursued constructive work toward
'direct militant mass politics' (Mathew, 2012: 597–606).

R. Srivatsan offers a critical evaluation of the *Constructive
Programme*. According to him, Gandhi proposes a
constructive social system by repairing the margins (items of
the *Constructive Programme*) while creating the centre of the
caste-Hindu adult health man. 'This apparent caricature of
categorisation has in fact a quiet logic to its structure. The
centre around which the defined groups, habits, failings and
afflictions fall cripplingly short, is the caste-Hindu, sober,
adult, healthy man, who takes stage as the norm of Indian

society. This evaluative core of a norm of what constituted a full bodied Indian citizen provides the implicit structure of a democratic sovereign body to rule post-colonial India' (Srivatsan, 2006: 434–35).

The interpretations above provide crucial insights for comprehending the text and its practices. However, the present reading provides an alternative by way of reading the *Constructive Programme* as 'extraparliamentary'. E.M.S. Namboodiripad used 'extraparliamentary activity' for the constructive programme (Namboodiripad, 2010: 153). Namboodiripad's critical assessment of Gandhi and his constructive programme indicates the power of extraparliamentary politics in a well thought out manner. Amidst Gandhi's intense touring to promote constructing programmes, Namboodiripad outlines five features: unlike 1921–22, avoiding political questions during 1924–28. Though he did not direct structural questions, he highlighted the misery of the downtrodden by way of studying each section of the society; khadi programme as capital-labour coordination; constructive programme as a plan of action; and integration of 'ostensibly non-political constructive programme' with 'avowedly political programme' (Namboodiripad, 2010: 63). This ostensibly non-political constructive programme becomes integrated with the avowedly political programme while maintaining its autonomy in both origin and expansion. This view can be inferred from his analysis of Gandhi, constructive programme and Swarajists.

On the one hand, in post-non-cooperation days, Gandhi allowed Swarajists to take full advantage of achieving swaraj while opening the negotiations with the British government and on the other hand, he intended to utilize ' . . . the energies of tens of thousands of selfless constructive workers to build up a network of organisations and thus preparing the country for another cycle of non-violent struggle if the negotiations were to end in failure' (Namboodiripad, 2010: 65). In other words, parliamentary activities cannot be robust without extraparliamentary activities. However, extraparliamentary activities do not originate from the space located within the parliamentary activities. Instead, it asserts its autonomy in a robust sense.

The *Constructive Programme* is to be linked with the notion of immanent text and the extraparliamentary for further development of text and practice. Since the immanent text urges for immediacy, it gets intertwined with the extraparliamentary due to urgent working by way of passing double exclusion of liberal political space. Double exclusion (a definite space of politics and constrained representation-based politics) is expounded and elaborated on in the following paragraphs. The study of the text is done chronologically to exhibit definite advances and crucial expansion of inclusion in the constructive programme while questioning the double exclusion (definite space and constrained representation), which prevents the resolution or heightening of contradictions.

Liberal Problematique

Reading Gandhi's *Constructive Programme* as extraparliamentary becomes crucial to rejecting the constrictive programme of the liberal political theory. The constrictive tendency of liberalism/liberal political theory allows democracy while normalizing fundamentalism, violence, communalism, caste atrocities, gendering and exploitation. In other words, liberalism and illiberalism can coexist together. There can be a liberal democracy and institutions with illiberal practices. This is the paradox of liberal democracy. Nevertheless, sometimes, democracy is used for anti-democratic practices. This mismatch must be answered unequivocally. One of the ways could be to understand the manifestation of politics. In other words, *how often politics is manifested* and *by what means politics is manifested* must become guiding norms for critical analysis.

These two spaces (often manifestation of politics and means of manifestation) in liberalism are marred by rigidities of deliberate protocols, norms and guarding rigidities of representation. The manifestation of politics becomes an occasional engagement. Means of manifestation of politics become the only 'authorized' and 'authenticated voice'. This is a sign of a constrictive tendency of politics that provides the 'occasional opportunity' for politics and permanent negation of non-authorized versions of politics.

Engaging with the *Constructive Programme* as extraparliamentary offers to cement the idea of permanent opportunity for 'politics' and inclusion of a non-authorized (heterodox) version of politics.

In other words, the construal of the *Constructive Programme* as extraparliamentary offers the permanency of politics, which does not require only occasions and authorized means of politics. Thus, rejecting the constructive programme of politics becomes crucial in this schema.

Gandhi's *Constructive Programme* is based on a non-binary universalistic normative emphasis. The non-binary universalistic normative concerns the issues to be expressed for addressing and readdressing in a dialectical sense. The issues and contradictions cannot be status quo or relapsed. This can be done on an everyday basis and by everyone.

The contents of the *Constructive Programme* may need a substantive addition or revision in the context of a slew of changes and alternatives. However, the idea of everydayness/everyone is a component par excellence for rejecting the occasional manifestation of politics and authorized notion of politics—the idea and practice of extraparliamentary offer such opportunities.

The idea of extraparliamentary is generally associated with social movements or activities associated with non-state actors. The extraparliamentary is subject to a slew of interpretations. This study uses the concept in a definite sense where extraparliamentary does not work in isolation from parliamentary politics. Engagement, however, is aimed at changing the latter by way of exposing serious limitations and politicizing everydayness. Extraparliamentary is 'political everydayness' for transformation. In the context of using it concerning Gandhi and Gandhian philosophy, the nearest use is by E.M.S. Namboodiripad is 'extraparliamentary activity'. He attributes it to the constructive programme in *The Mahatma and the Ism* (Namboodiripad, 2010: 163).

A conceptualization of the extraparliamentary needs to be defined in the context of limitations of liberal political theory or liberal constitution. The liberal political theory defines politics as a 'defined or designated space'. Some spaces are identified as 'political sites'. Consequently, the act and activities practised in *the* realm are called political activity—people's participation for political purpose in a particular domain to be entitled as a political act. Mere 'participation' is not a political activity in the liberal political theory or the liberal constitution. It is followed by *means* of participation in the political space in the form of political activity.

This way, there is a double definition of political activity or space. Firstly, a certain space is defined as a political space. Secondly, an agency or agencies is/are required to participate in the political space. This can also be called a double exclusion to identify space and representation by the agency. A slew of liberal concepts like state, party, civil society and governance are constructed around the double exclusion of people. It becomes more *problematic* when the otherwise marginalized political right becomes powerful solely due to the monopolization of both space and access to space which are crucial to the definition and practice of political. A relatively open space is also not de-isolated from the structural constraints.

Despite the significant development in liberalism from the 'social contract tradition' (Thomas Hobbes, John Locke and John Rawls) to the 'political liberalism' of John Rawls (overlapping consensus) and Charles Larmore (reasonable disagreement), the problem of definite space and constrained representation remains unresolved.

Along with the pursuance of possessive individualism in Hobbes and Locke (Macpherson, 1990), the political per se is reduced to either an artefact of the sovereign or the majority. For Hobbes, '[p]olitical (otherwise called bodies politic, and persons in law) are those, which are made by authority from the sovereign power of the commonwealth' (1998: 149). For Locke, '[w]hen any number of men have so consented to make one community or government, they are thereby presently incorporated, and make one body politic, wherein the majority have a right to act and conclude the rest' (1980: 52). This is followed by the obligation, '[a]nd thus every man, by consenting with others to make one body politic under one government, puts himself under an obligation, to every one of that society, to submit to the determination of the majority, and to be concluded by it' (Locke, 1980: 52). This majority in Locke, according to C. B. Macpherson, is propertied class because ' . . .only those with property were full members of civil society and so of the majority . . . Locke's consent of the majority is consent of the majority of property-owners' (Macpherson, 1990: 252).

J.S. Mill, Isaiah Berlin and John Rawls further compound the problem. In J.S. Mill, competence and participation are presented not without tension concerning representative government (1977; Thompson, 1979). 'The principle of participation constraints the principle of competence, just as the latter principle limits the former. Mill aims to "secure, as far as they can be made compatible", the advantage of government by the competent along with the advantage of government made responsible through participation by citizens. Thus, the two principles evidently are "coequal"' (Thompson, 1979: 10–11).

Despite this delicate defence in Mill or of Mill, 'coequal' seems floundering when the emphasis on 'plurality of votes' is outlined. According to Mill,

> When all have votes, it will be both just in principle and necessary in fact, that some mode be adopted of giving greater weight to the suffrage of the more educated voter; some means by which the more intrinsically valuable member of society, the one who is more capable, more competent for the general affairs of life, and possesses more of the knowledge applicable to the management of the affairs of the community, should, as far as practicable, be singled out, and allowed a superiority of influence proportioned to his higher qualifications.
>
> The most direct mode of effecting this, would be to establish plurality of votes, in favour of those who could afford a reasonable presumption of superior knowledge and cultivation (1977: 324).

In Isiah Berlin, the framework is constructed for 'freedom from' (negative liberty) over 'freedom to' (positive liberty). Herein politics becomes immune from everyday consideration of marginal groups for the arrival of negative liberty. 'But there is no necessary connection between individual liberty and democratic rule. The answer to the question "Who governs me?" is logically distinct from the question "How far does government interfere with me?" It is in this difference that the great contrast between the two concepts of negative and positive liberty, in the end, consists' (Berlin, 2016: 42). In John Rawls, pre-institutional exercise includes 'original positional'[1] in which people participate under 'veil of ignorance'[2] while having 'reflective equilibrium.'[3]

In other words, in Rawlsian original position, people meet together in an oblivious condition while representing diverse sections along with having crucial knowledge. This original position is crucial for the arrival and institutionalization of justice as fairness in the form of two principles of justice, i.e. the liberty principle and the equality principle (fair equality of opportunity (distribution of offices and positions sans consideration of background), and difference principle (justification of inequality only if benefit worse-off) (Rawls, 1999).

Two questions become important herein, i.e. how far is pre-institutional endeavour democratic? How far could it be democratic post-institutionalization in terms of available corrective mechanisms? Regarding the first, serious objections have been raised concerning the omission of diverse categories like gender[4] and class.[5]

This complicates the second question. Due to the first question, the second also remains problematic. If the 'problematic' passes on from pre-institutional arrangement to post-institutional setup, the remedy must be available. Rawls calls his formulation or his liberal alternative a near-just society/ system. It forbids any form of discrimination. In fact, Rawls barely recognises that there could be discrimination in his schema. However, he proposes civil disobedience to address infractions of the principle of justice as fairness (1999: 319, 322).

Civil disobedience applies to a nearly just society. '. . . [T]his theory is designed only for the special case of a nearly just society, one that is well-ordered for the most part but in which some serious violations of justice nevertheless do occur' (Rawls, 1999:319). Civil disobedience ' . . . may warn and admonish, it is not itself a threat' (Rawls, 1999:319). It works within the limits of the fidelity of laws. Civil disobedience ' . . . expresses disobedience to law within the limits of fidelity to law . . .' (Rawls, 1999:322).

Rawls insists on using civil disobedience against the infraction of substantial and clear injustice, which also obstructs the path of removing other injustices. 'Now if one views such disobedience as a political act addressed to the sense of justice of the community, then it seems reasonable, other things equal, to limit it to instances of substantial and clear injustice, and preferably to those which obstruct the path to removing other injustices' (Rawls, 1999: 326). He, therefore, reduces civil disobedience by addressing only infractions of the liberty principle and fair equality of opportunity of the equality principle. Civil disobedience is not permitted in the context of the difference (socioeconomic discrimination) principle of equality. 'For this reason [substantial and clear injustice which also obstructs the path of removing other injustice], there is a presumption in favor of restricting civil disobedience to serious infringements of the first principle of justice, the principle of equal liberty, and to blatant violations of the second part of the second principle, the principle of fair equality of opportunity' (Rawls, 1999: 326).The reasoning for rejecting the difference principle is as follows: 'By contrast infractions of the difference principle are more difficult to ascertain'[6] (Rawls, 1999: 327).

The 'grand' or comprehensive doctrine-led liberalism faced the charge of majoritarianism (and being indifferent to non-majoritarian opinions), propagation of one form of value, individualism and sheer autonomy, which are disconnected from a diverse section of society. Therefore, in place of overarching moral and abiding principles, 'Political Liberalism', by way of two crucial defenders of it, John Rawls and Charles Larmore, offers 'overlapping consensus' (Rawls, 1987: 1–25) and 'reasonable disagreements' (Larmore, 1990: 339–60), appeared as a distinctive alternative in the liberal political theory.

John Rawls (1987) outlines 'the idea of an overlapping consensus' for political liberalism. The political conception of justice is crucial for the arrival of an overlapping consensus, which means 'a consensus in which it is affirmed by the opposing religious, philosophical and moral doctrines likely to thrive over generations in a more or less just constitutional democracy, where the criterion of justice is that political conception itself' (Rawls, 1987: 1). He outlines two features of a political conception of justice: expressly framed to apply to the basic structure of society; and not derived from general or comprehensive doctrine (Rawls, 1987: 5). According to Rawls, for any workable conception of justice concerning the democratic regime, the envisaged liberalism will not be the liberalism of Kant and J.S. Mill (1987: 5). Liberalisms of Kant and Mill ' . . . are both general and comprehensive doctrines: general in that they apply to a wide range of subjects, and comprehensive in that they include conceptions of what is of value in human life, ideals of personal virtue and character that are to inform our thought and conduct as a whole' (Rawls, 1987: 6). Kant's idea of autonomy and enlightenment and Mill's idea of individuality are referred here. Since ' . . . two liberalism . . . comprehend far more than the political . . . [and] . . . [t]heir doctrines . . . are . . . not shared in a democratic society . . . [therefore] . . . [t]hey are not practicable public basis of a political conception of justice . . .' (Rawls, 1987: 6). Rawls proposes the third alternative, which is not based on comprehensive religious, philosophical and moral doctrines. This is based on intuitive ideas available in a democratic society. However, these intuitive ideas are not derived from religious, philosophical and metaphysical ideas (Rawls, 1987: 7).

It is important to achieve consensus; political philosophy must be autonomous from long-standing problems and controversies. Rawls defines his political liberalism against the strand of Hobbes (convergence of self and group interest and sustained by constitutional arrangement) and Kant and Mill-led liberalism (based on comprehensive moral doctrines) because the former lacks social unity and later lacks 'sufficient agreement'. Political liberalism is linked to overlapping consensus, which is imbued with pluralism. ' . . . [P]olitical liberalism is the view that under the reasonably favourable conditions that make constitutional democracy possible, political institutions satisfying the principles of a liberal conception of justice realise political values and ideals that normally outweigh whatever other values oppose them' (Rawls, 1987: 24). Against the two-specific objection to political liberalism like scepticism and indifference, and not acquiring enough support for the principles of justice, he suggests that both ' . . . objections are answered by finding a reasonable liberal conception of justice that can be supported by an overlapping consensus' (Rawls, 1987: 24).

Charles Larmore's Political Liberalism focuses on 'reasonable disagreement about the good life . . . [which is not] . . . 'pluralism' . . . [where the assertion is] . . . that there are many valid forms of human self-realization. This doctrine [political liberalism] is itself an affirmation about the nature of the good life. More relevant is the fact that whether the different forms of the good can be ranked, and if so how, is one of the items about which reasonable disagreement tends to thrive' (Larmore, 1990: 340). Larmore problematizes the idea of reasonable agreement and political neutrality, which is achieved through coercion rather than reason. In Kant and Mill, political neutrality does come through autonomy and individuality. Constitutional values would define the supreme value over controversial views. ' . . . Kantian and Millian conceptions of liberalism are not adequate solutions to the political problem of reasonable disagreement about the good life' (Larmore, 1990: 345) and romantic criticism of liberalism being 'individualist' and 'atomist'. This requires recasting liberalism into political liberalism. 'It is the attempt to understand how liberalism can be strictly a political doctrine and not a general "philosophy of man", not a "comprehensive moral ideal"' (Larmore, 1990: 345). 'The task of liberal theory today is to see how the principle of state neutrality can be justified without having to take sides in the dispute about individualism and tradition' (Larmore, 1990: 346). Individualism will be an important doctrine in liberal theory without extending it to all aspects of social life.

In political liberalism, as proposed by Larmore, '[p]rivate associations cannot violate the rights of citizens. Yet they can continue to organize their internal, extrapolitical affairs according to "illiberal" principles—principles which deny their members equal rights and require them to defer to traditionally constituted authority' (Larmore, 1990: 350). Quintessentially, '[p]olitical liberalism is a moral conception based on the norm of equal respect . . . [In it] . . . the norms of rational dialogue and equal respect, as well as the principle of neutrality they justify, are understood to be correct and valid norms and not merely norms which people in a liberal order believe to be correct and valid' (Larmore, 1990: 353).

Linda Hirshman invites attention to the problem of inclusivity of political liberalism, which cannot go uncontested. It appears to be the inclusion of merely diverse religious doctrines in the name of social diversity. According to Linda Hirshman, '[w]hile Rawls seeks to accommodate religious differences, he ignores the gender and racial demands of religion. Not surprisingly then each of his solutions to make room for religion raises tremendous problems for racial and gender justice' (1994: 1865).

Concerning liberalism, the debate must be understood in the context of Hanna Fenichel Pitkin's *The Concept of Representation* (1967) and Anne Philips's *The Politics of Presence* (1998). Pitkin proposes four types of representation (formalistic views of representation,[7] 'standing for': descriptive representation,[8] 'standing for': symbolic representation,[9] and substantive representation[10]) (Pitkin, 1967). Pitkin problematized the above four and traded with each carefully. However, her rejection of descriptive representation did not go unnoticed. According to Pitkin, ' . . . the best descriptive representative is not necessarily the best representative for activity or government' (Pitkin, 1967: 89). 'And the descriptive view can serve as a healthy corrective for the formalistic view, pointing to some of what the latter omits. But neither view by itself, nor yet a combination of the two views, is the whole story about representation' (Pitkin, 1967: 91).

Anne Philips highlights the difference between the 'politics of ideas' ('separation between "who" and "what" is to be represented, and the subordination of the first to the second' (Philips, 1998: 5) and 'politics of presence' (marginal section's direct presence/representation) while rejecting the rejection of descriptive representation by Pitkin. After that, she underlines the synthesis between the two. For her,

> . . .while the politics of ideas is an inadequate end vehicle for dealing with political exclusion, there is little to be gained by simply switching to a politics of presence. Taken in isolation, the weaknesses of the one are as dramatic as the failings of the other. Most of the problems, indeed, arise when these two are set up as exclusionary opposites: when ideas are treated as totally separate from the people who carry them; or when the people dominate attention, with no thought given to their policies and ideas. It is in the relationship between ideas and presence that we can best hope to find a fairer system of representation, not in a false opposition between one or the other (Philips, 1998: 24–25).

Iris Marion Young outlines the three conditions (interest, opinion and perspective) for feeling representation in the political process (Young, 2000: 134–38). The interest is linked with making life better. Young says, 'I feel represented when someone is looking after the interests I take as mine and share with some others' (Young, 2000: 134). As Anne

Philips suggested, opinion can be referred to as 'politics of idea'. ' . . . [I]t is important to me that the principles, values, and priorities that I think should guide political decisions are voiced in discussion' (Young, 2000: 134). Finally, perspective entails the significance of group-differentiated politics. 'I feel represented when at least some of those discussing and voting on policies understand and express the kind of social experience I have because of my social group position and the history of social group relations' (Young, 2000: 134).

Paraphrasing, Philips and Young suggest that constrained representation has to go for real democratic politics. In fact, liberalism and political liberalism offer multiple spaces regarding organizing spaces for associations and representation. Civil society, the public sphere, activities in political parties and pressure groups are ample spaces for forming multiple and multilayered associations. However, these spaces do not construct *political* sufficiently to influence people's decision-making directly. They become medium but not themselves a participant due to rigidities by defining and practising politics in constrained space and representation.

In other words, pluralism/reasonable disagreement is not decentralization due to a still unresolved and existing constraint of definite space as political and constrained representation in liberalism.

The double exclusion (a definite space and constrained representation) also operates through the further division of 'political equality' and 'economic inequality'. According to E.M. Wood, there is a separation between political and economic spheres in capitalism. The political does not decide or intervene in the 'economic sphere'. If there is any intervention by the 'political sphere', that is, the state, it is only to strengthen the 'immanent logic' of the economic sphere. For E.M. Wood, differentiation means several things:

> that production and distribution assume a completely 'economic' form, no longer (as Karl Polanyi put it) 'embedded' in extra-economic social relations, in a system where production is generally production for exchange; that the allocation of social labour and the distribution of resources are achieved through the 'economic' mechanism of commodity exchange; that the 'economic' forces of the commodity and labour markets acquire a life of their own . . . (2007: 28).

She sums up the differentiation further:

> the social functions of production and distribution, surplus extraction and appropriation, and the allocation of social labour are, so to speak, privatised and they are achieved by non-authoritative, non-political means. In other words, the social allocation of resources and labour does not, on the whole, take place by means of political direction, communal deliberation, hereditary duty, custom, or religious obligation, but rather through the mechanisms of commodity exchange (2007: 29).

Nevertheless, it does not entail the absence of the state or state becoming 'an extraneous actor in the production process'.

> To speak of the differentiation of the economic sphere in these senses is not, of course, to suggest that the political dimension is somehow extraneous to capitalist relations of production. The political sphere in capitalism has a special character because the coercive power supporting capitalist exploitation is not wielded directly by the appropriator and is not based on the producer's political or juridical subordination to an appropriating master. But a coercive of use, power and a structure of domination remain essential, even if the ostensible freedom and equality of the exchange between capital and labour mean that the 'moment' of coercion is separate from the 'moment' of appropriation (2007:19).

In fact, the state remains an important player in the differentiation and sustaining logic of the capitalist mode of production.

> Absolute private property, the contractual relation that binds producer to appropriator, the process of commodity exchange-all these require the legal forms, the coercive apparatus, the policing functions of the state. Historically too, the state has been essential to the process of expropriation that is the basis of capitalism. In all these

> senses, despite their differentiation, the economic sphere
> rests firmly on the political.
>
> Furthermore, the economic sphere itself has a juridical
> and political dimension. In one sense, the differentiation
> of the economic sphere means simply that the economy
> has its own juridical and political forms whose purpose is
> purely 'economic' (2007: 30).

The deriving theoretical postulation of capitalism into a liberal democracy, it can be stated that political equality is guaranteed unconditionally in the late liberal democracy. Political equality is ensured by guaranteeing one person one vote. However, this political equality is delinked from economic inequality, that is, privatization of an economic sphere by way of expropriation, exploitation, appropriation and accumulation. If political equality has to intervene, it has to only for sustaining economic inequality. The process becomes more complicated when 'political space' is also defined and constricted in terms of a domain and access to the domain. Political equality becomes an 'occasional opportunity' due to the space of the political open up occasionally and that too also by the *legitimate* agents.

Against the backdrop of the discussion above, it becomes categorical that political space is defined and granted through some technical mechanism. The political idea is made further available through invoking 'delegating' and 'representing'. The representative represents the politics of the people. The representative is also not allowed to make the decisions as a delegated representative but as a member of a collective of representatives. In liberal discourse, this space is known as a legislature, parliament, House of Commons, Senate, House of Representatives, People's House and so on.

Extraparliamentary

Extraparliamentary per se has invited meaningful attention in multiple ways. Primarily, deliberations about it are located in the context of political parties. As a result, there have been two-pronged debates: the competitive struggle between the parliamentary group and the extraparliamentary group within a political party; and the trust deficit with political parties and proposed alternatives. Moreover, since political parties are considered the important mechanism for the vehicle of representation and the legitimate occupants of parliamentary space, they become effective means of attention for analysis.

Robert Michel's preference for extraparliamentary control over a parliamentary group ends with a pessimistic note that a parliamentary group would emerge more powerful due to their linkages with policies and voters than the extraparliamentary group's connection with mere members. This may reduce the significant gap between the bourgeois and mass parties due to control over the electorate over members (Michels, 1962). For Maurice Duverger, this precise relation between the parliamentary group and the electoral would provide a co-equal role to the former with the extraparliamentary group (Duverger, 1964). Von Beyme observes that multiple factors and support from various corners will make the extraparliamentary group more powerful than the parliamentary group (Beyme 1985). These studies are the backdrop for the study of parliamentary and extraparliamentary power by Rachel Gibson and Robert Harmel. Rachel Gibson and Robert Harmel find in their study of total of nineteen parties; Denmark (9), Germany (4), the United Kingdom (4), and the United States (2) that there is a strong relationship between left ideology and extraparliamentary power.[11] 'The strong bivariate relationship between left ideology and extraparliamentary power supports a conclusion that socialist parties do tend to place more power outside parliamentary parties that do parties of the centre and right' (Gibson and Harmel, 1998: 649).

Trust deficit has been an important concern vis-à-vis political parties in the context of liberal democracies. It has invited attention in multiple ways. The absence of people's participation in the decision-making process is a crucial concern due to the confirmation of the choices of others. 'Arguably, citizens of representative "democracies" select their rules but they do not themselves rule, as any properly liberal democratic theory requires . . . [R]epresentative governments cannot allow for the aggregation of citizens' choices in the way adherents of popular sovereignty and therefore of popular control require' (Levine, 1981: 150). Therefore, in the Indian context, formulations like 'party-less democracy' (Narayan, 2009) and 'non-party political process' (Sheth, 1983: 1–24, 1984: 259–62 and 2004: 45–58), non-party organization (Kothari, 2005) are envisaged. For Narayan, '[p]artyless democracy is a long-term goal' (Narayan, 2009: 310). It ' . . . is a long-term objective' (2009: 326). In place of immediacy, Narayan stresses class society as a precondition for the arrival of partyless democracy. 'Partyless democracy is a concept common to Marxism and the Gandhian ideals. It has been the objective of the Sarvodaya movement from the very beginning. But it is a long term ideal and as I have often said in the recent past, I have come to believe that partyless democracy cannot be established before we succeed in achieving a classless society' (Narayan, 2009: 385).

According to Atul Kohli, the decline of the state's capacity to govern (promotion of development and accommodation of diverse interests) led to substantive activism outside the domain of established political channels (1990: 5). D.L. Sheth explores the alternative possibility in 'grass-roots' and micro-movements (1983: 1–24, 1984: 259–62 and 2004: 45–58). The new movements' new politics re-politicize development and reinvent participatory democracy. Concerning the re-politicization of development, the poor are not appealing to pre-modern nostalgia. Development is right, which is denied due to location disadvantageous to the power structure. There is a realization of abandoning the welfare state and centralization of economic and military power in the hand of a few powerful countries. Therefore, the formation of transnational alliances to democratize global power structures has become an important concern for micro-movements. Moreover, issues of development are discussed in the context of rights. For Sheth, liberal democratic theory becomes a site of political obligation while offering a very limited role in the decision-making process. Movement-politics envisage participatory or new discourse on democracy at grassroots, national and global levels: '(a) at the grass roots level through building peoples' own power and capabilities . . . (b) at the provincial and national level through launching nationwide campaigns and building alliances and coalitions for mobilising protests on larger issues . . . and creating organisational networks of mutual support and of solidarity among movements; (c) at the global level . . . creating a politics of counter-hegemonic globalisation' (Sheth, 2004: 56). In a nutshell, '. . . the long-term goal of the movements is to bring the immediate environment (social, economic, cultural and ecological) the people live in, within their own reach and control' (Sheth, 2004: 56).

Earlier, Rajni Kothari conceptualized the Indian democracy or the Indian political system as the Congress System. For Kothari, the Congress System or Indian system represented a system of one-party dominance. The Congress System consisted of 'a party of consensus' and 'parties of pressure'. Parties of pressure operate through a margin of pressure and are a crucial component of the system due to their presence within the party of consensus in the form of various factions having also linkages outside the party. The role of the margin outside the party ' . . . is to constantly pressurise, criticise, censure and influence it by influencing opinion and interests inside the margin and, above all, exert a latent threat that if the ruling group strays away too far from the balance of effective public opinion, and if the factional system within it is not mobilised to restore the balance, it will be displaced from power by the opposition groups'. Inbuilt corrective measures through factionalism within the party and ' . . . the idea of a latent threat from outside the margin of pressure are necessary parts of the one party dominance system.' (Kothari, 1964: 1162). In 1974, Kothari interpreted the Congress System, an empirical theory of a definite phase of institutional development, as ' . . . a conceptual framework for interpreting the dynamics of Indian politics from the perspective of the relationship between authority and opposition, between government and dissent, between a particular consensus and challenge to it when it becomes obsolete' (Kothari, 1974: 1053–54). Gradually he moved towards non-party formations. He emphasizes non-party politics while inviting attention to grassroots movements towards micro and macro issues. Non-party politics is a new historical phenomenon which occupies 'a specific political space'. 'Today's oppressed classes need to wage their struggles from outside the existing structures, not just by redefining the very concept and structure of politics with a view to empower people and transform people and transform society' (Kothari, 2005: 140).

Beyond the competitive struggle between the parliamentary group and the extraparliamentary group within a political party, and the trust deficit with political parties and proposed alternatives, studies have also shown the arrival of the complex phenomenon and inviting attention to look at grassroot differently along with the notion of democracy. Regarding the first, Neera Chandhoke's (2004: 308–30) 'revisiting the crisis of representation thesis' is an interesting study of Delhi. The important questions are about the crisis of political parties and the search for alternatives. In her study of Delhi, people have lost faith in the political parties to address their grievances and concerns. The decision-making forums are not addressing the basic needs of the people. This angst is rampant. However, it has not culminated in a search for new alternatives in the form of a non-governmental sector. Disenchantment with political parties has not galvanized them into non-party alternatives. The latter has not institutionalized the trust of people. Her five definite findings are as follows:

> In short, people (a) have little faith in any organisation, whether it belongs to the political or to the civil sphere, to either represent them and their interests or to help them resolve their day to day problems, (b) they by and large are convinced that no organisation is concerned with their problems, some of which are indeed severe because they pertain to the minimal conditions of life itself, (c) they would rather rely on personal associations in the neighbourhood or on their family to solve problems, and (d) with the help of their personal contacts or with the help of people who are familiar, they would rather approach the government directly. It appears that citizens would prefer to establish direct contact with the government than rely

on mediations that are provided by political parties and civil-society organisations (Chandhoke, 2004: 326–27).

Moreover, regarding the second, in one of the significant studies in the contemporary time led by Boaventura de Sousa Santos on 'Democratizing Democracy: Beyond the Liberal Democratic Canon', crises of liberal democracy and alternatives are explored in general and with particular reference to India, South Africa, Colombia, Mozambique, Putumayo and Baja Bota of Cauca, Uraba, San Jose de Apartado, Porto Alegre and Brazil (Santos, 2007). Santos proposes *participatory democracy* (a subaltern model of democracy as opposed to liberal, representative democracy), *alternative production system* (non-capitalist production of goods and services), *new labor internationalism* (more struggles along with 'extra-economic bonds'), *emancipatory multiculturalism, cultural citizenship and justice* (mutual intelligence and respect by translation work), and the *defence of biodiversity and the struggle for the recognition of rival knowledges* (Santos, 2007: xxx–xxxiii). Patrick Heller and T.M. Thomas Isaac (2007: 405–43) explore the interaction between participatory democracy and representative democracy in Kerala, India. They raise pertinent methodological points concerning the evaluation of democracy in the developing world. The focus has been on the regime in power, political parties and organized electoral political actors. 'What has been missing however is a deeper understanding of day-to-day democratic practices, and in particular the nature of the sub-national institutional field(s) on which both formal and informal political agents engage each other and the state' (Heller and Isaac, 2007: 405). Uncovering the multilayered surface of institutions makes the realization of degrees of democracy. 'Digging below the surface, moreover, one finds that within the unitary institutional domain marked by the boundaries of the Indian nation-state, there are marked degrees of democracy' (Heller and Isaac, 2007: 406). Empowered emancipatory governance backed by self-conscious and extensive experiments became possible due to the initiations of a slew of programmes by the Left in Kerala (Heller and Isaac, 2007: 406).

Against the backdrop of aforesaid debates and taking clues from the preceding paragraphs, I will attempt to summarize the crucial debates around faultlines of liberal political theory and the contour of extraparliamentary. There are five major concerns in liberal political theory and liberal democracy. Firstly, theoretically and practically, 'political equality' is treated in isolation. 'Theoretical political equality' is not attempted to be linked with a slew of other forms of equalities. Politics is envisaged as the domain in liberal discourse for implementing the notion of 'equality'. Since 'political equality' cannot stand alone because its location is also outside the domain of 'politics' itself, it faces further constriction and collapses.

Secondly, political equality is detached from economic inequality. The liberal justification has never been convincing on a normative level that is why in a political community, there is political equality but not socioeconomic equality. The rationale has always been for the apotheosis of liberty but without touching the question of miserable life conditions due to socioeconomic inequalities in the political community.

Thirdly, the value of political equality is further eroded by way of envisaging and practising 'politics' in a definite space. Politics and its equality have to be performed in the designated space. Otherwise, it compromises legitimacy.

Fourthly, political equality, which is operated through a definite space, needs the presence and function of 'being delegated' or 'delegation'. The access to define space is further complicated by delegation. This leads to the development of 'constrained representation'.

Fifthly, this condition and method provide a perfect backdrop and arrival of political majoritarianism. This happens due to both a definite space and constrained representation are decided by an 'empirical majority'. The empirical decision by the majority cannot be equivalent to 'access to all' (representation to all).

This paves the way for a 'political majority', which in the end does not compromise procedural–political equality but also leads to the marginalization of socioeconomic inequalities due to its dealing with economic equality and formation solely on 'empirical number'. In this framework, derision of, or deviation from, this political is not desired and is a violation of the people's general will.

The idea and praxis of the extraparliamentary contradict the aforesaid *modus operandi* (a particular way of doing) and *modus vivendi* (a way of living). Herein, the extraparliamentary has been used in a particular sense. It is not just a sporadic event or leisure activity organized in a designated, well-defined space. It is not a momentary, sudden or tentative fissure. It also cannot be reduced to some auxiliary activities. The 'extraparliamentary' connotes the context of serious limitations of the liberal-parliamentary–democracy model as endorsed by liberal political theory. In other words, extraparliamentary cannot be theorized by way of insulated separation of 'extra' from parliamentary or 'parliamentary' from 'extra'.

Methodologically, it adopts a 'centrifugal approach'. It does not abandon the opportunity and merits (like procedural universalism) of liberal political theory. On the contrary, it mobilizes existing resources for a heterodox alternative that is not feasible without 'being apart' to going 'out' for a better world. *Philosophically,* it provides an alternative lifeworld. *Politically,* there are challenges and possibilities for overcoming the faultlines of the liberal framework.

The extraparliamentary proposes the linkages between various forms of equalities. Political equality is not sustainable in the absence of socioeconomic equality. Furthermore, it makes the space for deliberative and participatory democratic alternatives. The definite space and constrained representation are to be converted into the de-definite space for politics and de-constrained representation in democracy. It helps to defy 'politics as mobilised being' and proposes 'politics as participatory being'. It helps to reject the arrival of the condition of empirical majoritarianism by making 'definite space' and 'constrained representation' as a criterion only channelized through political majority defunct while linking political equality with economic equality so later it must be channelized as removal of inequality and not appearing as 'othering' converted into political majoritarianism.

Right-wing populism and politics, religious fanaticism, traditionalist attack on individual rights, terrorism and revivalism cannot be categorized in the realm of 'extraparliamentary' primarily for two reasons. Firstly, they have no interest in engaging with the 'liberal conundrum'. They do not engage with liberal values. For example, debates over definite space/de-definite space, constrained representation/ deconstrained representation, separation or not separation between political equality and socioeconomic equality, and mobilized/participatory beings are meaningless or absolutely irrelevant. Secondly, they tend to resolve in a primordial sense. In this way, they precede even the 'universal proceduralism' of liberalism. They offer 'pre-liberal values', whereas the need is to offer a better framework than the existing one. Regression into the past cannot be construed as extraparliamentary. One has to engage with 'liberal fallacies' post this framework. Right-wing populism (making religion a central category by way of political power through 'otherness'), religious fanaticism (desire for everlasting supremacy), traditionist attack on individual rights (cultural supremacists), terrorism (violence as only theory and practice) and revivalism (replacing the future with the past) are distinct categories in their own right. These must not be conflated with the extraparliamentary realm.

The arduous mechanism of liberal political theory and liberal democracy by way of separating political equality and economic inequality, defining a space for political per se, and envisioning agents to have access to political space and further reducing the idea of delegation, representation and representative of the will of 'political majoritarianism' constitute the parliament per se. In this framework, derision of, or deviation from this political is not desired and is a violation of people's general will. Furthermore, this act is construed as extraparliamentary by the liberal state.

There could be many ways to fit into the extraparliamentary category. Actions could be extraparliamentary without questioning 'the liberal conundrum'. Right-wing popular politics, religious fanaticism, communitarian assault on individual rights, terrorism and revivalism, could also be categorized in the extraparliamentary category. The hollowness or severe deficiency in these groups is not the only non-engagement of a liberal conundrum but also taking to the political into 'identity question'. The alternative to the liberal conundrum cannot be a regression into pre-liberal days but going beyond the liberal edifice.

In this sense, the extraparliamentary can be defined as the construction of the space of political action or public action, which defies the logic of the particularities of space and authorized representatives of the space. The possibility of this way of 'the extraparliamentary' is explored by way of reading Gandhi's *Constructive Programme* in two senses: the idea of redefining 'space' for the political; and the issue of de-constrained representation. In other words, the rejection of the double rejection (space and representing) is explored in the *Constructive Programme*.

ACKNOWLEDGEMENTS

I express my deep gratitude to Amarendra Pandey, Anuradha Veeravalli, Ghanshyam Shah, Kunal Kishore, Lajwanti Chatani, M.P. Singh, N. Rajaram, Nitesh Choudhury, Premanand Mishra, Rityusha Tiwary, Smruti Ranjan Dhal, Sudarshan Iyengar and Vikram Amaravat for reading the text and making substantive and critical comments. In addition, on several occasions, I greatly benefitted from the comments of Manoranjan Mohanty, Bidyut Mohanty, Manindra Nath Thakur, Hilal Ahmed, Sadan Jha, Manoj Rai, Kamal Nayan Choubey, Sudhir Suthar, Shailaza Singh, Praveen Verma, Manas Kandi and Mohammad Naushad.

I am grateful to the Central University of Gujarat for granting me leave for the study. Prof. R.S. Dubey (vice chancellor, Central University of Gujarat) extended substantive academic and administrative requirements to pursue the study. Students, scholars and faculty of the university remained the critical source for starting the book. I am grateful to the Centre for Gandhian Thought and Peace Studies (CUG) for conducting the numerous debates that helped me write this book.

In addition, I would like to express my profound gratitude to the Centre for the Study of Developing Societies (CSDS) for awarding me a visiting fellowship that allowed me to continue working on this project. The everlasting faith that Awadhendra Sharan, director of CSDS, has shown in the book was made clear to me by his consistent encouragement and enthusiasm over it. Clarification on a variety of subjects was gained through conversations with Ananya Vajpeyi, Baidik Bhattacharya, Nishikant Kolge, Prabhat Kumar, Prathama Banerjee, Priyadarshini Vijaisri, Rakesh Pandey, Ravi Sundaram, Ravikant, Sanjay Kumar and Sanjeer Alam. Not only did Hilal Ahmed contribute a substantial amount of his time to the discussion on the content and form of the book but he also took a significant interest in the completion of the work and offered any and all assistance that was possible. At CSDS, Praveen Rai and Preethi Nambiar were quite helpful in academics and administrative support—both of you have my gratitude. My sincere thanks also go to Sachin, Ayodhya, and Vikas, along with the CSDS Library and its staff, who were a great help.

Premanka Goswami, the editor in charge at Penguin, offered some much-needed ideas regarding the reorganization of the arguments and the value of both the 'arguments' and 'access to arguments'. In addition to that, he graciously overlooked the multiple occasions on which I missed my deadlines. In conclusion, this book would not have been written if he had not been so consistently enthusiastic and encouraging throughout the process. The time that I spent working with him was something that I will always treasure. Aparna Abhijit, copy editor at Penguin, provided helpful comments, recommendations and edits.

NOTES

Introduction

1. Gandhi is the author of the text. The issues which were added by Gandhi both in the discourse and the *Constructive Programme* is discussed herein.
2. 'According to the law, I was to be on my trial, but truly speaking, Government was to be on its trial' (Gandhi, 2018: 637). Gandhi makes this statement in his *Autobiography*.
3. 'I venture to make this statement not in any way in extenuation of the penalty to be awarded against me, but to show that I have disregarded the order served upon me not for want of respect for lawful authority, but in obedience to the higher law of our being, the voice of conscience' (Tendulkar, 1957: 39–40).
4. See Footnote 3, page 4, CWMG XXIII. At this stage, the term constructive programme is used by the editorial team of CWMG.
5. Subjects Committee related to the Congress Constitution: It was the most important committee. As per the Article XVI:

(a) The new All India Congress Committee shall meet as Subjects Committee, under the President-elect at least two days before the Annual Congress.

(b) The Subjects Committee shall proceed to discuss the programme and shall frame resolution for being moved in the open session.

6. According to Sekhar Bandyopadhyay, '[i]t was through this constructive programme that Gandhi hoped to achieve true swaraj. But one important issue that this constructive programme did not touch was Hindu-Muslim unity' (Bandyopadhyay, 2015: 316).

7. In this letter, Gandhi responds to Jivanji Desai's suggestion to include *goseva* in the *Constructive Programme*.

8. Date at the end of the foreword is 13 November 1945. The term *foreword* is used in the text in place of the *preface*.

9. Manager of Navjivan Press.

10. Next, two questions/answers are omitted herein.

11. Next question/answer is omitted herein.

12. *Constructive Programme: Its Meaning and Place*, https://www.gandhiheritageportal.org/mahatma-gandhi-books/constructive-programme-its-meaning-and-place-gujarati#page/1/mode/2up, last accessed 25 June 2023.

13. Ibid.

14. 'This appeared in *Harijan* under the title "His Last Will and Testament"' (CWMG XC, 1984: 526).

15. 1910 edition is as follows: Gandhi, M.K. (1910). *Indian Home Rule*. Phoenix Natal: International Printing Press; the Following description was mentioned about the book: 'Being a Translation of "Hind Swaraj" (Indian Home Rule), Published in the Gujarati columns of *Indian Opinion*, 11th and 18th December 1909'.

16. *The Story of My Experiments with Truth Vol I* (Translated by Mahadev Desai) was published in 1927 by Navajivan Press, Ahmedabad. *The Story of My Experiments with Truth Vol II* (Translated by Mahadev Desai and Pyarelal Nair) was published in 1929 by Navajivan Press, Ahmedabad. *An Autobiography or the Story of My Experiment with Truth* (Translated by Mahadev Desai) was published in 1940 by Navajivan Press, Ahmedabad.

17. In Indian liberal political theory, violence is not considered an aberration. I am thankful to Ghanshyam Shah for this reminder.

18. In the context of using it concerning Gandhi and Gandhian philosophy, the nearest use is by E.M.S. Namboodiripad is 'extraparliamentary activity'. He attributes it to the constructive programme in *The Mahatma and the Ism* (Namboodiripad, 2010: 163).

19. It is maintained in a slew of studies that civil disobedience is one of the forms of Satyagraha. For example, in Karuna Mantena, '[c]ivil disobedience, noncooperation, the boycott, strike, and hartal (full work stoppage) are viable forms of satyagraha but only when embedded within a

robust politics of nonviolence' (Mantena, 2012: 462). Mantena further divides satyagraha into destructive satyagraha and constructive satyagraha and puts civil disobedience into the destructive satyagraha. According to her, '[d]estructive satyagraha revolves around the tactics of civil disobedience and noncooperation. It is a mode of militant and direct political action against unjust laws or an unjust political order, an order with which you are in, or place yourself in, an antagonistic relationship. By contrast, constructive nonviolent action is driven less by an urgency to resist, withdraw, or undo existing political authority than by the need to create political bonds and forms of association and authority on a voluntary and noncoercive basis' (Mantena, 2012: 465).

20. I am thankful to Anuradha Veeravalli for this suggestion.

Constructive Progamme: Its Meaning and Place

Introductory

1. L.S. Amery (1873–1955) was secretary of state for India and Burma (1940–55).

Communal Unity

1. The adjective 'communal' is used for shared meaning and shared living. In social sciences, particularly in the West, the adjective communal is used positively, which means 'collective'. In this chapter, the word 'communal' also entails a similar meaning. The term is absent in *An*

Autobiography or The Story of My Experiments with Truth, *Satyagraha in South Africa* and *Hind Swaraj*. Chapter 10 of *Hind Swaraj* is titled *The Condition of India (cont.): the Hindus and the Mahomedans*. *Satyagraha in South Africa* contains the word communalism once. In his other writings, associate use can be located in the context of the communal award (MacDonald award), communal organizations, communal questions, communal riots, communal tension, non-violence, anti-untouchability campaign, British rule in India, communal relations, communal harmony, communal propaganda, partition, communal discrimination, religion, Round Table Conference II, Simla Conference and swaraj.

Pledges and resolutions are essential mechanisms for Hindu–Muslim unity in *Autobiography*. In *Satyagraha*, he denies any Hindu–Muslim problem in South Africa. In *Hind Swaraj*, Mahomedans are used for Muslims. *Hind Swaraj* asserts that despite the religious differences, all are fellow countrymen since they have accepted India as their country.

2. Moreover, unlike the liberal discourse of secularism, which relegates 'secular discourse' only to statist discourse, Gandhi makes more problematic questions of 'communal unity' as a part of common discourse. Communal unity is not simply political unity but 'an unbreakable heart unity'. It is not a relationship governed solely by emotionless laws, but social relations play an important role here. Against a simplified definition of

representation in a liberal state, Gandhi urges for *merged representation,* in which others are intrinsically included. This merged representation exists in everydayness.

It should be followed by political unity, not otherwise.

3. Living unity is crucial, which cannot come from artificial institutions. This is a categorical message in all related contemporary writings.

In 1943, a book titled *Unity* (Series No. 3) contained a brief message (Source added by Abdul Ghaffar Khan along with chapters by Mahatma Gandhi, Maulana Abul Kalam Azad, Pandit Jawaharlal Nehru, the late Mahadevebhai Desai, Khwaja Ahmad Abbas and K.G. Mashruwala [Gupta, 1943]). Khan warns, '[b]eware of fanatics who make men insane and bloodthirsty in the name of religion' (Khan, 1943). The book's introduction culls out seventeen points on the subject from Gandhi, Nehru, Azad and others. For example, point 15 is: 'I do not want Swaraj even at the cost of weakest minority' (Gupta, 1943: viii).

Some of the compilations of Gandhi's work on community unity were also published. In 1949, *Communal Unity*, Gandhi as the author, a foreword by Rajendra Prasad and editor's note by Bharatan Kumarappa was published by Navajivan. According to Rajendra Prasad, '[c]ommunal unity requires that the people belonging to any, the particular group should have toleration, if not respect, for the religion, language and customs of others' (Prasad, 1949: iii). For Kumarappa, '[u]nlike political interdependence which could be had immediately the foreigner left, Hindu-Muslim unity demanded careful cultivation and nurturing through the years. It involved nothing less than a fundamental change in men's notions of religion and morality—the most conservative of all human spheres. It was, therefore, no mean undertaking' (Kumarappa, 1949: viii). The book contains 525 items and four addenda (Gandhi, 1949).

Other notable works include the following: M.K. Gandhi (1965). *The Hindu-Muslim Unity*, edited by Anand Hingorani. Bombay: Bharatiya Vidya Bhavan; S. Abid Husain (1969). *Gandhiji and Communal Unity*. New Delhi: Orient Longman and Gandhi Peace Foundation; M.K. Gandhi (1968). *Gandhi's India: Unity in Diversity*, selections prepared by the National Integration Sub-committee of the National Committee for Gandhi Centenary, foreword by Zakir Husain, Introduction by K. Santhanam. New Delhi: National Book Trust).

Removal of Untouchability

1. In *Hind Swaraj,* caste and untouchability are not mentioned. In *Autobiography,* caste, outcaste (in a different sense as to his own expulsion from his caste due to a proposed study in London) and untouchability are mentioned. He talks about untouchability in the context of the imperfection of Hinduism due to the practice of untouchability; separate kitchens in Congress session; Rebutting Swamy's request to wear a sacred thread during Kumbh Mela

(1912) since it was not allowed to countless Hindus; admission to the Ashram (Ahmedabad); Untouchability in Champaran; praising Gangabehn Majmundar for eradicating untouchability in 1917; the passing of a resolution on removal of untouchability (among other items) at Calcutta special session (1920) and confirmation at the Annual Session Nagpur. His visit to the untouchable's quarter in Rajkot during the plague; discrimination for a haircut; *dhedvado* (remote quarters in villages); rampant discrimination with untouchables in South Africa across all religions; Coolie being the equivalence of an untouchable in South Africa; joining of an untouchable family in the Ashram, and an economic and social crisis are an essential component of *Autobiography*. *Shudras* and *Panchama* are mentioned once and twice, respectively. Gandhi uses the term caste in his own location for his intra-community discrimination or description. *Satyagraha in South Africa* uses 'untouchability' or untouchable/Panchamas in a comparative sense, i.e. comparing Indian conditions in South Africa with Dalits' situations in India. (*Hind Swaraj, Autobiography, Satyagraha in South Africa*)

2. In popular Indian mythology, the curse is also known as *shap* or *abhsihap*. It can be used both as a noun and a verb. However, the usage herein entails 'severe indictment'.

3. The most critical interlocutors of Gandhi on caste and untouchability were B.R. Ambedkar and Jawaharlal

Nehru. Ambedkar did not differentiate between *varna*, caste and untouchability. The most crucial difference with Gandhi was on varna and its separation from untouchability. According to Ambedkar, a rights-based discourse that integrates social, economic and political rights is a must. Though the 'social question' remains vital in both, the division or not division between varna and untouchability is a contested zone. Ambedkar also refers to caste and untouchability as 'graded inequality'. For him, 'The caste system is marked not merely by inequality but is affected by the system of graded inequality. All castes are not on a par. They are one above the other. There is a kind of ascending scale of hatred and a descending scale of contempt' (Ambedkar, 2014: 167).

Despite the problematic nature of Gandhi's position on the separation between varna and untouchability, his contribution to four accounts is crucial. Firstly, he shifted the responsibility of untouchability onto the upper caste, or, in Gandhi's words, *Sanatani* Hindus. Secondly, in the discourse, discussion of the oppressor is also crucial. They also need to change. He suggested working among caste Hindus and called them sinners. Thirdly, he treated untouchability as a 'blot' and 'curse' on Hinduism, which is not without contestation due to negating 'materialism' of exploitation and humiliation. However, he uses 'religion' against caste Hindus for the practice of untouchability in the name of religion. Fourthly, he urges more action beyond 'political necessity' to end monstrous isolation.

4. In Gandhi's *'My Notes'* (2 August 1932, *Navajivan*), the term is used as 'Harijana'. On Gandhi's invitation to suggest a name in place of *Antyaja*, Jagannath Desai from Rajkot suggested Harijana. He suggested that this was widely used by 'the father of Gujarati poetry'. Footnote 1 suggests, as per the letter, its usage in villages and Narsinh Mehta's use for *Antyaja* devotees (CWMG XLVII, 1971: 245). The Harijan Sevak Sangh was established in 1932 (Constitution of the Harijan Sevak Sangh, 1935: 3). Gandhi also started Harijan (a weekly newspaper in English), Harijan Bandu (Gujarati), and Harijan Sevak (Hindi) in 1933. In the first issue of Harijan (11 February 1933), Gandhi explains the usage of the term *Harijan*. There was a complaint from 'untouchable correspondents' regarding the use of the term *Asprisya* (untouchable) in Navjivan. The suggestion also came from a 'untouchable' correspondent to use Harijan (a man of god) due to its strength derived from its use by the 'first known poet-saint of Gujarat'. In cases of relinquishing untouchability against the victim and sufferer by caste Hindus, all can be referred to as 'Harijans'. The former is already part of it, and the latter is imbued with conditionality (Gandhi, 1933: 7). This is Gandhi's parity pursuit. Though Gandhi does not mention the name Narsinh Mehta, 'the first known poet-saint of Gujarat' is widely accepted as the term for

Narsinh Mehta (CWMG XLVII, 1971: 245; Gandhi, 1995: 255).

The term has been subjected to severe criticism for metaphysical diversion, paternalism and omitting the struggle of Dalits. Nevertheless, on the other hand, the term 'Dalit' has gained massive popularity for denoting struggle, exploitation and solidarity.

5. Gandhi uses isolation in a very substantive sense. The closest concepts could be alienation and humiliation.

6. Gandhi's *Poorna Swaraj* is unthinkable without the eradication of untouchability. This is the arrival of freedom.

Prohibition

1. Prohibition refers here to the prohibition of intoxicants and narcotics. Gandhi stresses a non-violent solution. Prohibition per se is absent in *Hind Swaraj, Satyagraha in South Africa* and *Autobiography.* However, his disdain for wine is present in his *Autobiography.* He was allowed to go to England by his mother after taking three vows: 'not to touch wine, woman, and meat' (Gandhi, 2018: 104).

   Gandhi also demands total prohibition. Gandhi's formulation is also interesting in another aspect. 'The demand . . . for prohibition must go hand in hand with the demand for a corresponding reduction in military expenditure' (CWMG XXIX, 1968: 438). He also advised the Prohibition League of India to 'adopt a more forward policy and not treat total prohibition as a goal to be realized in the dim and distant future, but a national policy to be immediately adopted and enforced without the cumbersome process of taking a referendum' (CWMG XXIX, 1968: 439).

Temperance (abstinence) has invited definite attention. For Lucy Carroll, '[t]he temperance/prohibition agitation represents a fascinating chapter in the social and political history of India . . . it is generally dismissed (or elevated) as an example of the uniquely Indian process of "sanskritization" or as an equally unique component of "Gandhianism"—in spite of the fact that the liquor question has not been without political importance . . . And in spite of the fact that the temperance agitation in India in the late nineteenth century and well into the twentieth century was intimately connected with temperance agitation in England. Indeed, the temperance movement in India was organized, patronized, and instructed by English temperance agitators' (Carroll, 1976: 417).

Mark Lawrence Schrad's *Smashing the Liquor Machine: A Global History of Prohibition (2021)* is an essential book on the global temperance movement. According to Schrad, Gandhi used prohibitionism as resistance. This resistance mode was crucial against Britain's narco-military empire based on the trafficking of opium and alcohol. The proceeds were used to fund the military occupation. '. . . [M]erging of political power and economic profit from liquor and opium made the East India Company "perhaps the world's first 'narco-military' empire," according to historian David Washbrook' (Schrad, 2021: 202). Thus, it was important for Gandhi to work this aphorism: '. . . To make India free, make India dry' (Schrad, 2021: 202).

2. The Working Committee adopted C. Rajagopalchari's *Prohibition Campaign* (1929). Dr Ansari, Vallabhabhai Patel, Rajendra Prasad and C. Rajagopalachari became members of a committee for the implementation of this scheme (CWMG XL, 1970: 204). The *campaign* was circulated among provincial committees of the Congress. They were expected to respond quickly and effectively (CWMG XL, 1970: 415). The campaign consisted of fifteen items: appointment of a prohibition subcommittee, call for honorary workers and appoint drink secretary at Taluka, open membership for an Anti-Drink Sabha, adhering to the principle of non-violence by volunteer corps consisting of men and women, meeting on every second Sunday for total prohibition, everyday local meeting, organizing counter-attractions for diversion, pledge during the anti-drinking meeting, organizing a peaceful picketing of liquor and drug shop, influencing landholders to not give trees for tapping to manufacturers of intoxicants, dissuading people at auction sales of the right to vend drinks and drugs, gathering information by the taluka secretary on or before every Sunday and sending it to the Provincial Committee, taking a written pledge, appointment of A District Prohibition Secretary,

and total prohibition as a part of the election campaign (CWMG XL, 1970: 438–40).

In 1931, the *Indian Prohibition Manual,* a sixty-page book forwarded by Jawaharlal Nehru and authored by C. Rajagopalachari, was published by the Indian National Congress Prohibition Committee. Nehru emphasizes the importance of addressing the prohibition issue from fiscal and mental degeneration in a scientific manner. 'The greatest injury of intoxicants is the physical and mental degeneration of an individual or group. The question, therefore, must be approached in a scientific spirit' (Nehru, 1931).

Why Prohibition, a booklet with eight chapters written by Bharatan Kumarappa in 1952, made the case for alcohol prohibition.

In 1960, R.K. Prabhu compiled Gandhi's writings and published the twenty-two-page book *Prohibition at Any Cost* by M.K. Gandhi. 'Havoc wrought by the evil drink,' 'nothing short of total prohibition,' 'untenable plea of individual freedom,' 'cry of loss of revenue,' 'problem of illicit distillation,' 'Toddy and Nira,' and 'Need for Private Effort' (Gandhi, 1960) are the chapters that comprise the compilation.

Khadi

1. *Khadi* means clothes made of homespun yarn. It is also known as Indian coarse cloth. Broadly, it connotes self-sufficiency, interdependence, the fight against imperialism

and a substantive substitute for capitalism-led large-scale production. *Khadi* symbolizes economic freedom.

Khadi is not mentioned in *Hind Swaraj* or *Satyagraha*. In *Hind Swaraj*, he only uses handlooms once. He urges us to use it against machine-made goods. Khadi is mentioned extensively in the *Autobiography*. Chapter 39 is titled 'The Birth of Khadi'. Khadi is used in various ways, like personal choice, Punjab being an ideal place for khadi work, negligence of khadi, khadi as a positive substitute, promotion of khadi manufacturing in the Ashram, personal disposition for khadi, and establishing a living bond of relationship with exploited through khadi. Overall, in Gandhi's writings, some of the associated terms of khadi used by him are 'swadeshi', 'khaddar', 'spinning-wheel', 'swaraj', 'hand-spinning', 'charkha', 'handloom', and 'village industries'.

One of the earliest works on khadi was *Economics of Khaddar* (1928) by Richard B. Gregg. Verrier Elwin's booklet (published in 1931/reproduced in 1964), with a foreword by J.B. Kripalani, draws attention to the 'religious and cultural aspects of khadi' (Elwin, 1964a). *Economics of Khadi*, a collection of Gandhi's articles and speeches with a foreword from Rajendra Prasad, was published in 1941. The book contains 204 items. In 1955, Bharatan Kumarappa re-arranged several items from *Economics of Khadi* into seventeen themes and published *Khadi (Hand-Spun Cloth): Why and How* with Gandhi as the author. In the editor's note, he highlights the significance of *khadi* as true swaraj, the dignity of handlabour, bridging the gap between classes and a self-sufficient village economy (Kumarappa, 1955: v–vi).

Gandhi's engagement with *khadi* was absolute. He prepared a sale memo during the opening ceremony of Shuddha Swadeshi Bhandar (Kalbadevi, Bombay) on 1 October 1919. He also commented on P. Venkayya's proposal for the national flag. Venkayya published *A National Flag for India* in 1916. Amidst numerous suggestions, his need for an inclusive flag representing all religions stands out. 'We require . . . a flag which would command reverence from all our countrymen-Hindu, Mohamadan, Buddhist and Christian, Sikh and Jain, Parsee and Jew alike . . .' (Venkayya, 1916:19). Gandhi, in addition to some crucial changes, insisted on, initially suggested by Lala Hansraj, giving space to spinning wheel on the swaraj flag and it must be made of *khaddar* (CWMG XIX, 1966: 561–62). 1921 onwards, loincloth became an integral part of Gandhi. Onward the 1922 Ahmedabad Session of Congress, *khadi* became integral to the sessions. All India Khaddar Board (AIKB) was established in 1924 by the Kakinada (Cocanad then) session of Congress. On 22 September 1925, the All India Spinners' Association (AISA) was formed by the resolution of the Patna Session of Congress.

2. Khadi holds an important place in Gandhi's life. Khadi becomes extremely important by rejecting not only the well-accepted formulation of economic inequality in the liberal discourse or the liberal state, but also by breaking the discussion on merely political equality in which political space and agency are created. Khadi discourse in Gandhi takes the discussion beyond 'liberal political' while treating khadi as 'economic freedom' and 'economic equality for all'.

3. The idiom suggests the significance of the practical experience. *Proof* stands for 'test', not verification (Ayto, 2010: 276).

4. The swadeshi mentality has attracted considerable attention. In the context of Gandhi, it needs to be read as interdependence by way of economic autonomy. A counter-Gandhian reading of it is cultural absoluteness or supremacy.

5. This is an important phrase used by Jawaharlal Nehru in 1937 to celebrate 1 August all over India. This was an occasion to offer a 'camaraderie greeting' to Congress ministers. On this day, Nehru also remembers Lokmanya Tilak's death and the beginning of the non-cooperation movement. In this context, he makes the following statement: 'I trust that as an earnest of his sympathy and goodwill, every Indian who stands for India's freedom will wear khadi, the livery of our freedom, and will display and honour the National Flag' (published in *Harijan*, 31 July 1937) (CWMG LXV, 1976: 473).

Gandhi's 'Letter to Jawaharlal Nehru' (Segaon, Wardha, 30 July 1937) is appreciative of Nehru concerning the 'livery of freedom'. 'Your calling khadi "livery of freedom" will live as long as we speak the English language in India. It needs a first-class poet to translate into Hindi the whole of the thought behind that enchanting phrase. For me it is not merely poetry but it enunciates a great truth whose full significance we have yet to grasp' (CWMG LXV, 1976: 446).

6. Rather than making a few cities and British Imperialism survive on the exploitation of Indian villages, Gandhi emphasized making villages self-contained units, voluntarily linked with cities and the outside world for mutual benefits. Khadi offers the opportunity for this decentralization by way of 'the beginning of the khadi processes' and the decentralization of labour for the simpler and cheaper tools.

Khadi is also important for blurring the distinction between labour and intelligence. Overall, khadi is a euphemism for inviting attention to the situation where political equality and economic inequality are comfortably fitted.

7. Before A.I.S.A., the All India Khaddar Board was established in 1924. Jamnalal Bajaj (chairman), Vallabhbhai Patel, Maganlal Gandhi, Reva Shanker Jagjivan Jhaveri, Velji Nappu, Belgaumwalla, Shaukat Ali and Shankerlal Banker (secretary) served on the Board (Report of the Thirty-Eighth National Congress held at

Cocanada, 1924, 177–78). The Executive Council of the A.I.S.A. (1925) had the following members for five years: Mahatma Gandhi, Maulana Shaukat Ali, Rajendra Prasad, Satis Chandra Das Gupta, Maganlal K. Gandhi, Jamnalal Bajaj (treasurer), Shuaib Qureshi (secretary), Shankerlal G. Banker (secretary) and Jawaharlal Nehru (secretary). The association was located at Satyagraha Ashram, Sabarmati, Ahmedabad (CWMG XXVIII, 1968: 227–30).

8. Gandhi quotes this figure from the annual report (1940) of the All-India Spinners' Association (All India Spinners' Association, 1940; Gonsalves, 2012: 145). *Khadi Jagat* was started in July 1941 to disseminate khadi information under the editorship of Krishndas Gandhi. Earlier, he was the editor of *Maharashtra Khadi Patrika*. Gandhi's article in the inaugural issue was titled *Khadi Jagat.* He mentions 2,22,421 spinners (1, 67, 996 Hindus, 56,425 Muslims, 20,643 others (ginners, carders, weavers and washermen). He described the association as a representative of them and the wearer of Khadi (Gandhi, 1941: 4).

9. Gandhi launched the Champaran Satyagraha against the imposition of indigo cultivation, infamously known as the *tinkathiya* system (forced to grow on three parts out of twenty parts of land), on *raiyats* (tenant farmers) in 1917. The Champaran Agrarian Act of 1918 abolished the tinkathiya system. Gandhi successfully mobilized heterogeneous people while practising and experiencing constructive work in Champaran. The

following books are essential for understanding the
Champaran Satyagraha at the micro and macro levels:
Prasad, Rajendra (1928). *Satyagraha in Champaran*.
Madras: S. Ganeshan; Tendulkar, D.G. (1957). *Gandhi
in Champaran*. New Delhi: The Publication Division,
Ministry of Information and Broadcasting, Government
of India; Misra, B.B. (ed.) (1963). *Select Documents on
Mahatma Gandhi's Movement in Champaran: 1917–18*.
Patna: The Government of Bihar.

10. Literally, bow-shape spindle (*dhanush*/bow, *takli*/spindle).
It is even a much smaller version of the spinning wheel. It is
straightforward to operate and keep. Gandhi's technological
innovation was based on cost-effectiveness and human-
controlling machine, not otherwise.

11. Strings: There are two strings. One is thicker while the
other is thinner. The thicker string is used to join the two
wooden wheels or discs. The thinner one joins the smaller
disc to the spindle. I am grateful to Amarendra Pandey
for pointing out the literal and functional translation.

12. Gandhi was influenced by John Ruskin's *Unto This Last*.
He translated it into Gujarati as *Sarvodaya* (the welfare of
all) (Gandhi, 2018: 470–471). He summarizes it through
three components:

    1. That the good of the individual is contained in the
    good of all.

    2. That a lawyer's work has the same value as the barber's
    in as much as all have the same right of earning their
    livelihood from their work.

3. That a life of labour, i.e. the life of the tiller of the soil and the handicraftsman is the life worth living.

The first of these I knew. The second I had dimly realized. The third had never occurred to me. *Unto This Last* made it as clear as daylight for me that the second and the third were contained in the first. I arose with the dawn, ready to reduce these principles to practice' (Gandhi, 2018: 470–71).

Other Village Industries

1. Village industries per se are not discussed in *Hind Swaraj*, *Satyagraha in South Africa*, and *Autobiography*. The village is present in *Hind Swaraj* as 'small villages', and 'resentment against command'. In *Hind Swaraj,* Henry Sumner Maine's classic, *Village Communities in the East and West* (1871) is mentioned in appendices (one of twenty books to be read). Mains' argument about self-governing, self-contained republics, and self-sufficient Indian villages had attracted considerable attention in Gandhian schemes and postulations. In *Satyagraha,* village appears in the form of logistical support. In *Autobiography*, village is referred to as untouchability, lack of education and opening of schools in Champaran, village women, medical help, poverty, constructive work in villages, opening of Ashrams (Kochrab and Sabarmati), revenue assessment, principles of Satyagraha and hartal. Gandhi's discussion on 'other village industries' is incredibly significant. He takes the matter in the form

of what economists call 'agriculture-plus' in Indian villages, i.e. besides farming, non-farming livelihood is also important. Hand-grinding, hand-pounding, soap-making, papermaking, match-making, tanning, oil-pressing, etc. become immensely crucial for a complete village economy. 'Village-minded' in Gandhi should be construed as a fight against pauperism and starvation.

Accordingly, the All-India Village Industries Association (A.I.V.I.A., Headquarters: Wardha) was formed on 14 December 1934 (resolution by Gandhi was moved on 2 October 1934, to the AICC and passed on 27 October 1934, Bombay). Shrikrishnadas Jajooji (president and treasurer), J.C. Kumarappa (organizer and secretary), Gosibehn Captain, Khan Saheb, Shoorji Vallabhdas, Prafulla Ghosh, Lakshmidas Purushottam Asar and Shankerlal Banker had consented to form the association thus becoming foundation members and members of the first Board of Management: Rabindranath Tagore, J.C. Bose, P.C. Ray, C.V. Raman, Ramdas Pantulu, Jamal Mohamed Sahib, G.D. Birla, Purushottamdas Thakurdas, S. Pochkhanawalla, Sam Higginbottom, Jivraj Mehta, M.A. Ansari, Robert McCarrison, Rajabally, V. Patel, S. Subha Rao, B.C. Roy and Purushottam Patel consented to be a part of the Board of Advisors. Village reconstruction and decentralization were the central objectives (CWMG LIX, 1974: 449–53).

2. Henry Sumner Maine's classic, *Village Communities in the East and West* (1871), is an essential anchor in Gandhian discourse. Against the move of the South African Government to debar Indians from the franchise due to the absence of prior practice and experience, petitions were sent against it in this regard. 'Petition to Natal Assembly' (Durban, 28 June 1894; separately to Natal Legislative Council on 4 August 1894) quotes, inter alia, '. . . Sir Henry Summer Maine's *Village Communities,* where he has most clearly pointed out that Indian races have been familiar with representative institutions almost from time immemorial' (CWMG I, 1969: 129). *The Natal Mercury* rebutted this argument in its article 'Indian Village Communities'. It relied on arguments of Sir George Chesney's position in *The Nineteenth Century.* 'In a Letter to The Natal Mercury' on 7 July 1894, Gandhi rejected Chesney as a sole authority on India and requested to refer Maine (CWMG I,1969:144–45). 'Petition to Legislative Council, Transvaal' (10 June 1903), by Abdool Gandi (chairman, British Indian Association), against the attempt to disfranchise Indians due to the absence of any franchise system, or similar existence as such, quotes Maine's work in defence of the existence of self-government in India. 'Your petitioner begs leave respectfully to remind this Honourable House that the Indian nation has been used to Municipal self-government for ages past, as . . . Sir Henry Summer

Maine's works would show' (CWMG III, 1979: 399). Maine is also cited in 'Open Letter' (Gandhi, 19 December 1894) (CWMG I,1969: 170–88), 'Baroda: A Model Indian State' (Gandhi, *Indian Opinion*, 3 June 1905) (CWMG IV, 1960: 456–57), 'Speech at Y.M.C.A.'(Gandhi, 25 August 1925, Calcutta) (CWMG XXVIII, 1968: 107–109), 'Speech at Chatham House Meeting' (Gandhi, 20 October 1931, London) (CWMG XLVIII, 1971: 193–206), 'What It Means" (Segaon, 4 December 1939) (Gandhi LXXI,1978: 4–5) and 'Speech at Meeting of Deccan Princes' (Gandhi, 28 July 1946, Poona) (CWMG LXXXV, 1982: 76–81).

Gandhi's position on the village from this perspective has invited considerable contestation. However, his idea of village development has inspired several generations to initiate rural studies, transformation and reconstruction. Gandhi considered serving a village equivalent to achieving Swaraj. His '. . . idea of Village Swaraj is . . . a complete republic, independent of its neighbours for its own vital wants, and yet interdependent for many others in which dependence is a necessity' (Gandhi, 1962: 31). The ideal village will have perfect sanitation, ventilation, wells, village common, cooperative dairy, primary and secondary schools, Panchayats, intelligent human beings, no plague, no cholera, no smallpox and the importance of manual labour (Gandhi, 1962: 32–34). Basic principles of village swaraj contain 'supremacy of man [human]-full employment', 'body-labour', 'equality', 'trusteeship', decentralization', 'swadeshi', 'self-sufficiency', 'co-operation', 'satyagraha', 'equality of religions', 'Panchayati raj', and 'naitalim' (Gandhi, 1962: 34–43). Gandhi wrote these on different occasions. H. Vyas published a selection from Gandhi's writings and published it as *Village Swaraj* in 1962.

Village Sanitation

1. *Sanitation* is not mentioned in *Hind Swaraj*. In *Satyagraha*, sanitation is mentioned in the context of deliberation during Natal Indian Congress, Thambi Naidoo in charge of sanitation at Tolstoy Farm, and ignorance of sanitation laws during mobilization. Thambi Naidoo (1875–1933) was part of the first batch of prisoners in South Africa. Gandhi used 'the lion-like' epithet for him. In *Autobiography*, indifference to laws of sanitation, offering help to the sanitation department during the plague at Rajkot, disregarding of rules of sanitation at places of worship, criminal negligence of sanitation, negligence by Municipalities for Indian ghettos in South Africa, his sons pro-grounding for general sanitation, village sanitation in Champaran and sanitation issue at Kochrab Ashram in Ahmedabad due to plague nearby are adverted. In March 1935, he visited nearby Wardha and cleaned excreta and suggested converting it into rich manure (CWMG LX, 1974: 299).

2. Gandhi breaks the hiatus between intelligence and labour in several ways. This is vividly described in *Bahuroopee*

Gandhi (1964), written by Anu Bandopadhyaya with a foreword by Jawaharlal Nehru, which was written for children. R.K. Laxman did illustrations for the book. *Bahuroopee* stands for polymorphic. In other words, Gandhi played multiple roles. In the book, his roles are defined as toiler, barrister, tailor, washerman, barber, scavenger, cobbler, servant, cook, doctor, nurse, teacher, weaver, spinner, bania (the word is used to highlight frugal nature), kisan, auctioneer, beggar (begging for public cause), looter (bridging the disparity of income), jail-bird, general, author, journalist, painter–publisher, fashion–setter, snake charmer and priest (Bandopadhyaya, 1964).

3. The conjoining of village and sanitation is crucial to Gandhi. He decided to settle in and around villages.

4. Gandhi highlights the diversity of representation in Congress. Lawyers predominantly led the Congress leadership.

5. Overall, George Vivian Poore's (1843–1904) influence on Gandhi is noteworthy. '. . . I owe to Poore my knowledge of the cheapest and the most effective method of disposal of human excreta' (CWMG XXV, 1967: 461). 'I have said noting with regard to Western sanitation. In fact, I derived my idea of rural sanitation from Poore, an English doctor . . .' (CWMG LXV, 1976: 361). Poore was known as a scientist of sanitation or propagator of sanitation science who wrote *Colonial and Camp Sanitation* which remained a popular source for referring to sanitation.

Chapter I, 'the sanitation of Camps-Flies and the Science of Scavenging'(reprinted from the *Lancet,* 18 May 1901), discusses Salisbury plain, the burial of faeces, trenches, vegetation and cultivation, temporary camps, kitchen refuse, flies and their multiplication, chemical disinfectants and neatness. Chapter II, 'an Experiment in Sanitation – Collection of Rain Water – Disposal of Slop Water' (originally published in *Country Life,* 6 July 1901), deliberates on the country cottage, water analysis, straining for slop-water, filtration gutter, earth closet, dry urinals, the housing of animals and construction of wells (Poore, 1903).

Gandhi refers to Poore in 'Notes' (Young India, 26 December 1924) (CWMG XXV, 1967: 460–63), 'Speech at Chatham House Meeting' (London, 20 October 1931) (CWMG XLVIII, 1971: 193–206), 'History of the Satyagraha Ashram' (11 July 1932) (CWMG L, 1972: 188–207), 'Letter to Narandas Gandhi' (5/6 April 1933; 16 April 1933; 19 April 1933) (CWMG LIV, 1973: 309–11; 432; 453–55), 'Letter to N.' (6 April 1933) (CWMG LIV, 1973: 316–18), 'Advice to Students' (before 28 January 1935/8 February 1935, *Harijan*) (CWMG LX, 1974: 118–20), 'How to Begin? –III' (8 February 1935) (CWMG LX, 1974: 190–92), 'Manure Pits' (1 March 1935) (CWMG LX, 1974: 269–70), 'Letter to H.L. Sharma' (12 March 1935; 21 March 1935) (CWMG LX, 1974: 299, 322), 'Notes' (14 April 1935) (CWMG LX,1976: 417–19), and

'Interview to Capt. Strunk' (Segaon, before 3 July 1937) (CWMG LXV,1976: 360–62).

New Or Basic Education

1. A slew of words like new education or basic education or *Nayee Talim* and *Nai Talim* are used interchangeably in Gandhi's context of school education. Nayee Talim has invited considerable attention. For Gandhi, Nayee Talim includes craft, art, health and education. In *Hind Swaraj,* the eighteenth chapter is on education. He offers a critique of the overall British education system. He encourages the translation of important English books into Indian languages. In addition to one's language, an additional language should also be learnt. In *Satyagraha in South Africa*, he highlights the importance of the Natal Education Association (in *Autobiography,* it is mentioned as the Indian Educational Association) and teaching experiments at Tolstoy Farm. In *Autobiography*, physical training and mental training, good handwriting, multiple language schemas (Hindi, Sanskrit, Persian, Arabic, English and the vernacular), the role of parents, and character building are part of education.

2. Gandhi presided over the Broach Educational Conference in 1917. The All India National Education Conference, Wardha (22–23 October 1937), is significant for Nayee Talim. This conference took place under the presidency of Gandhi. The following resolutions were passed in the Wardha Conference: providing free and compulsory

education for seven years on a nationwide scale; mother tongue as medium of instruction; endorsing Gandhi's position that the process of education should centre around some form of manual and productive work; covering the remuneration of teachers by this education system. Wardha Conference constituted the Zakir Hussain Committee (Zakir Hussain [chairperson], K. G. Saiyidan, Kaka Kalelkar, Kishorelal Mashruwala, J.C. Kumarappa, Shrikrishnadas Jaju, Vinoba Bhave, Asha Devi and Aryanayakam [convener]) for the formulation of a scheme of basic education. The committee submitted its report on 2 December 1937.The main outlines of the seven-year course of basic education are *the basic craft* (spinning and weaving, carpentry, agriculture, fruit and vegetable gardening, leather work and local craft work), *mother tongue* (capacity to converse freely, speak lucidly on everyday interest topic, read, read aloud, use reference books and dictionaries, write legibly and correctly, describe in writing, write a personal letter and to acquaint with writings of standard authors), *mathematics, social studies, general science* (nature study, zoology, physiology, hygiene, physical culture (games, athletics, drill), chemistry, knowledge of stars, stories (of great scientists and explorers), *drawing, music* and *Hindustani* (to be acquainted with a common 'lingua franca'). Training of teachers was also suggested. Resolutions of the Wardha Conference were passed in the Haripura session (1938) of the Indian National Congress under the title of National

Education and paved the way for the formation of the All Indian Education Board/Hindustani Talimi Sangh (*Educational Reconstruction*, 1939).

Gandhi frequently interacts with Hindustani Talimi Sangh, especially in relation to the Congress, rural education, the promotion of khadi, the issue of requesting government assistance, integration with Harijan Ashram, merging with Charkha Sangh, co-education and workers' training in khadi production.

In 1938, J.B. Kripalani wrote *The Latest Fad [Basic Education]*. He listed ten principles of Basic Education: access to education at a certain minimal level to all and basic education is the universal minimum education; completion of education over the course of seven years, commencing at age seven; basic national education not focusing on the pre-school or post-school years at this time; mother tongue to teach the basic national education; incorporation of some form of handiwork or art into its methodology along with imparting intellectual education using craft's tool; learning craft methodically and scientifically with an eye toward effectiveness and useful outcomes; profitability of the cost's end product; commensuration of the work to pay the teacher's salary; covering the remaining costs associated with schools, including buildings, furniture, books, maps and all tools and equipment necessary for the craft being taught by the state; and commitment by the state using the craft's products to meet its own criteria or those of the municipal governments where the school is located (Kripalani, 1938: 72–73).

3. Gandhi links 'new or basic education' with the transformation of village children into model villagers. Though model villagers are not defined, it is meant to suit local contexts' needs. In place of mere 'skill' or market need for education, he finds its utility for local communities while bridging the gap between body and mind.

4. Marjorie Sykes was an important chronicler of Gandhi's education and Sevagram experiments. Marjorie Sykes played a crucial role in documenting Gandhi's educational initiatives and Sevagram experiments. She emphasizes the need for 'education for peace'. Gandhi's Nayee Talim, which teaches students how to organize a cooperative human society peacefully, is an example of non-violence in the educational setting. It is a vibrant attitude at the school, local and worldwide levels. To educate for peace, one must learn to constantly act in peace. To understand the path of peace, it is crucial to follow Nayee Talim's principles and practices (Marjorie, 1988).

   According to her, the perceptible shift can be discerned in Gandhi's vocabulary in the 1940s. He spoke not only of basic national education (minimum necessary equipment for the children) but also nayee talim (new education). On his seventy-fifth birthday (2 October 1944), he said that education must be extended beyond school, i.e. 'from conception to cremation' (Marjorie, 1988: 51).

This aspect is also present in Devi Prasad's analysis. Prasad terms *Bundiyadi Talim* as basic education. He cites Gandhi's explanation post-Quit India release from prison, where basic education was extended to everybody at every stage of life. Nayee Talim gives a wider scope. In 1947, truth and non-violence, along with individual and collective life, and true freedom, were included (Prasad, 2012).

In Krishna Kumar, basic education and *Nayee Talim* appear interchangeable. In Gandhi, nayee talim/basic education was a socializing strategy (Kumar, 2005: 121). Epistemologically, the idea of 'basic education' was completely new. It cannot fit inside the confines of older Indian educational systems (Kumar, 2005: 179). Akeel Bilgrami, in his foreword in Devi Prasad's book *Gandhi and Revolution* (2012), draws an immensely useful contribution of *Nayee Talim*. According to Bilgrami, 'Gandhi conceived of education as something that should be founded on *making*, not on learning, that it should involve the *body* and its habits as a path to the cultivation of virtue as well as to the development of skills and of understanding . . . Much is made by commentators on Gandhi of the affinities between him and Socrates. But I think there is nothing in the celebrated dialectical or dialogical method, quite like this link between the dispositions of the body and virtue, on which Gandhi rested his ideal of education. Nayee Talim . . . is a quite radical departure from even

the heterodoxies of a Socratic conception of education'
(Bilgrami, 2012: viii).

Adult Education

1. Adult education per se is absent in *Hind Swaraj,
   Satyagraha in South Africa* and *Autobiography*. Though it
   cannot be separated from education, yet it has a specific
   meaning for Gandhi. Ironically, 'adult education' is
   primarily ignored or reduced to methodological issues in
   the form of andragogy. Gandhi brings two crucial changes
   in this regard by exhibiting the significance of adult
   education and converting it into a site of the political.
   Firstly, there is an absence of realization of power to get
   rid of alien or imperialist rule. Gandhi elaborates on
   this point when discussing adult education and Indian
   villagers. Secondly, he links adult education with political
   education.

2. Concerning adult education, Gandhi appreciates the
   role of Frank Laubach and S.R. Bhagwat. 'I appreciate
   Prof. Laubach's immense labours in the way of making
   the alphabet easy and Prof. Bhagwat's great and practical
   contribution in the same direction' (CWMG LXV, 1976:
   235). Laubach wrote several books, including *Toward
   World Literacy the Each One Teach One Way* (Syracuse,
   N.Y.: Syracuse University Press, 1960).His *individual
   approach* (each one teach one) became highly popular.
   'Laubach method' stresses that 'you can teach, read, and
   write by using visual associations'. Prof. S. R. Bhagwat

was the chairman of the Provincial Board of Adult Education, Bombay. According to S.Y. Shah, 'Laubach was greatly influenced by Prof. S.R. Bhagwat's method of teaching a letter by making a story about its shape. But he observed that the method was time consuming and not easily adaptable in other languages. Taking a clue from Bhagwat, Laubach developed a new method of teaching the alphabet through pictures, words and syllables'(Shah, 2000: 19). Laubach asserted that while earlier approaches assisted adults in learning, they fell short of 'each one teaching one'. In particular, Bhagwat's picture-words-syllable lessons method is mentioned for its success. He emphasizes this lesson's advantages over earlier ones, including how simple it is for those who cannot read, how enjoyable pictures make learning, how new literary works are easier to understand other, and how pictures help us remember things (Laubach, 1940: 27).

Women

1. In *Hind Swaraj,* Gandhi highlights the women's condition. The working conditions for women in mills are appalling and they are forced to toil away in factories. In *Satyagraha in South Africa,* the issue of women is addressed by emphasizing black women as an equal partners in all aspects of life, the effects of British or European laws on them, the value of Boer women, British women and passive resistance, women at Tolstoy Farm, women in Satyagraha, women in jail and 127 women

in the Great March (he also refers to the number as 122). In *Autobiography*, Women's precarious conditions during the marriage, his admiration for the independence and vigour of Burmese women (during his Calcutta–Rangoon–Calcutta journey in January and February of 1902) as well as women's ashramites, praise for Punjabi women, Gangabehn Majmundar's role in eradicating untouchability and the use of khadi and the spinning wheel to provide work for women are all highlighted.

Gandhi raised or associated the women's question in the context of ahimsa, prohibition programme, picketing of liquor shops, spinning and weaving, wages, swadeshi, tolerance, literacy and their role in the national movement.

2. Kamaladevi Chattopadhyay (1903–88) is a crucial bridge between Gandhi and the gender question. She revived handicrafts, joined the international socialist feminist movement, participated in the International Alliance of Women (1929, Berlin), and worked with Margaret Cousins (founder and president of the All India Women's Conference). According to Yusuf Meherally, she was also the first woman to stand for legislative. As an ardent socialist, she presided over the All India Conference of the Congress Socialist Party and Satyawati Devi was the secretary of the reception committee at Meerut in 1936 (Meherally, 1947: 1–6).

Kamaladevi, in her book, *Indian Women's Battle for Freedom* (1983), elaborates on her discomfort with the 'male leaders' position on women's question. 'The main weakness of the male leaders of the time was their tendency to treat social evils as different malfunctioning constituents of society' (Chattopadhyay, 1983: 2). She was 'equally troubled by caste and economic differences, which continued to pose as a big question mark' (Chattopadhyay, 1983: 2). For Kamladevi, Gandhi bridges the gap through total change or a revolution or Sarvodaya. For women, the concept of a whole society, in which all components are interrelated and action-oriented decisions, is crucial. The first deputation and memorandum (1917) of Indian women to E.S. Montagu (the Secretary of State to India) stressed recognizing women as people in the schema of franchise conditions deliberations. The memorandum cites the petitions organized by Gandhi and signed by large numbers. She expressed her disagreement over the non-participation of women in the political direct action programmes. She tried to convince Gandhi to women's participation in Dandi March to break the salt law. In the absence of people from the Ashram, it was looked after by women, whereas men were active in political space. Women rejected this dichotomy. 'Their feelings were conveyed to him through a letter sent by Mrs Cousins: Division of sexes in a non-violent campaign seems unnatural and against all the awakened consciousness of the women of today . . . Women ask that no marches, imprisonment, no demonstrations organized for the benefit of India should prohibit women from a share in them' (Chattopadhyay,

1983: 105–06). Kamaladevi met Gandhi on the route during the Dandi March to convey the significance of this great march and value 'for the Indian women to liberate themselves in the process . . . They have been confined so long within their four walls, they seem hardly aware of the world which lies outside'(Chattopadhyay, 1983:106). Gandhi hoped for the emergence of women participation in large numbers eventually. Salt-breaking revolt reached every corner of the country. Women like men got the taste of liberation. 'As the men were being put behind bars, the women stepped out, providing mature, considered leadership, initiative, resourcefulness, beyond all expectations . . . [Gandhi] . . . commended them in these words: 'The role of women played in the freedom struggle should be written in letters of gold' (Chattopadhyay, 1983:107). Resolution on Fundamental Rights and Economic Programme (earlier drafting initiative taken by Nalinakshi Sanyal, Kamladevi and others, the preamble to the draft written by Nehru and approved by Gandhi) passed in the Karachi Session of Congress in 1931. It combined political freedom and socioeconomic rights. People's fundamental rights were combined with the secular state, adult suffrage, labour rights and women's rights with 'leave during maternity period' (Chattopadhyay, 1983:107–09). She quotes Gandhi regarding the minimum age of marriage and religious sanctions. 'I heartily endorse any movement to save innocent girls under age from man's lust. Even minimum age of 14 in my humble opinion is not permissible. *Sanskrit texts of doubtful authority cannot be invoked to sanctify a practice which in itself is immoral* (Chattopadhyay, 1983:113; original emphasis). For Gandhi, in addition to legislative reforms, a change of heart and social conscience are crucial against child marriage and discriminatory social laws (Chattopadhyay, 1983: 123).

In terms of gender violence, modern feminism presents a far more sophisticated, nuanced and necessary interpretation of patriarchy, which exhibits a monopoly of social and economic production and performativity. Gandhi does not provide a complete concept, but he does call attention to the politicization of women's space. It might be seen as the beginning of recognizing the issue rather than the end of the discourse—Gandhi challenges masculine identity via juxtaposition: 'Custom and law, founded by males, have repressed women.' According to one interpretation of Gandhi's theory, violence is a forerunner of masculinity. On the other hand, non-violence is the hallmark of female and male equality: 'In a nonviolent life plan, women have the same right to choose their destiny as men.' Furthermore, 'women have been trained to see themselves as men's slaves. Wives should be considered as honoured comrades engaged in a joint effort, not as dolls or objects of pleasure.' He suggests that, from the standpoint of an objective observer, women's legal and social position already demands radical reform. According to another interpretation, violence is a manifestation of patriarchy, while non-violence is a manifestation of equality. Although Gandhi could not construct a thorough critique of patriarchy and place patriarchy in the realms of social reproduction and material production, he politicizes women's issues for posterity.

3. His writing or letters concerning The All India Women's Conference (AIWC) (founded by Margaret Cousins [1878–1954; an Irish-Indian known for education and right to vote] in 1927) remains an essential component in this regard. Letters/comments/observations to the All-India Women's Conference highlight the following aspects: non-division on religious lines, seeking support for Village Industries Association, reminding the city women for care of women living in seven lakhs villages ('Letter to Amrit Kuar', 17 December 1934) (CWMG LX,1974: 4); becoming more representative by developing village instincts through khaddar and the village industry movements ('Interview to Mrs. C. Kuttan Nair', 8 January 1935) (CWMG LX,1974: 66); becoming *abla* (weak) to *sabla* (strong)('Message to the All-India Women's Conference', before 23 December 1936) (CWMG LXIV, 1976: 165); emancipation of women by women themselves, charkha and khaddar being important instrument for serving other poor women, bring Hindu–Muslim unity, eradicate untouchability ('Message to All-India Women's Conference', before 22 December 1938) (CWMG LXVIII, 1977: 230); appealing for the special obligation towards enforcing

the constructive programme ('Message to All-India Women's Conference', before 29 December 1941) (CWMG LXXV, 1979: 188); requesting delegation of Indonesian Women's League who were attending the All-India Women's Conference (Madras, 1947): 'Don't waver. Victory is in sight' ('Message to Indonesia', before 28 December) (CWMG XC, 1984: 307).

Gandhi highlighted the resolution passed by the standing committee of the All-India Women's Conference, which took place at Abbottabad in 1940. Three resolutions were opposition of Nazism and Fascism; means of non-violence in the lives of individuals, collectives and nations; and freedom of India, freedom of all nations and world democracy. He praised the Conference for Hindu–Muslim unity and rejecting the caste and religious distinctions (*Women's Role*, 27 July 1940) (CWMG LXXII,1978: 326–27). In 1941, Gandhi drafted the statement signed by Sarojini Naidu, Rameshwari Nehru, Vijaylakshmi Pandit, Amrit Kaur, Rani Lakshmibai Rajwade, Ammu Swaminathan and Radha Subbaroyan, which was sent as 'Reply to British Women's Appeal' on behalf of the All-India Women's Conference on 21 June 1941. British women's appeal was made in the context of the second world war for perceiving the war between forces of human slavery and human freedom. The statement rejects not only nazism and fascism but also British imperialism. It rejects the war as means of domination of non-European races. It

'. . . points out the anomaly of British women asking India, though a slave nation, to help the slave-owner in distress instead of asking the slave-owner to undo the wrong and cure himself of the initial sin and thus ensure the moral justness of his position' (CWMG LXXIV, 1978:116).

Education in Health and Hygiene

1. In liberal theory or state, some issues appear as policy papers, meaning they need to be read as 'government actions'. Therefore, government acts through committees and commissions and people are informed. In other words, they are sufficiently depoliticized due to reducing them as receivers of information concerning government acts. Even issues like 'education in health and hygiene' might appear in the state's policy papers, but in Gandhi, it is also a question which needs significant deliberation. It cannot be an apolitical defunct document. Gandhi stresses that '[y]our water, food and air must be clean', which can be a severe indictment of the state/government. The government's role is reduced to quality control of commodities called 'water', 'food' and 'air'. Gandhi politicizes it not only as 'personal cleanliness' but also for their surrounding.

2. Gandhi's education in health and hygiene is an elaborative scheme. In *Hind Swaraj,* health is explained for the proper use of hands and feet and the negative impact of artificial locomotion. Chapter twelve is on

doctors. In *Satyagraha in South Africa,* Gandhi mentions a booklet on health while bringing the significance of earth and water treatment along with fasting or change in diets. In *Autobiography,* he attributes the good condition of children due to his acquaintance with the subject. He experimented with bringing teachers' control of the kitchen for students' physical and moral health. He also describes his food habit and injuring his health. Gandhi's pamphlet, which is alluded to in *Satyagraha in South Africa,* is *A Guide to Health. A Guide To Health* is an English translation of his Gujarati articles published in *Indian Opinion.* These articles are written in Gujarati. The first publication trajectory of these articles can be located in *Indian Opinion* in 1913 under the title of *General Knowledge About Health* (relationship between mind and body, healthy state, our body, air, water, diet, eating pattern, exercise, attire, an intimate chapter, water treatments, earth cures, constipation, spare dysentery, piles, infectious diseases (smallpox, chickenpox, measles, plague, cholera, fast spreading dysentery, tumour fever), confinement, care of children, accidents (drowning, burns, Snake bites, scorpion and other stings)(CWMG XI, 1964: 428–30, 434–36, 441–43, 447–49, 453–55, 458–60, 463–66, 467–70, 472–75, 479–84, 492–94, 500–02, 507–10; CWMG XII, 1964: 4–7, 22–25, 38–40, 45–52, 62–64, 67–69, 73–75, 79–81, 97–99, 102–104, 110–112, 115–119, 129–132, 135–137, 142–145, 149–151,

152–153, 156–160, 163, 164–166). Controlling the palate is a critical aspect of all cures.

These articles were translated into Hindi and after that, translated from Hindi to English. *A Guide to Health* (first edition 1921; second edition revised: 1922, Madras: S. Ganesan) was translated from Hindi by A. Rama Iyer. In addition to the translator's note, the aforesaid contents are arranged under Introduction, Part 1: General, and Part II: Some Simple Treatments. The introduction is from *General Knowledge About Health-I* (*Indian Opinion*, 4 January 1913) and *General Knowledge About Health-II* (*Indian Opinion*, 11 January 1913). There may be variations due to the trajectory from Gujarati to English via Hindi. However, the content stays more or less similar.

As per Gandhi's preface to the *Key to Health* (Aga Khan Palace, Yeravada, 27 August 1942; initially written in Gujarati and subsequently translated by Sushila Nayyar into English in close reading by Gandhi; 1948, Navajivan Publishing House, Ahmedabad), there is no significant difference between two texts. He mentions earlier writing as the writing of 1906. Any change should be read in the context of 'the nature of progress'. Gandhi does not give reasons for *changing* name. However, he uses the key as a metaphor for unravelling the condition for 'health proper'. Part I comprises *the Human Body, Air, Water, Food, Condiments, Tea-Coffee and Cocoa, Intoxicants, Opium, Tobacco,* and *Brahmacharya*. Part II focuses on natural therapeutics (*Earth, Water, Akash/ether/sky, Sun,* and *Air*).

In Gandhi's health and hygiene schemes, Anna Kingsford (1846–88), Edward Maitland (1824–97), Tomas Allinson (1858–1918), and Louis Kuhne (1835–1901) are important interlocutors and reference points. They have been referred to and cited on multiple occasions. Kingsford's *The Perfect Way in Diet: A Treatise Advocating a Return to the Natural and Ancient Food of Our Race* (1981) is an important contribution in this regard. Gandhi refers to Kingsford and Maitland's *The Perfect Way or The Finding of Christ* on several occasions. The *Preface to the First Edition* (1881) points out that the book '. . . seeks to assure man that his best and most powerful friends on every plane are Liberty and Reason, as his worst enemies are Ignorance and Fear . . .' (Kingsford and Maitland, 1919a: viii). The revised edition stresses the importance of discovery and recovery in place of invention or compilation (Kingsford and Maitland, 1919b: i).

In *Autobiography,* Thomas Allinson is referred to several times. He is known for his works, *A System of Hygienic Medicine* (1886) and *The Advantage of Wholemeal Bread* (1889). He was removed from the medical register in 1892 for the position of anti-medical drug and also from the Vegetarian Society of the United Kingdom for supporting contraception. *A Book for Married Women* (1894) defends sexual equality in marriage, including contraception and family size. Despite disagreement on the use of contraception, Gandhi extended his support to Allinson. For Gandhi, despite the different moral positions, any vegetarian is entitled to membership in society. He met him personally. He appreciated Allinson's writings on health and hygiene, particularly a curative system through regulated dietary. 'From 1885 on, Allinson's column, Answers to Correspondents in the Weekly Times and Echo became popular and was subsequently published as Medical Essays' (1887–93) (Bae, 2022: 51). Allinson's medical essays (five volumes) are comprehensive. Volume one covers the management of infancy (food, bathing, exercise, sleep, clothing, walking, teeth, talking), health, longevity, the teeth, food, man's from his structure, brown bread, bread and bread making, the necessity for food, daily food, summer living, fruit, the truth about vegetarianism, fresh air, exercise, bathing, light, holidays, disease, unity of disease, constipation, biliousness, plethora (over-feeding), eczema (skin disease), pimples and blackheads, nervousness, autumnal diarrhoea, coughs and colds, chest complaints, deafness, vaccination, threadworms, roundworms, tapeworms, scabies or the itch, tobacco, why people drink, the results of drinking (wasting of life and force), diseases produced by drink, cure for the drink crave. Volume II elaborates on changes in our body and the healing power of nature. Volume III discusses health and wealth, no more death, youth, the necessity for ventilation, the management of children, hunger and appetite, the effects of fasting, perfect foods, green foods, suppers, unsuspected domestic poisons, thirst, perspiration, sea bathing, how to eat properly, how to eat fruit, how to judge bread, how to breathe properly, how to grow tall, how to keep warm, how I live, how persons have lived 100 years, how to improve memory, how to become beautiful and attractive, hay fever, flatulence, sleeplessness, varicose veins, boils and carbuncles, sebaceous tumours or cysts, winter cough, chilblains, mercurial diseases, and epilepsy or falling sickness. Volume IV encompasses varied issues ranging from new year resolutions; prevention is better than cure, health saving banks to against the use of knives and so on. Volume V discusses foods to sudden troubles like fits, strokes, fainting, etc. (Allinson, 1892).

Louis Kuhne also inspired Gandhi with his method of hydropathy. Kuhne is known for his book *The New Science of Healing or The Doctrine of the Unity of Diseases* (1899). He proposes his New Science of Healing against Allopathy (objection: poisoning patients with medicine), homoeopathy (objection: no clear fixed and clear principles of diets) and the earlier Natural Method (objection: lack of insight into the true nature of the disease and carrying old prejudices by way of adopting the orthodox system of diagnostics; unregulated diets) (Kuhne, 1899: 7–9). Kuhne's 'the New Science of Healing prescribes a non-stimulant system of dietetics based on natural laws and accurately and clearly defines' (Kuhne, 1899: 9). The book is organized into four parts. His remedial agents are steam baths, sun baths, friction, hip baths, friction sitz-baths and earth bandages. Gandhi, in *Autobiography*, praises hip baths and wholemeal bread as per Kuhne's recipe. In Gandhi's writings, a reference to Kuhne appears in the form of praising the restaurant in Johannesburg for adopting Kuhne's principle ('Letter to The Vegetarian', after 21 March 1903, Johannesburg) (CWMG III, 1979: 345), procuring his book (*Letter to A. J. Bean*, 5 March 1906, Johannesburg; *Letter to Chhaganlal Gandhi*, 1 September 1906, Johannesburg) (CWMG V, 1961: 216 & 409), praising Shaukat Ali for taking Kuhne's treatment (*Letter to Shaukat Ali*, Sabarmati, 23 February 1925) (CWMG XXVI, 1967: 191), remembering Hanumantharao for practising Kuhne's hydropathy (*A Servant of India*, Young India, 25 March 1926) (CWMG XXX, 1968: 171), advising G.D. Birla for visiting institutions of Kuhne in Germany for his health ('Letter to G.D. Birla', Nandi Durg, 1 June 1927) (CWMG XXXIII, 1969: 412), advising Nehru for Kuhn treatment to Kamala Nehru ('Letter to Jawaharlal Nehru', 17 June 1928) (CWMG XXXVI, 1970: 427), appreciating the benefit of Kuhne's method ('Letter to Yvonne Privat', 27 April 2933) (CWMG LV, 1973: 43), extending Kun's diet besides Juicy fruits, Kellogg and Carrington ('Letter to Hiralal Sharma', 14 April 1934), (CWMG LVII, 1974: 390), trying to buy a copy of Kuhne (*Letter to Sharda*

G. Chokhawala, August 10, 1941) (CWMG LXXIV, 1978: 228), significance of hip-bath and size bath in *Key to Health*, Kuhne's treatment for tumour ('Letter to Rampra B. Sadvas', Panchgani, 14 June 1945) (CWMG LXXX, 1980: 325), taking nature cure to the people (*Dr Mehta's Institution,* New Delhi 24, 1946) (CWMG LXXXIV, 1981: 196–97), advising mud-pack ('Letter to Ramprasad Vyas', Mussoorie, 4 June 1946) (CWMG LXXXIV, 1981: 283), using Kuhne Bath for removing the cause of miscarriage ('Letter to Manilal and Sushila Gandhi', before 1 January 1928) (CWMG XXXV,1969: 460), mentioning Kuhne method in *General Knowledge about Health* and choosing vegetarianism on physiological ground ('Letter to "The Natal Mercury"', Durban, 3 February 1896) (CWMG I, 1969: 294), significance of hip-bath ('Letter to Haribhau Upadhyaya', 13 April 1937) (CWMG LXV, 1976: 78) and suggesting Rajendra Nath Barua or following the instruction of Kuhne's *Science of Healing* ('Letter to Rajendra Nath Barua', February 1935) (CWMG LX, 1974: 175).

Overall, Gandhi's Health Swaraj must be considered for giving autonomy and rights to the body for self-correction and without being subject to external control.

Provincial Languages

1. Gandhi invites attention towards languages in *Hind Swaraj*. He defines India as a nation. The idea of a nation is not without having differences. People travelled

across India while learning one another's language. This
helped to mitigate aloofness. Gandhi gives importance
to the mother tongue for reducing their dependency
on translation. He emphasizes teaching morality
in the mother tongue to English-educated people.
The relationship between inter-languages (different
languages) and inter-religions (different religions) is
crucial. He approves the translation of valuable English
books into numerous Indian languages. His rejection
of English as domination or slavery (both in theory and
empirical) is absolute. Around this time (13 November
1909, *Indian Opinion*), the cultivation of the Indian
language became an important task for him. He praised
two Gujarati poems written on *Satyagraha* and *Fakir* and
their uniqueness which cannot be translated into English.
He appreciates Lloyd George for acquainting Welsh
children to their own language. 'How much more need
is there for Indians to preserve their languages than for
the Welsh to preserve theirs, and how much more keen
should we be?' (CWMG IX, 1963: 492). In *Satyagraha
in South Africa,* his praise for multiple languages in South
Africa is noteworthy. He also highlights the complexity of
teaching at Tolstoy Farm to multilingual students. He also
suggests, in *Autobiography*, the place of Hindi, Sanskrit,
Persian, Arabic, English and the vernacular language in
the higher education curriculum. He highlights the close
relationship between language and the mother tongue's
significance.

2. Gandhi emphasizes the mother tongue and links it with swaraj. According to him, '[s]waraj should not mean the imposition of one language on those who speak different languages. Primary importance ought to be given only to the mother language. Only secondary importance can be given to Hindi, the common language of India. Real inspiration and elevation can come only through the mother tongue' (CWMG LXIII, 1976: 222).

3. Gandhi in his 'Speech at Benares Hindu University' (6 February 1916) urged the university for adopting students' language as medium of instruction (CWMG XIII, 1964: 211). For him medium of instruction in mother tongue is a non-negotiable principle. Foreign languages can be taught as an optional subject. He, in 'Introduction to Vernaculars as media of instruction' (1 February 1917) terms the question of media of instruction as national importance and neglect of vernaculars as national suicide (CWMG XIII, 1964:336). In all provinces, medium of instruction should be the mother tongue. Two to three Indian languages should also be learned (CWMG XII, 1964: 359). The eleventh item of the *History of the Satyagraha Ashram* deals with education, wherein 27 aspects are elaborated. He emphasizes on mother tongue for education, along with the teaching of Hindu–Urdu as the national language for children before learning of letters (CWMG L, 1972: 233).

4. The legitimacy of sovereignty, political institutions and constitution are based on people's consent acquired

through constructed and restricted political spaces. It becomes almost like a positivist endeavour, meaning a mere record of participation in liberal political space is ipso facto considered consent. However, an empirical record of participation is a misleading exercise due to the possibility of not understanding the language of statecraft. Ironically, there can be statecraft even if people do not comprehend its meaning. In this backdrop, Gandhi's discussion of provincial languages becomes crucial. Gandhi locates fissures between the educated classes and politically minded classes and the masses due to the prioritization of the English language over mother tongues. 'The masses can make no solid contribution to the construction of Swaraj. It is inherent in Swaraj . . . that every individual makes his own direct contribution . . . The masses cannot do this fully unless they understand every step with all its implication. This is impossible unless every step is explained in their own languages' (Gandhi, 1948:19–20). Gandhi makes the language question a question of a legitimate understanding of peoples' sovereignty by rejecting positivist consent. His defence of the provincial language and Hindustani (Hindi–Urdu) must be understood in this context.

National Language

1. In *Hind Swaraj*, he identifies Hindi as a universal language of India. Gandhi's Hindi can be written in Devanagari or Persian. This is crucial in the context of Hindu–Muslim

relations. He identifies English as the ruler, which needs rejection by making Hindi a common language. The epithet national language is also present here. Later on, the subtle shift from Sanskritized Hindi or Persianized Urdu is categorically visible in Gandhi. Eventually, Hindustani (written in Devanagari and Persian scripts) became especially important in his lexicon. Hindustani is used on multiple occasions in *Satyagraha in South Africa*. In the text, he underlines that H.O. Ali and Thambi Naidoo spoke Hindustani at ease. He highlights the importance of the mother tongue and Hindustani, the lingua franca of India. In *Autobiography*, in the backdrop of his participation and address at a joint conference of Hindu–Mussalmans on the Khilafat Questions (November 1919), he terms Hindi–Urdu alone as the lingua franca of India. During the war conference in Delhi, he also sought permission from the viceroy to speak in Hindi-Hindustani. He was congratulated for being well-spoken in Hindustani.

Gandhi's *Thoughts on National Language* (collections of his articles originally published in Gujarati in 1945, in Hindi in 1947 and in English in 1956) and Tara Chand's *The Problem of Hindustani* (1944) are essential sources for deliberation. Gandhi's engagement with Tara Chand on national language/Hindustani is well known. According to Tara Chand, 'India is a composite country; it has many races, many religions, many cultures, many languages. Indian nationality cannot be sort of unitary homogeneous society and civilization which obtains in England, France, Italy or Germany. A common Indian *lingua franca* must reflect the composite character of the Indian nation, and therefore all endeavours to make that language the national language of India which rests upon the exclusive basis of one cultural tradition is fraught with strife and destined to fail'(Chand, 1944: 123).

2. The resolution of the Kanpur Congress is as follows:

   Resolution VIII: Hindustani (Amendment to Constitution)

   This Congress resolves that Article XXXIII of the Constitution be amended as follows:

   The proceedings of the Congress shall be conducted as far as possible in Hindustani.

   The English language or any provisional language may be used if the speaker is unable to speak Hindustani or whenever necessary. Proceedings of the Provincial Congress Committee shall ordinarily be conducted in the language of the Province concerned. Hindustani may also be used.

   Indian National Congress, Kanpur, 1925(Gandhi, 1956: 21).

3. Gandhi mused over the suggestion of the editor of the *Indian World*, a monthly published from Calcutta, regarding the need for a common language in India. Achieving nationhood is impossible through English due to its minuscule speakers. Hindustani appears to be the

best alternative due to its derivation from Sanskrit and Persian, liked by Hindus and Muslims, spoken by fakirs and sanyasis, thus spreading it widely, and its nature is very sweet, polite and spirited. Mother tongue and Hindustani should be taught in every school in India (18 August 1906, *Indian Opinion*) (CWMG V, 1961: 396–97). In 1917, Gandhi's Speech at the Second Gujarat Educational Conference (20 October 1917, Broach [present Bharuch]) as the president of the conference outlined the five criteria of a national language: easy learning for government officials; serving ability as a medium of religion, economic and political intercourse across India; spoken by a large number of people; easy learning for every Indian; not counting temporary and passing circumstance for choosing a national language. On all these counts, Gandhi rejects English. He recommends Hindi for this status, the language of Hindus and Muslims. He rejects the difference between Hindi and Urdu. The difference is due to the educated class's led intervention. 'That is, educated Hindus Sanskritize their Hindi with the result that Muslims cannot follow it. Muslims of Lucknow Persianize their Urdu and make it unintelligible to Hindus . . . To the masses both these languages are foreign and so they have no use for them . . . Write it in the Urdu script and call it Urdu, or write it in the Nagari script and call it Hindi' (CWMG XIV, 1965: 24).

His 'Address at Convocation Hindi Prachar Sabha' (12 June 1936, Bangalore), rejected any difference between Hindi, Urdu or Hindustani and suggested all three words denote only one language (CWMG LXIII, 1976: 53). He asserts the significance of vernaculars' place which Hindi cannot replace. He proposes Hindi only 'as a medium of inter-provincial intercourse. Therefore, Hindi propaganda should not only not interfere with the progress of vernaculars, but it must enrich them' (CWMG LXIII, 1976: 300–01). For Gandhi, 'Speech at Akhil Bharatiya Sahitya Parishad' (24 April 1936, Nagpur), 'The reason why Hindi is qualified by the word 'Hindustani' is that words originating from the Persian Idiom may not be shunned in that language' (CWMG LXII, 1975: 347).

Gandhi insists, in Hindustani, Hindi and Urdu (19 October 1938, Utmanzai), that 'India of the future will be a perfect and happy blend of both [Hindi and Urdu]' (CWMG LXVIII, 1977: 25). He also proposes, Hindi+Urdu = Hindustani (2 February 1942, Sevargram), the fusion of both languages to become 'a common interprovincial speech' called Hindustani. Thus in place of 'Hindustani=Hindi+Urdu', the alternative is Hindustani=Hindi=Urdu (CWMG LXXV, 280).

Gandhi conceived of the Hindustani Prachar Sabha (on 5 May 1942 in Wardha and later in Mumbai). Jawaharlal Nehru, Zakir Hussain, Kakasaheb Kalelkar, Shrimann

Narayan Agrawal, two sisters, Perinben Captain and Goshiben Captain (both granddaughters of Dadabhai Naoroji), Morarjibhai Desai and others were associated with Sabha. In a note to Perin Captain (Hon. Secretary, Hindustani Prachar Sabha, May 1942), Gandhi points out that 'Hindi is incomplete without Urdu' (CWMG LXXVI, 1979: 175). A happy and natural fusion of Hindi and Urdu is a must for living Hindustani (CWMG LXXVI: 338). Gandhi's long reply to Raihanabehn Tyabjee's letter (Hindustani written in Nagari Only, 1 November 1947, New Delhi) is important. She suggested that Gandhi keep only the Nagari script for Hindustani as the inter-provincial language while excluding the Urdu script to reject the policy of appeasement and separatist tendency. Gandhi rejected her suggestion and insisted on two scripts for Hindustani. He states that '[i]mprovement is possible only when fanaticism has died out . . . The beauty of Hindustani is that it has no quarrel either with Sanskrit or with Arabic words' (CWMG LXXXIX, 1983: 448).

Overall, Hindi/Urdu/Hindustani are very crucial and debated and discussed by Gandhi in the context of Devanagari script, Muslims, regional languages, students, and Tamils, medium of communication, the national language, opposition to it, dictionary, grammar, Congress engagement propagation, South India, Hindustani Culture Society, All India Hindustani Prachar Conference, Hindustani Prachar Samiti

(Gujarat), Hindustani Sabha, Hindustani Seva Dal and Hindustani Talimi Sangh.

The urge for a national language has not been without nuanced criticism and political opposition in modern India. The imposition of one dominant language invites attention towards the marginalization of numerous languages and political patronage. Gandhi's position on the national language is nuanced. He prefers provincial languages over national languages. In the choice of two, the former would prevail. Gandhi wanted a common lingua for the political community. The possibility of a common lingua is not without certain inherent dangers. However, Gandhi was more concerned with the deliberative form of political community in which massive participation and deliberation by all are quintessential features. This is crucial for rejecting positivist consent preferred by modern nation-states in which mechanical and procedural consent are always prioritized and practised. The possibility of a common lingua without the hegemony of a national language needs a wider debate, everyday caution and constant willingness to learn each other's languages. At least in the context of language and religion or religious chauvinism concerning language, he proposes a non-binary model of Hindi and Urdu or Hindustani. It helps to avoid religious appropriation or communal binary of languages. Gandhi aims to avoid language chauvinism while avoiding religious fissures.

Economic Equality

1. Gandhi proposes a non-violent economy in which economic equality, *apagriha* (non-possession), no distinction between economics and ethics, availability of food–cloth–sufficient work universally by control of masses of 'the means of production of the elementary necessaries of life', free availability and no monopolization of means of production of the elementary necessaries by country nation groups, true economics as justice, economics as dismal science for promoting amassed wealth at the expense of weak, equalization of the status of the working class, decentralization as non-violent, centralization as force, *sarvodaya* (welfare of all), and socialism as economic equality are essential features.

   Gandhi's position on capitalism is a nuanced one. He stresses the abolition of capitalism, not capital and capitalists (CWMG XLVIII,1971: 245–47). His position on the abolition of capitalism is categorical. In the absence of capitalism, capital and capitalists seem an infeasible proposition. Despite this, Gandhi does not take a direct call on the 'abolition' of capital and capitalists. Probably this is due to 'violence attach[ed] to it'. However, in this absence of whole, parts would also disappear. Gandhi's lecture, 'Does Economic Progress Clash with Real Progress?' at a meeting of the Muir Central College Economic Society (Allahabad, 22 December 1916) stresses on moral progress as real progress while terming economic progress as material advancement without limit'. In 'Economic Constitution of India' (15 November 1928, *Young India*), Gandhi advocates control of 'the means of production of the elementary necessaries of life' by the masses.

In 1944, Shriman Narayan Agarwal outlined the *Gandhian Plan of Economic Development for India*. For Narayan, simplicity, non-violence, sanctity of labour and human values are the fundamentals of Gandhian economics (Agarwal, 1944: 15–29). In *Economy of Permanence* (1945), J.C. Kumarappa divides five 'types of economies in nature' in which economy of nature is the highest form: parasitic economy, predatory economy, economy of enterprise, economy of gregation, and economy of service. In *Gandhian Economic Thought* (1951), he suggests that the principles underlying the Gandhian economy are truth and non-violence. In this backdrop, Gandhi was working for the development of economy of service. In *Small is Beautiful*, E.F. Schumacher reminds us about the famous Gandhi's statement: 'As Gandhi said, the poor of the world cannot be helped by mass production, only by production by the masses' (Schumacher, 1973: 145).

2. Economic inequality belongs to the realm of violent formation, and economic equality belongs to the realm of non-violent formation. For non-violent formation, the 'eternal conflict between capital and labour' must be abolished. In Gandhi's framework, the violent formation

could be treated as 'exploitation,' which is undoubtedly based on capitalist production. The only solution is to replace a more democratic and decentralized mode of production in which privatization of the means of production and surplus accumulation are prohibited. This is categorical in Gandhi's teachings. Nevertheless, this is based on identifying the problem, which Gandhi rightly identifies as a conflict between capitalists and workers. The proposed solution seems to be at odds with identifying the problem. Two remarks are important in this regard. First, he sees the solution as 'the levelling down of the few rich, in whose hands the bulk of the nation's wealth is concentrated on the one hand, and the levelling up of the semi-starved, naked millions on the other'. Secondly, he 'adheres to . . . his doctrine of trusteeship in spite of the ridicule that has been poured upon it'.

The identification aspect of the problem should be given more importance than the solution aspect on two grounds. Firstly, the voluntary giving away of property or trusteeship is a sign of the capitalist mode of production since there can be an abdication of voluntary property or the idea of trusteeship only when there is private capital. Secondly, since Gandhi treats overall inequality as a violent formation, the first ground becomes untenable.

Overall, Gandhi deserves credit for defining violent formation as undesirable and stating that post-swaraj equality is impossible to achieve. It will not appear out of anywhere one fine morning. In this way, he makes economic equality an everyday political project—an unthinkable project in liberal political theory.

Kisans

1. Champaran Satyagraha (1917, Bihar) was the first significant movement against the oppression of *nilaha sahib* (white planters engaged in indigo cultivation), who were forcing peasants to grow indigo plants on three parts out of twenty parts, i.e., three *katthas out* of one bigha (twenty katthas). This was also referred to as the *tinkathiya* system. The Champaran Satyagraha is crucial for linking peasants' questions with the national movement (though Gandhi avoided reference to the Congress) and promoting disobedience against unjust laws based on systemic studies and testimonies. Peasants' testimonies became crucial grounds for a principled position and evolving local leadership. Thirty years later, in a message to Bihar on 19 December 1947, Gandhi appealed to Bihar to maintain peace amidst communal strife in India while reminding '. . . history of India's freedom movement began with the Champaran Satyagraha' (CWMG XC, 1984: 260).

2. Kheda Satyagraha (1918, Gujarat) peasant protest over-assessment of the land revenue in the backdrop of famine impact. Gandhi's 'Letter to Collector, Kheda' (26 February 1918) was based on an investigation of crop conditions. After starting the investigation by Gandhi

and his co-workers, a report of 425 villages (out of 600 villages) was made available. Gandhi investigated thirty villages (CWMG XIV, 1965: 215). 'Letter to People of Kheda' (6 June 1918, Satyagraha Camp, Nadiad), jointly written by Gandhi and Vallabhbhai Patel, is a painful summation of the Kheda Satyagraha. However, they state that '[b]y their courage the people of Kaira [Kheda] have drawn the attention of the whole of India' (CWMG XIV, 1965: 418).

3. Bardoli Satyagraha (1928, Gujarat): started against the government's raising tax rates by 22 per cent amidst natural calamities. Gandhi extended his full support to Bardoli Satyagraha and appreciated people's resilience against both heavenly and earthly calamities. 'The land of many who owned it was washed away by the last years' floods and it is covered with sand-heaps. If Gujarat bravely withstood that calamity sent by a heavenly power, led Bardoli bravely go through this sent by an earthly one and keep to its pledge'(Desai, 1929: 59).The thirteenth chapter of *Story of Bardoli: Being A History of the Bardoli Satyagraha of 1928 and its Sequel* by Mahadev Desai is named *The Peasants' Sardar*. Vallabhbhai Patel was the chief Anchor of the Satyagraha. According to Patel,

'If any one is fit to walk with his head erect on this earth, it is the peasant. He is the producer, the others are parasites . . . The whole world depends on . . . agriculturalist and the labourer . . . and you are the worst abused people on earth. I am grieved at the woeful state of helplessness to which you have been reduced. You shudder at the sight of a worthless Government peon who can compel you to do his bidding. The Government taxes you according to its sweet will, and you have no voice in it. There is a soil rate, a water rate, a special irrigation rate and a special subsoil water, even the improvements that you make at your cost and by your labour are taxed. You toil in the fields even as your own bullocks do from morning until evening, in biting cold, in scorching heat and drenching rain. You grapple with scorpions and wade through mud and raise a crop of rice must be taxed. Why are you so fear-stricken? Why are you so inarticulate? I feel deeply ashamed and humiliated at your plight. I shall feel myself blessed and all my labours fulfilled when I see you come to your own and walk erect like men' (Desai, 1929: 68–69).

4. Borsad Satyagraha (1923, Gujarat): against the punitive cess for not cooperating with the government against a dacoit, Babar Deva. The Satyagraha was successful, and the punitive cess was withdrawn in 1924 (CWMG XXIII, 1967: 381).

5. Regarding peasants (kisans), Gandhi makes an interesting comment based on peasant movements organized in Kheda, Bardoli and Borsad. His comments about the success of these movements are important. 'The secret of success lies in a refusal to exploit the kisans for political purposes outside their own personal and felt grievances.' In other words, there cannot be peasant politics without peasants. There cannot be a

referential politics of peasants without a substantive issue of peasants. Peasant issues cannot be without peasant substantive. In an 'Interview to N.G. Ranga' (29 October 1944), Gandhi underlined the power, including political power for peasants in Democratic Swaraj at all levels (CWMG LXXVIII, 1979: 246). On 29 January 1948, 'Speech at Prayer Meeting', he stated that '[i]f the man who produced foodgrain out of the earth becomes our Chief, our Prime Minister, the face of India will change' (CWMG XC, 1984: 525).

Labour

1. Anusuyaben Sarabhai (1985–72) came closer to the Fabian Society and its programmes while studying at the London School of Economics. In 1914, she started a school for children of mill workers in Ahmedabad. In 1916, Anasuyaben Sarabhai and Shankarlal Banker initiated *Majoor Mitra Mandal* (Friends of Labourers Society). On 25 February 1920, the *Majoor Mahajan Sangh* (Textile Labour Association, Ahmedabad, popularly known as TLA) was founded with Anusuyaben as president for life (Breman, 2004: 38–44). In fact, '. . . in combination the words *major* and *Mahajan* represented the partnership, as envisaged by Gandhi, between employee and employer' (Barot 1997: viii cited in Breman, 2004: 44–45). Gandhi emphasized service in place of leadership to Anasuyaben. 'A trade union leader should act like a *Sevak* and not as *Sardar*'(Barot 1997: 53 cited in Breman, 2004: 45).

2. In Gandhi, labour, among other things, appears in three forms. Firstly, the notion of 'bread-labour' is crucial in his schema. *From Yeravda Mandir: Ashram Observances* (1935) (English translation of Gandhi's weekly letters to the Satyagraha Ashram during his incarceration in Yeravda Central Prison in 1930), contains chapter nine on 'bread-labour'. T.M. Bondaref (Timofey Bondarev), Tolstoy, Ruskin are important interlocutors. He also cites *Gita* and *Bible* in this regard. Gandhi interprets the third chapter of *Gita* as follows: '. . . he who eats without offering sacrifice eats stolen food. Sacrifice here can only mean Bread Labour' (Gandhi, 1935: 50). 'Rain comes from sacrifice' (verse 14, Gita) is interpreted by him as 'the necessity of bodily labour' and 'labouring enough for one's food' and 'labouring enough for one's food as *yajna* in *History of the Satyagraha Ashram'* (CWMG L, 1972: 215). From *Bible (Genesis 3: 19),* the quote is as follows: 'In the sweat of thy brow shalt thou eat thy bread.' This also influenced Bondarev, who wrote *The Triumph of the Farmer or Industry and Parasitism* and advocated '. . . that it was each person's moral and religious duty to earn their bread through physical labour, regardless of their social station' (Bartlett, 2010: 496). Bondarev's manuscript, *Industry and Idleness or the Glory of the Agriculturist*, was printed by Tolstoy. It was preserved unpublished at a Minusinski museum. G.I. Uspensky read it and wrote about it in *Ruskaya Misl* in 1884. Tolstoy read it and subsequently connected with Bondarev through V.S. Lebedev and L.N.

Zhebynev, political prisoners exiled in the area. Tolstoy published the text in *Ruskaya Beseda* in 1888, but the censors confiscated it. In 1890 and 1896, the manuscript was published in French and English abroad (Green, 1986: 198).

Gandhi refers to Bondarev and gives credit to him for the concept of bread labour. 'Strictly speaking, bread labour is not a word of Tolstoy's coining. He took it from another Russian writer Bondarif' (CWMG XXVIII, 1968: 431). Gandhi refers to bread labour in the context of Bondarev as 'bodily labour' (*Discourses on the Gita,* 15 April 1926) (CWMG XXXII, 1969: 159), 'preach and practice' or 'blurring distinction between manual and intellectual work' (*Varnadharma and Duty of Labour-III,* 20 February 1930) (CWMG XLII, 1970: 489–90), 'earn bread by laboring his/her own hands' ('Letter to Narandas Gandhi', 16 September 1930) (CWMG XLIV, 1971: 149), 'must work in order to live' (*History of the Satyagraha Ashram*, 11 July 1932) (CWMG L, 1972: 214), 'bread labour being God's law for all mankind' ('Letter to F. Mary Barr and Duncan Greenlees', 8 March 1933) (CWMG LIV, 1973: 9), 'common labour with the body'/'closet cooperation' (*Ahimsa in Practice,* 23 January 1940) (CWMG LXXI, 1978: 131), 'to earn our bread by the sweat of our brow' *Speech at Prayer Meeting* (September 23, 1946) (CWMG LXXXV, 1982: 362), 'necessity of physical labour'/'body labour' (*Question Box: Intellectual and*

Manual Work, February 6, 1947)(CWMG LXXXVI, 1982: 436–37).

Secondly, labour as equality is an important consideration in Gandhi. In *Autobiography* (Part IV, Chapter XVIII), Gandhi attributes three features of Ruskin's *Unto This Last,* which was paraphrased and translated into Gujarati as *Sarovodaya* ('the welfare of all'): good of the individual is intertwined with the good of all; equal value of labour; and worthiness of a life of labour. In other writings, Gandhi proposes the anti-utilitarian notion of equality by striving for ' . . . the greatest good of all and . . . [dying] . . . in an attempt to realise the ideas . . . He/she/they] will serve [himself/herself/themselves] with the rest, by . . . dying . . . The utilitarian to be logical will never sacrifice himself' (Gandhi, 1954: 4). He also connotes Sarvodaya as a true democracy, i.e. '. . . the humblest and lowest Indian as being equally the rules of India with the tallest in the land . . . No one would . . . harbour any distinction between community and community, caste and outcaste. Everyday would regard all as equal with oneself and hold them together in the silken net of love . . . Everyday would know how to earn an honest living by the sweat of one's brow and make no distinction between intellectual and physical labour'(Gandhi, 1954: 4–5).

Thirdly, the relationship between capital and labour is a crucial consideration in Gandhi. Since he emphasizes *ahimsa* or non-violence, therefore antagonism per se is avoided. However, he calls capital labour's servant, which cannot be the latter's master. He proposes some concrete form: (a) labour should have its own unions; (b) Education, both general and scientific, of both men and women, should be regularly undertaken through night schools; (c) Children of labourers should be educated after the basic education style; (d) There should be a hospital, a creche and a maternity home attached to every centre; (e) Labour should be taught the science of conducting a successful non-violent strike' (Gandhi, 1970: 79). For Gandhi, '[l]abour, united and morally and intellectually trained, would any day superior to capital' (Gandhi, 1970: 80).

He also makes the Ahmedabad Labor Union a model for all of India to copy. His appreciation for it comes primarily from three reasons: engaging in multiple activities like having hospitals, a school for the children of mill hands, classes for the adults, a printing press, a khadi depot, and residential quarters; not participating in the party politics of the Congress; governing relations between mill owners and labour through voluntary arbitration. The last two points are important for discussion. Gandhi's direct involvement in the Ahmedabad labour strike and his politics also played a crucial role in 'voluntary arbitration'. Voluntary arbitration is a non-starter concept in the capitalist mode of production. What made it work was the immense interest generated due to the immense politicization of the issue, thanks to many modes of politics, including Gandhi. Ultimately, 'voluntarily arbitration' takes place in a violent formation because, in a non-violent formation, the division of labour and capital is absent. In other words, Gandhi makes a tentative proposal for 'voluntarily arbitration' based on his own analysis of economic equality because the arrival of non-violent formation is greatly desired.

Adivasis

1. This is where a slew of activists, directly or indirectly or critically influenced by Gandhi or Gandhian methods, devoted a lifetime to arrive at the categorical positions or ambiguous stands, resolutions or non-resolutions of adivasis questions. Ownership of natural resources, protections against usurpation and pauperization and substantive representations (political and cultural) have been the core area of the adivasis movements. 'Gandhians and Adivasis Questions' conversed and diverged as well on aforesaid issues. In addition to Gandhi's comments, writings and visits to Chhota Nagpur (1917, 1925, 1927, and 1941), people like Indulal Yagnik (1892–1972), Amritlal Thakkar (1869–1951), Sumant Mehta (1877–1968), Narhari Parikh (1891–1957), Jugatram Dave (1892–1985), Verrier Elwin (1902–64), and B.G. Kher (1888–1957) are some of the important interlocutors towards Gandhian position on economic conditions, cooperative societies, agriculture, prohibition, land conversation, cultural assertion, resistance methodology,

rights discourse and excluded or partially excluded adivasis areas clause under the Constitution of India, 1935.

Gandhi and Elwin's relations are well-documented based on the critical admiration of convergence and divergence. Elwin, in his autobiography *The Tribal World of Verrier Elwin* (1964), highlights the influence of Gandhi and Tagore. 'There have always been two sides to me—one side, the world-renouncing, was captivated by Gandhi, but the other side of world-affirmation I found in Tagore' (Elwin, 1964b: 340). According to Elwin, '[f]or Gandhi, my affection never wavered, but I allowed the differences between us to keep me away from him' (Elwin, 1964b: 85). Khadi programme, prohibition, philosophy of sex relations, and excessive emphasis on diet are cited as reasons for differences. Regarding the khadi programme, he suggests that '. . . khadi programme was not suitable for our tribes. I have always been a strong supporter of handloom weaving, but spinning, for very poor people and in places where cotton did not grow, seemed to me artificial and uneconomic' (Elwin, 1964b: 85).

K.S. Singh presents a critical appreciation of Gandhi towards tribal mobilization at two levels. 'First, the Mahatma, his personality and his message seemed to carry forward and deepen the process of sanskritisation started by the tribal *bhagats* in the latter half of the nineteenth century' (Singh, 1977: 393). One may notice the shift in the *Constructive Programme*, where Gandhi makes 'service' a point of engagement. Second, '. . . the Gandhian reconstruction programme started the process of the politicisation of the tribals, nurtured a generation of tribal leaders and provided a common political platform for the tribals and non-tribals, thus bringing the first into the mainstream of national politics' (Singh,1977: 393).

2. According to David Hardiman, Gandhi was drawn closer to tribal issues during the Non-Cooperation Movement. The Bhils and the Kaliparaj were two of the most concerned groups. The Bhils were the most significant tribal community in western India. The Kaliparaj were located in South Gujarat. The term 'Kalipara' (the black people) was used derogatorily by non-adivasis for local adivasi communities. Indulal Yagnik and Amritlal Thakkar, among others, raised funds for food distribution. Hostel (the Bill Ashram) and organization (the Bhil Seva Mandal) were started. This also led to a campaign against the term 'Kaliparaj' to be replaced by 'Raniparaj' (people of the forest). Sumant Mehta was a leading figure. Adivasis Mahashabha (1938) was established in Jharkhand for constitutional rights. Similarly, under the presidency of B.G. Kher, the Adivasi Seva Mandal was also established. Hereafter, the adivasi term became important for Gandhi. Gandhi rejected terms like 'animist,' 'aboriginal,' etc. and used terms like 'Raniparaj' and 'Girijan' in the 1920s and 1930s. In 1938, Elwin changed the name of his organization to the Bhumijan Seva Mandal. Bhumijan means 'people of the soil'. Elwin

formulated his concept, prioritizing Bhumijan as an 'attachment to earth' and construing adivasi as a 'place of residence'. Bhumijan could not become popular. The Adivasi Mahasabha coined and popularized the term 'adivasi' in Jharkhand. Amritlal Thakkar used it constantly and became an ardent advocate of it. Gandhi used the term often and thought that Thakkar had created it. Due to the displacement by outsiders argument, the 'original inhabitants' formulation was not acceptable to Hindu nationalists; thus, the adivasis were construed as imperfectly integrated classes or backward Hindus to be integrated. Gandhi rejected this position and used the term 'adivasi' throughout his life (Hardiman, 2003: 123–54).

3. Amritlal Vithaldas Thakkar was associated with the *Servants of India Society* (1914), the *Bhil Seva Mandal* (1922), the *Harijan Sevak Sangh* (1932), *Adim Jati Sewa Mandal* (1946) and the *Bharatiya Adim Jati Sevak Sangh* (1948). He also headed the *Excluded and Partially Excluded Areas (Apart from those in Assam) Sub-Committee* (one of the four subcommittees of the *Advisory Committee on Fundamental Rights, Minorities and Tribal and Excluded Areas,* headed by Vallabhbhai Patel) of the Constituent Assembly of India.

In *The Problem of Aborigines in India* (1941), Thakkar states that adivasis ' . . . were the original sons of the soil and were in possession of our country before the Aryans poured in from the North-West and North-

East passes, conquered them with their superior powers and talents and drove them from the plains to the hills and forests' (Thakkar, 1941: 2). He examined the difficulties into the following categories: a) poverty, b) illiteracy, c) ill-health, d) inaccessibility of the areas inhabited by tribals, f) faults in administration and g) lack of leadership. Overall, he dismisses Kalipraja as a racist and disdainful category. He offered a critique of Elwin on shifting cultivation. For him, eradicating the exploitative system of Bethi (forced work) and bonded slavery was imperative. The anti-poverty programme depended mainly on prohibition. There was a need to teach youngsters in their mother tongue. Residential schools were an important component of education. People would suffer if educational resources were scarce. The immediate need in adivasi areas was for medical aid, and additional connectivity through infrastructure was required. He pointed out that an authoritative and dictatorial administration was making self-government nominal. He requested that tribal panchayats not be encroached upon. Adivasis were underrepresented in the legislature and on municipal boards. He opposed the isolationist approach to adivasi empowerment (Thakkar, 1941: 7–26).

4. 'The harvest is rich, but the labourers are few': The verse is from the New Testament (The Holy Gospel of Jesus Christ, according to St Matthew (Matthew 10:37); The Holy Gospel of Jesus Christ, according to St Luke (Luke

10:2). There are variations in words, but the essence remains similar. For example, in *the New Oxford Annotated Bible* (2010), the verse of Matthew 10:37 is: 'Then he [Jesus] said to his disciples, 'The harvest is plentiful, but the laborers are few' (Coogan et al., 2010: 1760) under *the Gospel According To Matthew. Under the Gospel According To Luke, the verse Luke 10: 2 is* 'He said to them, 'The harvest is plentiful, but the laborers are few" (Coogan et al., 2010: 1849–50). Gandhi, in *Autobiography,* states his liking for the New Testament, particularly the *Sermon of the Mount* and compared it with Gita. *The Sermon of the Mount* (five, six and seven chapters of *The Gospel According To Matthew).* Particularly verse 38 ('You have heard that it was said, "An eye for an eye and a tooth for a tooth".'), 39 ('But I say to you, Do not resist an evildoer. But if anyone strikes you on the right cheek, turn the other also'), 40 ('and if anyone wants to sue you and take your coat, give your cloak as well'), 41('and if anyone forces you to go one mile, go also the second mile'), 42 ('Give to everyone who begs from you, and do not refuse anyone who wants to borrow from you'), 43 ('You have heard that it was said, "You shall love your neighbor and hate your enemy".') and 44 ('But I say to you, Love your enemies and pray for those who persecute you')(Coogan et al., 2010: 1754) are significant in this regard.

5. Gandhi refers to the adivasis as the original inhabitants, as do contemporary sociologists. He also describes the dilemma of the political community, which also thrives

on anonymity and does not live together substantively. For Gandhi, 'even the most knowledgeable of us cannot know everything there is to know about men and their condition because our country is vast and the races so diverse'. He adds that 'after discovering this for oneself, one realises how difficult it is to live up to our claim of being one nation unless each unit has a living consciousness of being one with every other'. As a result of modern development, the adivasis have been subjected to a series of attacks, including dispossession and displacement. Gandhi's 'living consciousness of being one with every other' is a powerful rebuke to those who treat the adivasi question as an anthropological pursuit and to classes that live off surpluses generated by displacing adivasis.

Lepers

1. The modern equivalent of the leper is leprosy, also known as Hansen's disease, caused by the bacillus (bacterium), Mycobacterium leprae. According to modern scientific findings, leprosy is an infectious disease. It is contagious in extreme circumstances and undoubtedly undeserving of segregation of the infected to the point of ostracization. Gandhi's position and Gandhian discourse also developed along with this line. For Gandhi, 'leprosy is no contamination. We must learn the laws governing infectious and contagious disease and obey them' (CWMG LXXXV, 1982: 297). Moreover, the leper '. . . word has been discarded now. Any person having this

particular disease caused by lepra Bacillus is a "leprosy patient" and not a leper' (Mehendale, 1971: vii).

In *Autobiography*, Gandhi describes coming into contact with a leprosy patient in South Africa. Ladha Maharaj of Bileshvar is also referred to as a patient of leprosy. T.N. Jagadisan, a leprosy patient who started Kasturba Kushta Nivaran Nilayam in 1946 in Tamil Nadu, describes Gandhi's approach as the balanced confluence of scientific temper and compassionate feeling (Jagadisan, n.d.). His brief book *Mahatma Gandhi: Answers the Challenge of Leprosy* (1965) contains Gandhi's encounter with a group of leprosy patients in South Africa; admiration for Christian missionaries for serving leprosy patients; admiration of 'martyrdom' of Father Damien (who devoted his life to leprosy patients; Gandhi writes in *Unity and Minister* in July 1905); visit to leprosy hospitals run by the Mission to Lepers and visit to Purulia Leprosy Home and Hospital in 1925 and subsequent visit to Cuttack Leprosy Home and Chandkhuri Leprosy Home; friendship with A. Donald Miller (secretary of the Mission to Lepers) and active support to establish an indigenous leprosy home at Dattapur, Sevagram, sending Manohar Diwan to the Purulia home for initial training and starting of Maharogi Seva Mandal; compassionate treatment to satyagrahis who were leprosy patients concerning Champaran, Dandi march and later his service to Parchure Shastri in Yeravada Jail (1932) and Sevagram Ashram. Gandhi also gave the message to the

First All-India Leprosy-Workers' Conference, Wardha (3 October–1 November 1947): 'This Conference has met at Wardha to consider the problems of those suffering from leprosy. It is a good omen. I hope we will not forget that disease of the mind is far more dangerous than physical illness. If there is requisite purity of mind, the bodily diseases will disappear of their own accord' (Jagadisan, 1965: 4).

2. Madhav Mehendale's *Gandhi Looks at Leprosy* focuses on three components, 'deeds not words' (Gandhi's slew of substantive actions), 'words follow deeds' (Gandhi's engagement with others), and 'in the footsteps of the Mahatma' (vivid description of the Gandhi Memorial Leprosy Foundation). Besides multiple activities and appreciation of others, Gandhi also endorses a booklet (*Leprosy Diagnosis, Treatment and Prevention* by Dr Muir) published by the Indian Council of the British Empire Leprosy Relief Association. Mehendale compares Gandhi's views with the Gandhi memorial Leprosy Foundation's policy on six accounts: On Prevention—Gandhi's prevention includes sanitation, cleanliness and hygiene and so on. The foundation uses prevention in the modern sense, that is, immunization and detection of leprosy in the earlier stages. Primary prevention includes immunization and secondary prevention (since 1949) has been the use of power drugs to treat the disease; On approach to Patients in the Villages: Gandhi pointed out that true ordinary

medical treatment is reaching out to the ailing patient and not otherwise. The foundation became the first institution to start door-to-door surveys for the detection, health education and treatment of cases; On Health Education: health education is important in both. The SET (Survey, Education and Treatment) method is considered very effective in controlling the disease; On the beggar problem: Gandhi proposes an immediate palliative and discovery of the root cause of it. Extending the argument for beggar-leprosy-patients, reaching the root of the problem is suggested in the activities of the Foundation; On Opening Colonies for the Services of Humanity: Gandhi did not consider the opening of the leper asylums, colonies as the best way of serving humanity. The Foundation also adopted the method of reaching villagers in their own villages. Mehendale finds a symmetrical collaboration between Gandhi's idea and the work of the foundation (Mehendale, 1971: 40–48).

Sanjeev Kakar's study throws a significant light on this regard. Gandhi's engagement with the question of lepers/leprosy is a triumph of the 'secularisation of leprosy'. Gandhi's own position evolved through exposure to the discourse on the bacteriology of modern science and the rejection of religious interpretation of leprosy. Gandhi started to visit the leprosy institution in India in 1925. His writings in *Young India* and *Harijan* are self-evident. Post-1934, Gandhi was influenced by modern medicine concerning leprosy. This was a secular form of knowledge as advocated and contributed to the Indian Auxiliary of the British Empire Leprosy Relief Association (BELRA). BELRA, founded in 1927, was an outcome of a collaborative effort of the colonial state, medical missionaries and Indian doctors. BELRA's approach and methodology (all forms of leprosy not contagious; treatment in early stage; visiting villages, collaborating with local bodies for treatment; humane perspective; non-coercive attitude; focus on prevention, diet and improvement of sanitation) was very much closer to Gandhi's schema. Gandhi visited Maharogi Seva Mandal (the first leprosy home and hospital on the Gandhian principles) in 1944. In 1946, leprosy was included in the activities of the Kasturba Gandhi National Memorial Trust. The transition of understanding leprosy from hereditary (colonial medicine), then the discovery of leprosy bacillus by Armauer Hansen, the replacement of environmental theories with a bacteriological understanding of disease causation, the death of Father Damien de Veuster causing uproar on contagious diseases in London 1889, and appointment of the Leprosy Commission of India (1889) gave ample exposure to Gandhi as a student in London (1888–91). Gandhi was the lone voice in discussing the sexual rights of lepers. In 1934, he met Dr Isaac Santra (a very prominent leprosy expert) at the Sambalpur Leper Asylum. Gandhi endorsed BELRA booklet's *Leprosy: Diagnosis,*

Treatment and Prevention by Dr Ernest Muir in *Harijan*, 7 September,1935. Under the charge of Manohar Dewan, the Mahayogi Seva Mandal was established at Wardha in 1936. Gandhi extended full support to Parchure Shastri, a leprosy patient at Sevagram. The First All India Leprosy Workers' Conference (MSM, Wardha, 30 October to 1 November 1947) was a point of shared ideals paving the path of joining of Gandhi with Donald Miller, Santra, T.N. Jagadisan, Cochrane, Manohar Dewan and many more. Gandhian discourse on leprosy is an outcome of collective effort of Vinoba Bhave, A.V. Thakkar, Monohar Dewan and Baba Raghav Das. In Gandhi, it is crucial to understand *the shift from his article Lepers Blessings* (Indian Opinion, 1908) to the days of 'secularization of leprosy' (Kakar, 2020: 25–41).

In a nutshell, Gandhi invites attention to the precarious condition of leprosy patients because they have not been paid attention. There is heartless negligence of lepers. For him, leprosy patients cannot be chained and unaccounted for in Independent India. What makes it significant in this regard are two points: Gandhi is asking to take care of those who are minuscule in number. There has to be a political concern in everydayness since the government is administered by way of majoritarianism; secondly, it is crucial to invite attention to those groups who may face discrimination within the discrimination.

The last Sunday in January is designated as World Leprosy Day. Anti-Leprosy Day/World Leprosy Day is marked in India on 30 January, the day of Gandhiji's martyrdom.

Students

1. For Gandhi, students' role in the constructive programme is supreme. In his address or communication to students, the constructive programme appeared as one of the most critical signposts for attaining swaraj. In 'Speech at Jamia Millia Islamia' (2 November 1927), Gandhi invites students to some of his core components of the constructive programme like Hindu–Muslim unity, khadi, charkha and respect for women (CWMG XXXV, 1969: 208–11).

   Speech at Hindu University (25 September 1929) refers to khadi, *Daridranarayana,* identifying with striving million people by spreading the message of the spinning wheel through becoming expert of spinners, wearing khadi and financial contributions, charkha, issue of untouchability and purity of hearts (CWMG XLI, 1970: 461–63). His 'Convocation Address at Kashi Vidyapith' (25 September 1929, Banaras) reminds the student about the struggle for swaraj (CWMG XLI, 1970: 463–66). 'Speech at Meeting of Students' (11 September 1931, Marseilles) reminds students that 'No people on earth can be finally subjected without their co-operation voluntary or involuntary' (CWMG XLVII, 1971: 421). In 'Message to U.P. Students' (17 December 1947), Gandhi suggests moral upliftment for awakening and self-reliance for free from anxiety. He makes two very substantive arguments. Universities must be guided by craft. In swaraj, all are brothers and sisters, and no place for high/low status and religion is a private affair. This is a remarkable statement and position. 'Let there be no Hindus, no Parsis, no Christians and no Jews. We should realize that we are only Indians, and *that religion is a private matter*' (CWMG XC, 1984: 249, emphasis added).

2. Gandhi divides educational institutions between government schools and national schools. In the context of the non-cooperation movement and civil disobedience, students were urged to withdraw from government schools. Against the government-schools-led objective of mere job creation, '[t]he objective of national schools being swaraj, independence and self-reliance, along with literary instruction, students should be trained with a view to developing their moral and manual fibre. National schools should teach such things as would further the cause of swaraj' (CWMG XXV, 1967: 446). Moreover, the spinning wheel teaching of Hindi and Urdu, the presence of all religions and are crucial components of national schools for winning swaraj. Closing down of national schools that boycott untouchables will serve the country. Gandhi underlines the distinction between government schools and national schools. 'Therein lies the test for the

organizers, teachers and students. That distinction is the conscpicous feature of non-co-operation, but without this distinctive feature it cannot be called non-co-operation' (CWMG XXV, 1967: 447). This is to remember that '[t]he general impression about non-co-operating students is that they should be upright, fearless, self-controlled, hardworking and patriotic' (CWMG XXVI, 1967: 150).

3. Highest military-ranked officer in China.

4. Gandhi's 'Speech at Bihar Students' Conference' (Bhagalpur, 1917) highlights the significance of learning in the mother tongue, health and inter-religious learning. He links the learning in the mother tongue (in this context Hindi) with more comprehensive social communication and dissemination of knowledge and thinking with family and surroundings, which may be hampered if English is used as a medium of instruction (CWMG XIV, 1965: 131–39). According to Gandhi, '[s]o long as our languages do not acquire the power to express all our thinking and remain incapable of serving as the medium of communication for the various sciences, the nation will not get modern knowledge. It is self evident:

a. that the entire body of our people need this knowledge;

b. that it will never be possible for all our people to understand English;

c. that, if only an English-educated individual can acquire new knowledge, it is possible for all the people to have it.

This means that if the first two propositions are correct, there is no hope for the masses. For this position, however, the blame does not lie with the languages' (CWMG XIV, 1965: 132).

5. In his 'Speech at Bihar Students' *Conference* (Bhagalpur, 1917) concerning students' participation in politics, he highlights two aspects of politics: theoretical study and political activity. He advocates participation in the former and denies it in the latter. 'They may attend political meetings or the sessions of the Congress in order to learn the science of politics. Such gatherings are useful as object-lessons. Students should have complete freedom to attend them and every effort should be made to get the recent ban on them removed' (CWMG XIV, 1965: 137). Up to this time, serving the nation was construed as focusing on study, health and utilization of study for the service of the country.

6. Gandhi advises students not to participate in 'party politics.' ('Party politics' is not the sole realm of politics. Thus, Gandhi develops the idea of extraparliamentary.) It should not be considered 'anti-politics' per se. Gandhi was redefining the domain of politics by creating unbounded space and unrestricted representation. In this way, politics was writ large everywhere. The most important aspect of the constructive programme was the politicization of issues and spaces and the redefinition of politics. In general, constructive programme issues became a central part of students' lives. Remarkably, he himself politicizes

students' space by asking them to join in non-cooperation and civil disobedience and question majoritarianism and exclusivist nationalism. Therefore, it can be construed that he was against the participation of students in the discriminatory party of electoral politics. He championed everyday resistance by constructing new political spaces. He opposed the imposition of 'Vande Mataram' or the national flag on others. Gandhi sufficiently politicizes students' space against institutionalized exclusion.

Place of Civil Disobedience

1. Gandhi proposes *Satyagraha* as an effective means of resistance and transformation. Gandhi shifted to the notion and practice of *Satyagraha* from earlier formulation and practice of 'passive resistance'. Civil disobedience is one of the forms of *Satyagraha*. According to Gandhi,
'Civil disobedience is civil breach of unmoral statutory enactments. The expression was . . . coined by Thoreau to signify his own resistance to the laws of a slave state. He has left a masterly treatise on the duty of civil disobedience . . . Thoreau limited his breach of statutory laws to the revenue law, i.e., payment of taxes, whereas the term 'civil disobedience' as practised in 1919 covered a breach of any statutory and unmoral law. It signified the resister's outlawry in a civil, i.e., non-violent manner. He invoked the sanctions of the law and cheerfully suffered imprisonment. It is a branch of satyagraha' (CWMG XIX, 1966: 466).

Gandhi is refereeing to the essay 'On the Duty of Civil Disobedience' (1849) by Henry David Thoreau. Gandhi also published a summary of Thoreau's ideas as 'Duty of Disobeying Laws-1' (*Indian Opinion*, 7 October 1907) and 'Duty of Disobeying Laws-2' (*Indian Opinion*, 14 October 1907)(CWMG VII, 1962: 217–18; 228–30). Some of the powerful reminders in the essay became the vantage point in civil disobedience discourse, people movements and the conceptualization of deliberative democracies: 'Can there not be a government in which majorities do not virtually decide right and wrong, but conscience?' (Thoreau, 1903: 9); 'It is not desirable to cultivate a respect for the law, so much as for the right' (Thoreau, 1903:9); The mass of men serve the state thus, not as men mainly, but as machines, with their bodies (Thoreau, 1903: 9).

2. Gandhi, on multiple occasions, stressed conjoining on civil disobedience and the constructive programme reiterated in the *Congress Working Committee Resolution* (passed on 13 December 1945 in Calcutta). 'The Working Committee is of [the] opinion that civil disobedience, mass or any other, meant for the attainment of freedom, is inconceivable without the adoption of the constructive programme on the widest scale possible by the masses of India' (CWMG LXXXII, 1980: 201). In other words, Gandhi reminds us that without a constructive programme, civil disobedience remains ineffective. The immense significance of different realms of spaces being

converted into political space will contribute to the overall development of the political community.

Appendices

1. As discussed in the previous pages regarding the first appendix, Gandhi had expressed his desire to include 'improvement of livestock' in a letter to Jivanji Desai on 16 January 1946. This was added as Appendix 1 (or item 19) posthumously in March 1948. Some significant changes from the 1946 letter are as follows: change of sentence formation, cow service in place of cow protection, and 'improvement of livestock' in place of 'improvement of cattle' as the title for the appendix. These changes were executed at the editorial level since evidence of Gandhi's further suggestions is unavailable. Nevertheless, this appendix is crucial for Gandhi's theorization on the issue. As discussed earlier, in responding to Desai's suggestion to *goseva as one more item in the Constructive Programme*, Gandhi's response is as follows: 'You are right; cow service (*goseva*) should be included as one more item in the *Constructive Programme*. I would phrase it as improvement of cattle' (Gandhi, 1948: 30). In this way, Gandhi develops a non-sectarian critique of anthropocentrism. He rejects communal standpoints toward anthropocentrism.

2. The second appendix (or twentieth issue) is 'Congress Position'. As discussed earlier, Gandhi discussed 'Congress Position' on 27 January 1948. The available

records do not suggest his consent to include it in the *Constructive Programme*. Moreover, it should be read along with the 'Draft Constitution of Congress', which he wrote on 29 January 1948. The Congress Position does not reflect 'extra-parliamentary' politics, but the 'Draft Constitution of Congress' offers a nuanced understanding of 'extra-parliamentary' politics along with a final summation of Gandhi before his assassination. Therefore, methodologically, the Congress Position should be delinked from the *Constructive Programme* in terms of text and its interpretation.

However, it does not diminish the value of the Congress Position. The rejection of it in totality will be an erroneous reading of it. It offers how parliamentary politics should act. It is important to note that Gandhi does not reject or devalue 'organized politics'. On the contrary, he led and expanded its scope and reach. His defence of Congress is a defence of organized politics. He writes that the 'Indian National Congress . . . cannot be allowed to die . . . It can only die with the nation. A living organism ever grows, or it dies' (Gandhi, 1948: 30). In other words, there is a need for organized politics. Nevertheless, as it happens, liberal political theory or liberal state reduces equality in political realms and unfreedom in other realms. 'The Congress has won political freedom, but it has yet to win economic freedom, social and moral freedom' (Gandhi, 1948: 30). Gandhi highlights the limits of the political equality project of liberalism to expand the scope of organized politics for constructive space as a political space and questioning social-economic inequality. Expanding the scope of organized politics beyond liberal spaces poses a challenge to transforming the capitalist state, which thrives on the comfortable yet untenable division of political equality and socioeconomic inequality and getting constant legitimacy from constructed political space and limited access to it.

* * *

Afterword

1. 'It seems reasonable to suppose that the parties in the original position are equal. That is, all have the same rights in the procedure for choosing principles; each can make proposals, submit reasons for their acceptance, and so on' (Rawls, 1999: 17)

2. 'The principles of justice are chosen behind a veil of ignorance. This ensures that no one is advantaged or disadvantaged in the choice of principles by the outcome of natural chance or the contingency of social circumstances' (Rawls, 1999: 11).

3. 'It is an equilibrium because at last our principles and judgments coincide, and it is reflective since we know to what principles our judgments conform and the premises of their derivation' (Rawls, 1999: 18).

4. Susan Okin problematizes Rawls's neglect of gendered structure and advances his ideas for addressing

questions of all sexes. On the one hand, 'Rawls himself neglects gender . . .[and] does not consider whether or in what form the family is a just institution' (Okin, 1989: 108). On the other hand, '[t]he original position, with the veil of ignorance hiding from its participants their sex as well as their other particular characteristics, talents, circumstances, and aims, is a powerful concept for challenging the gender structure' (Okin, 1989: 108–09).

Carol Pateman challenges 'sexless' representation of participants in original position. 'Rawls' parties merely reason and make their choice . . .The representative is sexless. The disembodied party who makes the choice cannot know one vital 'particular fact', namely, its sex. Rawls' original position is a logical construction in the most complete sense; it is a realm of pure reason with nothing human in it . . . Rawls' participants in the, original contract are, simultaneously, mere reasoning entities, and "heads of families", or men who represent their wives' (Pateman, 1988: 43)

5. C.B. Macpherson (1973) and Kai Nielsen (1978) are important. According to Macpherson, '[t]he central concern of *A Theory of Justice* remains the justification of unequal life prospects for members of different social classes' (1973: 341).

6. Rawls reduces the socio-economic condition of minorities at the mercy of the majority. Vinit Haksar aptly highlights this.

'Rawls thinks that as long as our civil and political liberties are secure, the normal political processes can be relied upon to correct injustices automatically in fields like social justice. But he is being too optimistic here. For a minority, even though it has the liberty to vote, freedom of speech, etc., may be outvoted and economically and socially exploited by a majority for long periods over issues such as income, housing and education. It may be argued that in a near-just society a majority would not do this for long, but we must remember that we are assuming that the Rawlsian majority is capable of lapses from justice. Indeed we have seen that unless we make this and other assumptions there will be no place for civil disobedience at all. The majority, the authorities, and the courts are assumed to be capable of conniving (intentionally or through "false consciousness") against the interests of the minority' (Haksar, 1976: 170–71).

7. 'The basic features of the authorization view are these: a representative is someone who has been authorized to act' (Pitkin, 1967: 38).

8. '[D]escriptive representation', in which a person or thing stands for others 'by being sufficiently like them' (Pitkin, 1967: 80).

9. 'Descriptive likeness is not the only basis on which one thing can be substituted for another, can represent by "standing for". Symbols, too, are often said to represent something to make it present by their presence, although

it is not really present in fact. This kind of representing too, can be taken as central and definitive, and all other kinds, including political representation, can then be interpreted in terms of it and approximated to it. We may call this the "symbolic representation" or "symbolization" view, and writers who adopt it, "symbolization theorists"' (Pitkin, 1967: 92).

10. 'We need representation precisely where we are not content to leave matters to the expert; we can have substantive representation only where interest is involved, that is, where decisions are not merely arbitrary choices' (Pitkin, 1967: 212).

11. The seven indicators in question form are as follows:

   a. 'To what extent is *parliamentary candidate selection* controlled by the extraparliamentary party?

   b. To what extent is the extraparliamentary party directly involved in the *selection of the official parliament group leader* of the party?

   c. Is there a requirement that the party's *MPs rotate out of office* after a particular period of time, and if so, is it taken seriously?

   d. Who, if anyone, is responsible for *disciplining parliamentary representatives* who deviate from the extraparliamentary party's policy positions?

   e. To what extent is the parliamentary group required to *conform to the extraparliamentray organization's policy positions?*

f. To what extent is the extraparliamentary party (as opposed to the parliamentary group) responsible for formulating the party's *public positions on policy?*

g. Who is *the primary leader of the party,* officially and in fact, the parliamentary or the extraparliamentary leader?'(Gibson and Harmel, 1998: 638–9; original emphasis).

REFERENCES

Agarwal, S.N. (1944). *Gandhian Plan of Economic Development for India*. Bombay: Padma Publications.

Agarwal, S. N. (1945). *Constructive Programme for Students*. Bombay: Padma Publications.

Agarwal, S. N. (1953). *Constructive Programme for Congressmen*. New Delhi: All India Congress Committee.

All India Spinners' Association (1940). *Annual Reports, 1925–1940*. Ahmedabad: The Association.

Allinson, T.R. (1892). *Medical Essays*. London: F. Pitman.

Ambedkar, B.R. (2014). 'Thoughts on Linguistic State'. In *Dr. Babasaheb Ambedkar Writings and Speeches, Volume One*, ed. Vasant Moon, pp. 137–201. New Delhi: Dr. Ambedkar Foundation, Ministry of Social Justice and Empowerment, Govt. of India.

Ayto, J. (2010). *Oxford Dictionary of English Idioms*. Oxford: Oxford University Press.

Bandopadhyaya, A. (1964). *Bahuroopee Gandhi*. Bombay: Popular Prakashan.

Bae, M. (2022). 'Locating Hygienic Medicine within the Intellectual History of Hygiene: Cases of E. W. Lane and

T. R. Allinson'. *History and Philosophy of the Life Sciences,* *44* (51), 1–25.

Bandyopadhyay, S. (2015). *From Plassey to Partition and After: A History of Modern India.* Hyderabad: Orient Blackswan.

Barot, N.M. (1997). *The Gandhian Path in Trade Unionism.* Ahmedabad: Navinchandra M. Barot.

Bartlett, R. (2010). *Tolstoy: A Russian Life.* London: Profile Books.

Berlin, I. (2016). 'Two Concepts of Liberty'. In *The Liberty Reader,* ed. David Miller, pp. 33–57. New York: Routledge.

Beyme, K. (1985). *Political Parties in Western Democracies.* Aldershot: Gower.

Bilgrami, A. (2012). Foreword to *Gandhi and Revolution,* by Devi Prasad, pp. vii–xiii. New Delhi: Routledge.

Breman, J. (2004). *The Making and Unmaking of an Industrial Working Class: Sliding Down the Labour in Ahmedabad, India.* New Delhi: Oxford University Press.

Brown, J. M. (2008). *Mahatma Gandhi: The Essential Writings.* Oxford: Oxford University Press.

Carroll, L. (1976). 'The Temperance Movement in India: Politics and Social Reform'. *Modern Asian Studies, 10*(3) 417–47.

Chand, T. (1944). *The Problem of Hindustani.* Allahabad: Indian Periodicals Ltd.

Chandhoke, N. (2004). 'Revisiting the crisis of representation thesis: The Indian Context'. *Democratisation, 12* (3), 308–30.

Chattopadhyay, K. (1983). *Indian Women's Battle for Freedom*. New Delhi: Abhinav Publications.

Choudhary, M. (1966). *Freedom for the Masses*. New Delhi: Central Gandhi Smarak Nidhi.

Coogan, Michael D. et al (Eds.) (2010). *The New Oxford Annotated Bible: New Revised Standard Version with the Apocrypha*. New York: Oxford University Press.

CWMG I (1969). Petition to 'The Natal Assembly', pp. 128–32. New Delhi: The Publication Division: Ministry of Information and Broadcasting, Government of India.

CWMG I (1969). Letter to 'The Natal Mercury', pp. 144–45. New Delhi: The Publication Division: Ministry of Information and Broadcasting, Government of India.

CWMG I (1969). Letter to 'The Natal Mercury', pp. 292–95. New Delhi: The Publication Division: Ministry of Information and Broadcasting, Government of India.

CWMG I (1969). Open Letter, pp. 170–88. New Delhi: The Publication Division: Ministry of Information and Broadcasting, Government of India.

CWMG III (1979). Petition to 'Legislative Council, Transval', pp. 399–400. New Delhi: The Publication Division: Ministry of Information and Broadcasting, Government of India.

CWMG III (1979). Letter to 'The Vegetarian', p. 345. New Delhi: The Publication Division: Ministry of Information and Broadcasting, Government of India.

CWMG IV (1960). Baroda: A Model Indian State, pp. 456–57. New Delhi: The Publication Division:

Ministry of Information and Broadcasting, Government of India.

CWMG V (1961). India for Indians, pp. 396–97. New Delhi: The Publication Division: Ministry of Information and Broadcasting, Government of India.

CWMG V (1961). Letter to A. J. Bean, p. 216. New Delhi: The Publication Division: Ministry of Information and Broadcasting, Government of India.

CWMG V (1961). Letter to Chhaganlal Gandhi, pp. 408–09. New Delhi: The Publication Division: Ministry of Information and Broadcasting, Government of India.

CWMG VII (1962). Duty of Disobeying Laws 1 & 2, pp. 217–18, 228–30. New Delhi: The Publication Division: Ministry of Information and Broadcasting, Government of India.

CWMG XI (1964). London, pp. 488–92. New Delhi: The Publication Division: Ministry of Information and Broadcasting, Government of India.

CWMG XI (1964). New Delhi: The Publication Division: Ministry of Information and Broadcasting, Government of India.

CWMG XII (1964). New Delhi: The Publication Division: Ministry of Information and Broadcasting, Government of India.

CWMG XIII (1964). Introduction to 'Vernaculars as media of instruction', pp. 336–37. New Delhi: The Publication Division: Ministry of Information and Broadcasting, Government of India.

CWMG XIII (1964). Our System of Education, pp. 358–59. New Delhi: The Publication Division: Ministry of Information and Broadcasting, Government of India.

CWMG XIII (1964). Speech at Benares Hindu University, pp. 210–16. New Delhi: The Publication Division: Ministry of Information and Broadcasting, Government of India.

CWMG XIV (1965). Second Gujarat Educational Conference, pp. 8–36. New Delhi: The Publication Division: Ministry of Information and Broadcasting, Government of India.

CWMG XIV (1965). Speech at Bihar Conference, pp. 131–39. New Delhi: The Publication Division: Ministry of Information and Broadcasting, Government of India.

CWMG XIV (1965). Letter to Collector, Kheda, pp. 215–16. New Delhi: The Publication Division: Ministry of Information and Broadcasting, Government of India.

CWMG XIV (1965). Letter to People of Kheda, pp. 416–19. New Delhi: The Publication Division: Ministry of Information and Broadcasting, Government of India.

CWMG XIX (1966). The National Flag, pp. 561–62 Ahmedabad: Navajivan Trust.

CWMG XIX (1966). Congress Resolution on Non–Co–Operation, pp. 576–78. New Delhi: The Publication Division, Ministry of Information and Broadcasting, Government of India.

CWMG XIX (1966). Satyagraha, Civil Disobedience, Passive Resistance and Non–co–operation, pp. 465–67. New

Delhi: The Publication Division: Ministry of Information and Broadcasting, Government of India.

CWMG XX (1966). To Gujaratis, pp. 48–51. Delhi: The Publication Division, Ministry of Information and Broadcasting, Government of India.

CWMG XXII (1966). Interview to 'The Bombay Chronicle', pp. 404–08. New Delhi: The Publication Division, Ministry of Information and Broadcasting, Government of India.

CWMG XXIII (1967). My Disappointment, pp. 4–10. New Delhi: The Publication Division, Ministry of Information and Broadcasting, Government of India.

CWMG XXIII (1967). Gujarat Efforts, pp. 381–83. New Delhi: The Publication Division, Ministry of Information and Broadcasting, Government of India.

CWMG XXV (1967). Non–Co–Operating Students, pp. 444–47. New Delhi: The Publication Division: Ministry of Information and Broadcasting, Government of India.

CWMG XXV (1967). Notes, pp. 460–63. New Delhi: The Publication Division, Ministry of Information and Broadcasting, Government of India.

CWMG XXV (1967). Presidential Address at Belgaum Congress, pp. 471–489. New Delhi: The Publication Division: Ministry of Information and Broadcasting, Government of India.

CWMG XXVI (1967). About Students, pp. 148–50. New Delhi: The Publication Division: Ministry of Information and Broadcasting, Government of India.

CWMG XXVI (1967). Letter to Shaukat Ali, pp. 190–91. New Delhi: The Publication Division: Ministry of Information and Broadcasting, Government of India.

CWMG XXVI (1967). My Notes, pp. 360–62. New Delhi: The Publication Division: Ministry of Information and Broadcasting, Government of India.

CWMG XXVII (1968). Speech at All–Bengal Hindu Sammelan, pp. 10–11. New Delhi: The Publication Division, Ministry of Information and Broadcasting, Government of India.

CWMG XXVII (1968). Speech at Bengal Provincial Conference, Faridpur, pp. 27–35. New Delhi: The Publication Division, Ministry of Information and Broadcasting, Government of India.

CWMG XXVII (1968). Speech at Public Meeting, Calcutta, pp. 4–9. Delhi: The Publication Division, Ministry of Information and Broadcasting, Government of India.

CWMG XXVII (1968). Talk with Untouchable, pp. 12–16. Delhi: The Publication Division, Ministry of Information and Broadcasting, Government of India.

CWMG XXVII (1968). Letter to 'The Statesman', pp. 462–64. New Delhi: The Publication Division, Ministry of Information and Broadcasting, Government of India.

CWMG XXVIII (1968), The constitution of the All-India Spinners' Association, pp. 227–30. New Delhi: The Publication Division: Ministry of Information and Broadcasting, Government of India.

CWMG XXVIII (1968). Speech at Y.M.C.A., pp. 107–09. New Delhi: The Publication Division: Ministry of Information and Broadcasting, Government of India.

CWMG XXVIII (1968). A Hotch–Pot of Questions, pp. 431–34. New Delhi: The Publication Division: Ministry of Information and Broadcasting, Government of India.

CWMG XXIX (1968). Total Prohibition, pp. 437–39. New Delhi: The Publication Division, Government of India.

CWMG XXX (1968). A Servant of India, pp. 171–72. New Delhi: The Publication Division: Ministry of Information and Broadcasting, Government of India.

CWMG XXXII (1969). Discourses on the Gita, pp. 94–376. New Delhi: The Publication Division: Ministry of Information and Broadcasting, Government of India.

CWMG XXXII (1969). Kathiawar Political Conference, pp. 421–23. New Delhi: The Publication Division, Ministry of Information and Broadcasting, Government of India.

CWMG XXXIII (1969). Letter to G.D. Birla, pp. 411–12. New Delhi: The Publication Division: Ministry of Information and Broadcasting, Government of India.

CWMG XXXV (1969). Letter to Manilal and Sushila Gandhi, pp. 460–61. New Delhi: The Publication Division: Ministry of Information and Broadcasting, Government of India.

CWMG XXXV (1969). Speech at Jamia Millia Islamia, Delhi, pp. 208–11. New Delhi: The Publication Division:

Ministry of Information and Broadcasting, Government of India.

CWMG XXXVI (1970). Letter to Jawaharlal Nehru, p. 427. New Delhi: The Publication Division: Ministry of Information and Broadcasting, Government of India.

CWMG XXXVII (1970). Speech at Bardoli, pp. 162–69. New Delhi: The Publication Division, Ministry of Information and Broadcasting, Government of India.

CWMG XXXVIII (1970). Speech on Resolution on Nehru Report, Calcutta Congress–I, pp. 267–73. New Delhi: The Publication Division, Ministry of Information and Broadcasting, Government of India.

CWMG XXXVIII (1970). Speech on Resolution on Nehru Report, Calcutta Congress–II, pp. 283–96. New Delhi: The Publication Division, Ministry of Information and Broadcasting, Government of India.

CWMG XXXVIII (1970). Speech on Constructive Programme, Calcutta Congress-III, pp. 311–14. New Delhi: The Publication Division, Ministry of Information and Broadcasting, Government of India.

CWMG XXXVIII (1970). Then and Now, pp. 354–55. New Delhi: The Publication Division, Ministry of Information and Broadcasting, Government of India.

CWMG XL (1970). Appendix II: Prohibition Campaign, pp. 439–40. New Delhi: The Publication Division, Government of India.

CWMG XL (1970). Prohibition Campaign, p. 204. New Delhi: The Publication Division, Government of India.

CWMG XL (1970). Prohibition Campaign, p. 415. New Delhi: The Publication Division, Government of India.

CWMG XLI (1970). Speech at Hindu University, pp. 461–63. New Delhi: The Publication Division: Ministry of Information and Broadcasting, Government of India.

CWMG XLII (1970). Varnadharma and Duty of Labour-III, pp. 488–90. New Delhi: The Publication Division: Ministry of Information and Broadcasting, Government of India.

CWMG XLIV (1971). Letter to Narandas Gandhi, pp. 147–50. New Delhi: The Publication Division: Ministry of Information and Broadcasting, Government of India.

CWMG XLVII (1971). My Notes, pp. 243–46. New Delhi: The Publication Division: Ministry of Information and Broadcasting, Government of India.

CWMG XLVII (1971). Speech at Meeting of Students, Marseilles, pp. 421–22. New Delhi: The Publication Division: Ministry of Information and Broadcasting, Government of India.

CWMG XLVII (1971). Indian State and Satyagraha, pp. 103–06. Delhi: The Publication Division, Ministry of Information and Broadcasting, Government of India.

CWMG XLVIII (1971). Interview of Charles Petrasch and others, pp. 241–48. New Delhi: The Publication Division: Ministry of Information and Broadcasting, Government of India.

CWMG XLVIII (1971). Speech at Chatham House Meeting, pp. 193–206. New Delhi: The Publication Division, Ministry of information and Broadcasting, Government of India.

CWMG L (1972). History of Satyagraha Ashram, pp. 188–236. New Delhi: The Publication Division: Ministry of Information and Broadcasting, Government of India.

CWMG LI (1972). Letter to Ambalal, pp. 395–96. New Delhi: The Publication Division, Ministry of Information and Broadcasting, Government of India.

CWMG LII (1972). Statement on Untouchability–X, pp. 151–55. New Delhi: The Publication Division, Ministry of Information and Broadcasting, Government of India.

CWMG LIV (1973). Letter to F. Mary Barr and Duncan Greenlees, pp. 9–10. New Delhi: The Publication Division: Ministry of Information and Broadcasting, Government of India.

CWMG LIV (1973). Letter to N., pp. 316–18. New Delhi: The Publication Division, Ministry of information and Broadcasting, Government of India.

CWMG LIV (1973). Letter to Narandas Gandhi, pp. 309–11. New Delhi: The Publication Division, Ministry of information and Broadcasting, Government of India.

CWMG LIV (1973). Propaganda v. Construction, pp. 206–09. New Delhi: The Publication Division, Ministry of Information and Broadcasting, Government of India.

CWMG LV (1973). Letter to Yvonne Privat, pp. 42–43. New Delhi: The Publication Division: Ministry of Information and Broadcasting, Government of India.

CWMG LVII (1974). Letter to Hiralal Sharma, p. 390. New Delhi: The Publication Division: Ministry of Information and Broadcasting, Government of India.

CWMG LVIII (1974). Letter to Vallabhbhai Patel, pp. 403–06. New Delhi: The Publication Division: Ministry of Information and Broadcasting, Government of India.

CWMG LIX (1974). Statement to the Press, pp. 3–12. New Delhi: The Publication Division: Ministry of Information and Broadcasting, Government of India.

CWMG LIX (1974). A.I.V.I.A.-Object and Constitution, pp. 449–53. New Delhi: The Publication Division: Ministry of Information and Broadcasting, Government of India.

CWMG LX (1974). Letter to Rajendra Nath Barua, p. 175. New Delhi: The Publication Division: Ministry of Information and Broadcasting, Government of India.

CWMG LX (1974). Advice to Students, pp. 118–20. New Delhi: The Publication Division, Ministry of Information and Broadcasting, Government of India.

CWMG LX (1974). Advice to Villagers, pp. 299–300. New Delhi: The Publication Division, Ministry of Information and Broadcasting, Government of India.

CWMG LX (1974). How to Begin?–III, pp. 190–92. New Delhi: The Publication Division, Ministry of Information and Broadcasting, Government of India.

CWMG LX (1974). Interview to Mrs. C. Kuttan Nair, pp. 66–69. New Delhi: The Publication Division, Ministry of Information and Broadcasting, Government of India.

CWMG LX (1974). Letter to Amrit Kaur, p. 4. New Delhi: The Publication Division, Ministry of Information and Broadcasting, Government of India.

CWMG LX (1974). Letter to H.L. Sharma, p. 322. New Delhi: The Publication Division, Ministry of Information and Broadcasting, Government of India.

CWMG LX (1974). Manure Pits, pp. 269–70. New Delhi: The Publication Division, Ministry of Information and Broadcasting, Government of India.

CWMG LX (1974). Notes, pp. 417–19. New Delhi: The Publication Division, Ministry of Information and Broadcasting, Government of India.

CWMG LXII (1975). Speech at Akhil Bharatiya Sahitya Parishad, pp. 344–47. New Delhi: The Publication Division: Ministry of Information and Broadcasting, Government of India.

CWMG LXII (1975). Speech at Gandhi Seva Sangh Meeting–IV, pp. 229–34. New Delhi: The Publication Division, Ministry of Information and Broadcasting, Government of India.

CWMG LXIII (1976). Convocation Address at Hindi Prachar Sabha, pp. 51–54. New Delhi: The Publication Division: Ministry of Information and Broadcasting, Government of India.

CWMG LXIII (1976). Letter to G.S.N. Acharya, pp. 300–01. New Delhi: The Publication Division: Ministry of Information and Broadcasting, Government of India.

CWMG LXIII (1976). More Cobwebs, pp. 221–24. New Delhi: The Publication Division: Ministry of Information and Broadcasting, Government of India.

CWMG LXIV (1976). Message to the All–India Women's Conference, p. 165. New Delhi: The Publication Division, Ministry of information and Broadcasting, Government of India.

CWMG LXV (1976). Letter to Haribhau Upadhyaya, p. 78. New Delhi: The Publication Division: Ministry of Information and Broadcasting, Government of India.

CWMG LXV (1976). Letter to Jawaharlal Nehru, pp. 445–46. New Delhi: The Publication Division, Ministry of Information and Broadcasting, Government of India.

CWMG LXV (1976). Appendix VIII: Livery of Freedom, p. 473. Letter to Jawaharlal Nehru. New Delhi: The Publication Division, Ministry of Information and Broadcasting, Government of India.

CWMG LXV (1976). Interview to Capt. Strunk, pp. 360–62. New Delhi: The Publication Division, Ministry of information and Broadcasting, Government of India.

CWMG LXV (1976). Speech at Tithal, pp. 233–35. New Delhi: The Publication Division, Ministry of information and Broadcasting, Government of India.

CWMG LXVI (1976). Workers of Kathiawar, pp. 21–24. New Delhi: The Publication Division, Ministry of Information and Broadcasting, Government of India.

CWMG LXVIII (1977). Hindustani, Hindi and Urdu, pp. 23–25. New Delhi: The Publication Division: Ministry of Information and Broadcasting, Government of India.

CWMG LXVIII (1977). Message to All–India Women's Conference, p. 230. New Delhi: The Publication Division, Ministry of Information and Broadcasting, Government of India.

CWMG LXIX (1977). Talks With Co–Workers, Rajkot pp. 273–78. New Delhi: The Publication Division, Ministry of Information and Broadcasting, Government of India.

CWMG LXIX (1977). Answers to Questions at Gandhi Seva Sangh Meeting–I, pp. 206–17. New Delhi: The Publication Division, Ministry of Information and Broadcasting, Government of India.

CWMG LXIX (1977). Speech at All–India Village Industries Board Meeting, Brindaban, pp. 237–39. New Delhi: The Publication Division, Ministry of Information and Broadcasting, Government of India.

CWMG LXIX (1977). Statement on Travancore, pp. 322–25. New Delhi: The Publication Division, Ministry of Information and Broadcasting, Government of India.

CWMG LXXI (1978). Ahimsa in Practice, pp. 129–32. New Delhi: The Publication Division: Ministry of Information and Broadcasting, Government of India.

CWMG LXXI (1978). What it means, pp. 4–5. New Delhi: The Publication Division: Ministry of Information and Broadcasting, Government of India.

CWMG LXXII (1978). Implications of Constructive Programme, pp. 378–81. New Delhi: The Publication Division, Ministry of Information and Broadcasting, Government of India.

CWMG LXXII (1978). To the Readers, pp. 450–51. New Delhi: The Publication Division, Ministry of Information and Broadcasting, Government of India.

CWMG LXXII (1978). Women's Role, pp. 326–27. New Delhi: The Publication Division, Ministry of information and Broadcasting, Government of India.

CWMG LXXIII (1978). Appeal to Congress Workers, pp. 387–88. New Delhi: The Publication Division, Ministry of Information and Broadcasting, Government of India.

CWMG LXXIII (1978). Discussion with Kishorelal Mashruwala, pp. 174–76. Delhi: The Publication Division, Ministry of Information and Broadcasting, Government of India.

CWMG LXXIII (1978). Fragment of Letter to Abdul Ghaffar Khan, pp. 35–36. New Delhi: The Publication Division, Ministry of Information and Broadcasting, Government of India.

CWMG LXXIV (1978). Reply to British Women's Appeal, pp. 114–16. New Delhi: The Publication Division, Ministry of information and Broadcasting, Government of India.

CWMG LXXIV (1978). Letter to Sharda G. Chokhawala, p. 228. New Delhi: The Publication Division: Ministry of Information and Broadcasting, Government of India.

CWMG LXXV (1979). Constructive Programme, p. 263. New Delhi: The Publication Division, Ministry of Information and Broadcasting, Government of India.

CWMG LXXV (1979). Adivsasis, pp. 299–300. New Delhi: The Publication Division, Ministry of Information and Broadcasting, Government of India.

CWMG LXXV (1979). Dhanush Takli, pp. 272–73. New Delhi: The Publication Division, Ministry of Information and Broadcasting, Government of India.

CWMG LXXV (1979). Hindi+Urdu = Hindustani, pp. 278–80. New Delhi: The Publication Division: Ministry of Information and Broadcasting, Government of India.

CWMG LXXV (1979). Message to All–India Women's Conference, p. 188. New Delhi: The Publication Division, Ministry of Information and Broadcasting, Government of India.

CWMG LXXV (1979). Constructive Programme and Government, p. 236. New Delhi: The Publication Division, Ministry of Information and Broadcasting, Government of India.

CWMG LXXV (1979). Notes: Adivasis, pp. 210–11. New Delhi: The Publication Division, Ministry of Information and Broadcasting, Government of India.

CWMG LXXV (1979). Statement to the Press, pp. 55–62. New Delhi: The Publication Division, Ministry of Information and Broadcasting, Government of India.

CWMG LXXV (1979). Constructive Programme: Its Meaning and Place, pp. 146–66. New Delhi: The Publication Division, Ministry of Information and Broadcasting, Government of India.

CWMG LXXV (1979). Letter to Jawaharlal Nehru, p. 145. New Delhi: The Publication Division, Ministry of Information and Broadcasting, Government of India.

CWMG LXXV (1979). Statement to the Press, pp. 136–38. New Delhi: The Publication Division, Ministry of Information and Broadcasting, Government of India.

CWMG LXXVI (1979). Note to Perin Captain, p. 175. New Delhi: The Publication Division: Ministry of Information and Broadcasting, Government of India.

CWMG LXXVI (1979). Urdu Examination, pp. 337–38. New Delhi: The Publication Division: Ministry of Information and Broadcasting, Government of India.

CWMG LXXVII (1979). Statement to the Press, pp. 429–30. New Delhi: The Publication Division, Ministry of Information and Broadcasting, Government of India.

CWMG LXXVIII (1979). Interview to N.G. Ranga, pp. 246–52. New Delhi: The Publication Division: Ministry of Information and Broadcasting, Government of India.

CWMG LXXVIII (1979). Hints for Constructive Workers, pp. 218–21. New Delhi: The Publication Division, Ministry of Information and Broadcasting, Government of India.

CWMG LXXIX (1980). Statement to the Press, p. 334. New Delhi: The Publication Division, Ministry of Information and Broadcasting, Government of India.

CWMG LXXIX (1980). Speech at A.I.S.A Meeting–I, pp. 296–300. New Delhi: The Publication Division, Ministry of Information and Broadcasting, Government of India.

CWMG LXXIX (1980). Speech at Prayer Meeting, pp. 348–50. New Delhi: The Publication Division, Ministry of Information and Broadcasting, Government of India.

CWMG LXXX (1980). Letter to Rampra B. Sadvas, pp. 324–25. New Delhi: The Publication Division: Ministry of Information and Broadcasting, Government of India.

CWMG LXXXII (1980). Congress Working Committee Resolution, pp. 200–01. New Delhi: The Publication Division: Ministry of Information and Broadcasting, Government of India.

CWMG LXXXII (1980). Discussion with Midnapur Political Workers, pp. 333–35. New Delhi: The Publication Division, Ministry of Information and Broadcasting, Government of India.

CWMG LXXXII (1980). Letter to Jivanji D. Desai, pp. 174–75. New Delhi: The Publication Division, Ministry of Information and Broadcasting, Government of India.

CWMG LXXXII (1980). Letter to Jivanji D. Desai, pp. 348–49. New Delhi: The Publication Division, Ministry of Information and Broadcasting, Government of India.

CWMG LXXXII (1980). Letter to Jivanji D. Desai, pp. 428–30. New Delhi: The Publication Division, Ministry of Information and Broadcasting, Government of India.

CWMG LXXXII (1980). Letter to R. G. Casey, p. 167. New Delhi: The Publication Division, Ministry of Information and Broadcasting, Government of India.

CWMG LXXXIII (1981). Answers to Questions at Constructive Worker's Conference, Madras, pp. 38–39. New Delhi: The Publication Division, Ministry of Information and Broadcasting, Government of India.

CWMG LXXXIV (1981). Dr. Mehta's Institution, pp. 196–97. New Delhi: The Publication Division: Ministry of Information and Broadcasting, Government of India.

CWMG LXXXIV (1981). Letter to Ramprasad Vyas, p. 283. New Delhi: The Publication Division: Ministry of Information and Broadcasting, Government of India.

CWMG LXXXV (1982). Leprosy and Contamination, pp. 296–97. New Delhi: The Publication Division: Ministry of Information and Broadcasting, Government of India.

CWMG LXXXV (1982). Speech at Meeting of Deccan Princes, pp. 76–81. New Delhi: The Publication Division: Ministry of Information and Broadcasting, Government of India.

CWMG LXXXV (1982). Speech at Prayer Meeting, pp. 362–63. New Delhi: The Publication Division: Ministry of Information and Broadcasting, Government of India.

CWMG LXXXVI (1982). Question Box: Intellectual and Manual Work, pp. 436–37. New Delhi: The Publication

Division: Ministry of Information and Broadcasting, Government of India.

CWMG LXXXVIII (1983). A Letter, p. 355. New Delhi: The Publication Division, Ministry of Information and Broadcasting, Government of India.

CWMG LXXXIX (1983). Hindustani Written in Nagari Only, pp. 446–449. New Delhi: The Publication Division: Ministry of Information and Broadcasting, Government of India.

CWMG LXXXIX (1983). Right or Wrong, pp. 144–47. New Delhi: The Publication Division, Ministry of Information and Broadcasting, Government of India.

CWMG LXXXIX (1983). Speech at Prayer Meeting, pp. 363–67. New Delhi: The Publication Division, Ministry of Information and Broadcasting, Government of India.

CWMG XC (1984). Congress Position, pp. 497–98. New Delhi: The Publication Division, Ministry of Information and Broadcasting, Government of India.

CWMG XC (1984). Message to Indonesia, p. 307. New Delhi: The Publication Division, Ministry of information and Broadcasting, Government of India.

CWMG XC (1984). Message to U.P. Students, p. 249. New Delhi: The Publication Division: Ministry of Information and Broadcasting, Government of India.

CWMG XC (1984). Speech at Prayer Meeting, pp. 523–26. New Delhi: The Publication Division: Ministry of Information and Broadcasting, Government of India.

CWMG XC (1984). Discussion at Constructive Works Committee Meeting, pp. 215–21. New Delhi: The Publication Division, Ministry of Information and Broadcasting, Government of India.

CWMG XC (1984). Draft Constitution of Congress, pp. 526–28. New Delhi: The Publication Division, Ministry of Information and Broadcasting, Government of India.

CWMG XC (1984). Worthy of Reflection, pp. 479–81. New Delhi: The Publication Division, Ministry of Information and Broadcasting, Government of India.

CWMG XC (1984). Message to Bihar, p. 260. New Delhi: The Publication Division: Ministry of Information and Broadcasting, Government of India.

Dalton, D. (2012). *Mahatma Gandhi: Nonviolent Power in Action*. New York: Columbia University Press.

Das, S. (Ed.) (2022). *Gandhi and the Champaran Satyagraha*. Delhi: Primus Books.

Dasgupta, A. K. (1996) *Gandhi's Economic Thought*. London: Routledge.

Datta, B. K. (1946). *The Indian Revolution and the Constructive Programme*. Foreword by Rajendra Prasad. Calcutta: Saraswaty Library.

Desai, M. (1929). *History of the Bardoli Satyagraha of 1928 and its Sequel*. Ahmedabad: Navajivan Publishing House.

Duverger, M. (1964). *Political Parties: Their Organisation and Activity in the Modern State*. London: Methuen.

Educational Reconstruction (1939). Wardha: Hindustani Talimi Sangh.

Elwin, V. (1964a). *Religious and Cultural Aspects of Khadi*. Thanjavur: Sarvodalaya Prachuralaya.

Elwin, V. (1964b). *The Tribal World of Verrier Elwin: An Autobiography*. Delhi: Oxford University Press.

Gandhi, M.K. (1928). *Satyagraha in South Africa*. Trans. Valji Govindji Desai. Madras: S. Ganeshan.

Gandhi, M.K. (1933). 'Why "Harijan"?'. *Harijan*, 1 (1), 7.

Gandhi, M.K. (1935). *From Yeravda Mandir: Ashram Observances*. Trans. Valji Govindji Desai. Ahmedabad: Jivanji Dahyabhai Desai at Navajivan Karyalaya.

Gandhi, M.K. (1941). 'Khadi Jagat'. *Khadi Jagat, 1*(1), 4–6.

Gandhi, M.K. (1948). *The Constructive Programme: Its Meaning and Place*. Ahmedabad: Navajivan Publishing House.

Gandhi, M.K. (1949). *Communal Unity*. Ed. Bharatan Kumarappa. Ahmedabad: Navajivan Publishing House.

Gandhi, M.K. (1954). *Sarvodaya*. Ed. Bharatan Kumarappa. Ahmedabad: Navajivan Publishing House.

Gandhi, M.K. (1956). *Thoughts on National Language*. Ahmedabad: Navajivan Publishing House.

Gandhi, M.K. (1960). *Prohibition at Any Cost*. Comp. R. K. Prabhu. Ahmedabad: Navajivan Publishing House.

Gandhi, M.K. (1962). *Village Swaraj*. Comp. H.M. Vyas. Ahmedabad: Navajivan Publishing House.

Gandhi, M.K. (1970). *Capital and Labour*. Ed. Anand T. Hingorani. Bombay: Bharatiya Vidya Bhavan.

Gandhi, M.K. (1997). *Hind Swaraj and Other Writings*. Ed. Anthony J. Parel. Cambridge: Cambridge University Press.

Gandhi, M.K. (2018). *An Autobiography or the Story of My Experiments with Truth*. Trans. Mahadev Desai and introduced with notes by Tridip Suhrud. Gurgaon: PRHI.

Gandhi, R. (1995). *The Good Boatman: A Portrait of Gandhi*. New Delhi: Penguin Books.

Gibson, R. and Harmel, R. (1998). Party Families and Democratic Performance: Extraparliamentary vs. Parliamentary Group Power. *Political Studies, XLVI*, 633–50.

Gonsalves, P. (2012). *Khadi: Gandhi's Mega Symbol of Subversion*. New Delhi: SAGE.

Green, M. (1986). *The Origins of Nonviolence: Tolstoy and Gandhi in their Historical Settings*. London: Pennsylvania State University Press.

Greg, R.B. (1928). *Economics of Khaddar*. Madras: S. Ganeshan.

Gujaral, M. L. (1985). *Thus Spake Bapu or Dialogues between Gandhi's Spirit and the Scribe*. New Delhi: Gandhi Peace Foundation.

Gupta, J.P. (Ed.). (1943). *Unity*. Bombay: Hamara Hindostan Publications.

Haksar, V. (1976). Rawls and Gandhi on Civil Disobedience. *Inquiry: An Interdisciplinary Journal of Philosophy, 19* (1–4), 151–92.

Hardiman, D. (2003) *Gandhi in His Time and Ours: The Global Legacy of His Ideas.* Ranikhet: Permanent Black.

Heller, P. and Isaac, T M. T. (2007). 'The Politics and Institutional Design of Participatory Democracy: Lessons from Kerala, India'. In *Democratising Democracy: Beyond the Liberal Democratic Canon (Reinventing Social Emancipation)*, ed. Boaventura de Sousa Santos, pp. 405–43. London: Verso.

Hirshman, L. R. (1994). 'Is the original position inherently male–superior?'. *Columbia Law Review*, *94* (6), 1860–81.

Hobbes, T. (1998). *Leviathan.* Ed. C. A. Gaskin. New York: Oxford University Press.

Jagadisan, T.N. (1965). *Mahatma Gandhi: Answers the Challenge of Leprosy.* Madras.

Jagadisan, T.N. (n.d.). *Gandhi's Approach to Leprosy.* New Delhi: Hind Kusht Nivaran Sangh.

Johnson, R. L. (Ed.). (2006). *Gandhi's Experiments with Truth: Essential Writings by and About Mahatma Gandhi.* Oxford: Lexington Books.

Kakar, S. (2020). 'Gandhi's Evolving Discourse on Leprosy'. In *M.K. Gandhi, Media, Politics and Society: New Perspectives*, ed. Chandrka Kaul. *Cham,* Switzerland: Palgrave Macmillan.

Khan, A.G. K. (1943). Title unavailable. In *Unity*, ed. J.P. Gupta. Bombay: Hamara Hindostan Publications.

Kingsford, A. and Maitland, E. (1919a). Preface to *The Perfect Way or the Finding of Christ,* first edition, pp. i–viii. New York: Macoy Publishing & Masonic Supply Co.

Kingsford, A. and Maitland, E. (1919b). Preface to *The Perfect Way or the Finding of Christ*, revised edition, pp. i–xii. New York: Macoy Publishing & Masonic Supply Co.

Kohli, A. (1990). *Democracy and Discontent: India's Growing Crisis of Governability*. Cambridge: Cambridge University Press.

Kothari, R. (1964). 'The Congress "System" in India'. *Asian Survey*, 4(12), 1161–73.

Kothari, R. (1974). 'The Congress System Revisited: A Decennial Review'. *Asian Survey*, 14 (12), 1035–54.

Kothari, R. (2005). *Rethinking Democracy*. Hyderabad: Orient Longman.

Kripalani, J. B. (1938). *The Latest Fad [Basic Education]*. Allahabad: Allahabad Law Journal Press.

Kuhne, L. (1899). *The New Science of Healing or the Doctrine of the Unity of Diseases*, forming the basis of a Uniform Method of Cure, without Medicines and without Operations, translated by Kenneth Romanes. Leipsic: Louis K.

Kulkarni, G., Swami, C.K.N. and Khan, N. (1945). *The Constructive Programme: Its Perspectives and Dynamics*. Bombay: Bombay Provincial Congress Committee.

Kumar, K. (2005). *Political Agenda of Education: A Study of Colonialist and Nationalist Ideas*. New Delhi: SAGE.

Kumarappa, B. (1949). Introduction to *Communal Unity*, by M.K. Gandhi, pp. viii–xiv. Ahmedabad: Navajivan Publishing House.

Kumarappa, B. (1952). *Why Prohibition*. Ahmedabad: Navajivan Publishing House.

Kumarappa, B. (1955). *Khadi (hand–spun cloth): Why and How.* Ahmedabad: Navajivan Publishing House.

Kumarappa, J.C. (1945). *Economy of Permanence.* Varanasi: Sarva Seva Sangh Prakashan.

Kumarappa, J.C. (1951). *Gandhian Economic Thought.* Bombay: Vora & Co.

Larmore, C. (1990). 'Political Liberalism'. *Political Theory*, *18* (3), 339–60.

Laubach, F. C. (1940). *India shall be Literate.* Nagpur: National Christian Council.

Levine, A. (1981). *Liberal Democracy: A Critique of its Theory.* New York: Columbia University Press.

Locke, J. (1980). *Second Treatise of Government.* Ed. C.B. Macpherson. Cambridge: Hackett Publishing.

Macpherson, C. B. (1973). 'Rawls' Models of Man and Society'. *Philosophy of the Social Sciences*, *3*(4), 341–47.

Macpherson, C.B. (1990). *The Political Theory of Possessive Individualism: Hobbes to Locke.* New York: Oxford University Press.

Mantena, K. (2012). 'Another Realism: The Politics of Gandhian Nonviolence'. *American Political Science Review*, *106* (2), 457–70.

Mathew, B. (2012). 'Mahatma Gandhi's Constructive Programme: Some Reflections'. *Proceedings of the Indian History Congress*, *73*, 597–606.

Mehendale, M.S. (1971). *Gandhi Looks at Leprosy.* Bombay: Bharatiya Vidya Bhavan.

Meherally, Y. [Ed.] (1947). Introduction to *At the cross-roads*, by Kamaldevi, pp. 1–6. Bombay: The National Information and Publications Ltd.

Mehta, V. (2013). *Mahatma Gandhi and His Apostles*. New Delhi: Penguin.

Michels, R. (1962). *Political Parties: A Sociological Study of the Oligarchical Tendencies of Modern Democracy*, Trans. by E. Paul and C. Paul with an introduction by S. M. Lipset. New York: Free Press.

Mill, J.S. (1977). 'Considerations on Representative Government'. In *Essays on Politics and Society: Collected Works of John Stuart Mill, volume xix,* ed. J. M. Robson and introduction by Alexander Brady. Toronto: University of Toronto Press.

Naess, A. (1958). 'A Systematisation of Gandhian Ethics of Conflict Resolution'. *The Journal of Conflict Resolution, 2* (2), 140–55.

Naidu, M.V. (2006). 'Indian Democracy: A Case Study in Conflict Resolution and Peace Building'. *Peace Research, 38*(2), 71–97.

Namboodiripad, E.M.S. (2010). *The Mahatma and the Ism*. New Delhi: LeftWord Books.

Narayan, J. (2009). 'My Objective Remains Unchanged: Changes in Tactics Only', 3 August 1974. In *Jayaprakash Narayan: Selected Works, Volume Ten (1972–1979),* ed. Bimal Prasad, pp. 226–330. New Delhi: Manohar and Nehru Memorial Museum & Library.

Narayan, J. (2009). 'On the Happenings in Bihar' on 4 November Again, Patna, 11 November 1974. In

Jayaprakash Narayan: Selected Works, Volume Ten (1972–1979), ed. Bimal Prasad, pp. 383–86. New Delhi: Manohar and Nehru Memorial Museum & Library.

Narayan, J. (2009). 'Youths will Bring About a Revolution', Allahabad, 29 June 1974. In *Jayaprakash Narayan: Selected Works, Volume Ten (1972–1979),* ed. Bimal Prasad, pp. 308–10. New Delhi: Manohar and Nehru Memorial Museum & Library.

Nehru, J. (1931). Foreword to *Indian Prohibition Manual,* by C Rajagopalachari. Madra: S. Ganeshan.

Nielsen, K. (1978). 'On the Very Possibility of a Classless Society: Rawls, Macpherson, and Revisionist Liberalism'. *Political Theory, 6* (2), 191–208.

Okin, S.M. (1989). *Justice, Gender and the Family.* New York: Basic Books.

Panikkar, K.N. (2009). 'Culture as a Site of Struggle'. *Economic and Political Weekly, 44(7),* 33–41.

Parekh, B. (1989). *Gandhi's Political Philosophy: A Critical Examination.* London: Macmillan.

Parekh, B. (1997). *Gandhi: A Very Short Introduction.* New Delhi: Oxford University Press.

Parel, A.J. (Ed.) (1997). *M.K. Gandhi: Hind Swaraj and Other Writings.* Cambridge: Cambridge University Press.

Parel, A.J. (2011). 'Gandhi and the State'. In *The Cambridge Companion to Gandhi,* eds. Judith M. Brown and Anthony Parel, pp. 154–72. Cambridge: Cambridge University Press.

Pateman, C. (1988). *The Sexual Contract.* Stanford: Stanford University Press.

Philips, A. (1998). *The Politics of Presence.* Oxford: Oxford University Press.

Pitkin, H.F. (1967). *The Concept of Representation.* Berkeley: University of California Press.

Poore, G.V. (1903). *Colonial and Camp Sanitation.* Bombay: Longmans, Green, and Co.

Prasad, D. (2012). *Gandhi and Revolution.* New Delhi: Routledge.

Prasad, R. (1942). *Constructive Programme—Some Suggestions.* Ahmedabad: Navajivan Publishing House.

Prasad, R. (1949). Foreword to *Communal Unity*, by M.K Gandhi, pp. iii–vii. Ahmedabad: Navajivan Publishing House.

Rajagopalachari, C. (1931). *Indian Prohibition Manual.* Madra: S. Ganeshan.

Rawls, J. (1987). 'The Idea of an Overlapping Consensus'. *Oxford Journal of Legal Studies, 7* (1), 1–25.

Rawls, J. (1999). *A Theory of Justice.* Cambridge, Massachusetts: The Belknap Press of Harvard University Press.

Report of the Thirty–Eighth National Congress Held at Cocanada (1924). Cocanada: Printing Works: General Secretary Reception Committee.

Santos, B.S. (Ed.). (2007). *Democratising Democracy: Beyond the Liberal Democratic Canon (Reinventing Social Emancipation).* London: Verso.

Sarkar, S. (2014). *Modern India: 1885–1947.* Delhi: Pearson.

Schrad, M. L. (2021). *Smashing the Liquor Machine: A Global History of Prohibition.* London: Oxford University Press.

Schumacher, E.F. (1973). *Small is Beautiful: Economies as if People Mattered.* London: Harper Torchbooks.

Shah, S. Y. (2000). 'Contribution of Frank Laubach to the Development of Adult Education in India (1930–70)'. In *Adult Education in India Selected Papers*, eds. C. J. Daswani and S. Y. Shah, pp. 16–33. New Delhi. United Nations Educational, Scientific and Cultural Organization.

Sheth, D. L. (1983). 'Grass–roots Stirrings and the Future of Politics'. *Alternatives, 9* (1), 1–24.

Sheth, D. L. (1984). 'Grass-roots initiatives in India'. *Economic and Political Weekly, 19*(6), 259–62.

Sheth, D.L. (2004). 'Globalisation and New Politics of Micro–Movements'. *Economic and Political Weekly, 39* (1), pp. 45–58.

Singh, K.S. (1977). 'Presidential Address'. *Proceedings of the Indian History Congress, 38*, 373–97.

Singh, P. (1944). *Gandhi's Constructive Programme.* Lahore: Paramount Publications.

Srivatsan, S. (2006). 'Concept of "Seva" and the "Sevak" in the Freedom Movement'. *Economic and Political Weekly, 41*(5), 427–38.

Suhrud, T. (2011). 'Gandhi's Key Writings: In Search of Unity'. In *The Cambridge Companion to Gandhi*, eds. Judith M. Brown and Anthony Parel, pp. 71–92. Cambridge: Cambridge University Press.

Sykes, M. (1988). *The Story of Nai Talim: Fifty Years of Education at Sevagram, 1937–1987: A Record of Reflections.* Sevagram, Wardha: Nai Talim Samiti.

Tendulkar, D.G. (1957). *Gandhi in Champaran*. Delhi: The Publication Division, Ministry of Information and Broadcasting, Government of India.

Tendulkar, D.G. (1962). *Mahatma, Volume Six*. Delhi: The Publication Division, Ministry of Information and Broadcasting, Government of India.

Terchek, R. J. (2011). 'Conflict and Nonviolence'. In *The Cambridge Companion to Gandhi*, eds. Judith M. Brown and Anthony Parel, pp. 117–34. Cambridge: Cambridge University Press.

Thakkar, A. V. (1941). *The Problem of Aborigines in India*, R.R. Kale Memorial Lecture. Pune: Gokhale Institute of Politics and Economics.

Thompson, D.F. (1979). *John Stuart Mill and Representative Government*. Princeton: Princeton University Press.

Thoreau, H.D. (1903). *On the Duty of Civil Disobedience*. London: The Simple Life Press.

Veeravalli, A. (2016). *Gandhi in Political Theory: Truth, Law and Experiment*. New York: Routledge.

Venkayya, P. (1916). *A National Flag for India*. Masulipatam: P. Venkayya.

Weber, T. (2004). *Gandhi as Disciple and Mentor*. Cambridge: Cambridge University Press.

Wood, E.M. (2007). *Democracy against Capitalism: Renewing Historical Materialism*. New Delhi: Cambridge University Press.

Young, I. M. (2000). *Inclusion and Democracy*. New York: Oxford University Press.

Scan QR code to access the
Penguin Random House India website